Japanese Diplomacy in th

This book provides a detailed examination of Japan's diplomatic relations in the 1950s, an important decade in international affairs when new structures and systems emerged, and when Japan established patterns in its international relationships which continue today. It examines the process of Japan's attempts to rehabilitate itself and reintegrate into a changing world, and the degree of success to which Japan achieved its goals in the political, economic and security spheres. The book is divided into three parts, each containing three chapters: Part I looks at Japan in the eyes of the Anglo-American powers; Part II looks at Japanese efforts to gain membership of newly forming regional and international organizations; and Part III considers the role of domestic factors in Japanese foreign policy making. Important issues are considered including Japanese rearmament and the struggle to gain entry into the United Nations. In contrast to much of the academic literature on post-war Japanese diplomacy, generally presenting Japan as a passive actor of little relevance or importance, this book shows that Japan did not simply sit passively by, but formed and attempted to instigate its own visions into the evolving regional and global structures. It also shows that although Japan did not always figure as highly as its politicians and policy makers might have liked in the foreign policy considerations of other nation states, many countries and organizations did attach a great deal of importance to rebuilding relations with Japan throughout this period of readjustment and transformation.

Iokibe Makoto is President of the National Defense Academy and Emeritus Professor of Modern Japanese Political and Diplomatic History in the Graduate School of Law and Politics at Kobe University. He is one of Japan's leading specialists of Japanese foreign relations, particularly with the US. He is the author of several award-winning books, including *The Occupation Era: Prime Ministers and the Rebuilding of Postwar Japan, 1945–1952* (Yomiuri Shinbunsha, 1997), and *A Diplomatic History of Postwar Japan* (Yuhikaku, 1999).

Caroline Rose is senior lecturer in Japanese Studies and currently head of the Department of East Asian Studies at the University of Leeds. She has published two monographs on Sino-Japanese relations and articles on Japanese history education, Chinese and Japanese nationalism, and Sino-Japanese relations in the East Asian context.

Tomaru Junko is professor in the School of Political Science and Economics at Waseda University. Her publications include *The Postwar Rapprochement of Malaya and Japan, 1945–61* (Macmillan, 2000, awarded the Masayoshi Ohira Memorial Prize in 2001).

John Weste held lectureships in Japanese Studies at the University of Durham (1995–2004) and Leeds (2004–06). He studied in Japan at the University of Tsukuba and obtained his PhD from Cambridge. His publications cover areas including post-war Japanese rearmament and Anglo-Japanese relations

Routledge Studies in the Modern History of Asia

Japanese Diplomacy in the 1950s

From isolation to integration

**Edited by Iokibe Makoto,
Caroline Rose, Tomaru Junko,
and John Weste**

Routledge
Taylor & Francis Group

LONDON AND NEW YORK

First published 2008
by Routledge
2 Park Square, Milton Park, Abingdon, Oxon, OX14 4RN

Simultaneously published in the USA and Canada
by Routledge
711 Third Avenue, New York, NY 10017

Routledge is an imprint of the Taylor & Francis Group, an informa business

First issued in paperback 2011

Typeset in Times New Roman by Prepress Projects Ltd, Perth, UK

British Library Cataloguing in Publication Data
A catalogue record for this book is available from the British Library

Library of Congress Cataloging in Publication Data
Japanese diplomacy in the 1950s: from isolation to integration / edited by Iokibe Makoto...[et al.].
        p. cm.— (Routledge studies in the modern history of Asia series; 49)
Includes bibliographical references and index.
1. Japan—Foreign relations—1945–1989. I. Iokibe, Makoto, 1943–
DS889.5.J48 2008
327.52009'045—dc22
                        2007031087

ISBN10: 0-415-37296-8 (hbk)
ISBN10: 0-415-67391-7 (pbk)
ISBN10: 0-203-09925-7 (ebk)

ISBN13: 978-0-415-37296-1 (hbk)
ISBN13: 978-0-415-67391-4 (pbk)
ISBN13: 978-0-203-09925-4 (ebk)

Contents

x   *Contents*

Contributors

Kweku AMPIAH gained his PhD from St. Antony's College, Oxford. He has held posts at the universities of Sterling and Edinburgh as lecturer in Japanese Studies. He is currently working at the Department of East Asian Studies, University of Leeds, as a lecturer in Japanese studies. His first book, *The Dynamics of Japan's Relations with Africa: South Africa, Tanzania and Nigeria*, was published by Routledge in 1997. His second book, *The Moral and Political Implications of the Bandung Conference of 1955: The Reactions of the US, the UK and Japan*, was published in 2007.

Robert D. ELDRIDGE joined the School of International Public Policy, Osaka University, in 2001 as an associate professor. His field is Japanese political and diplomatic history, and, in addition to that subject, he teaches US–Japan relations. He earned his PhD in Political Science from Kobe University in 1999. Prior to joining Osaka University, he worked as a Research Fellow at the Suntory Foundation (Osaka), the Research Institute for Peace and Security (Tokyo), and the Institute of Asian Cultural Studies at International Christian University, Japan. From 2004–2005, he served as a scholar-in-residence at the headquarters of US Marine Corps Forces Pacific at Camp Smith, Hawaii. He is the author of numerous works including *The Origins of the Bilateral Okinawa Problem* (Garland, 2001) and *The Return of the Amami Islands* (Lexington, 2004).

IOKIBE Makoto is President of the National Defense Academy and Emeritus Professor of Modern Japanese Political and Diplomatic History in the Graduate School of Law and Politics at Kobe University. He is one of Japan's leading specialists of Japanese foreign relations, particularly with the US. He has served as a member on various government advisory groups, such as the Council on Security and Defense Capabilities and the New Japan-China Friendship Committee for the 21st Century. He is the author of several award-winning books, including *US Occupation Policy towards Japan* (Chūō Kōronsha, 1985), *The Japanese-American War and Postwar Japan* (Osaka Shoseki, 1989), *Japan and the Changing World Order* (PHP, 1991), *The Occupation Era: Prime Ministers and the Rebuilding of Postwar Japan, 1945–1952* (Yomiuri Shinbunsha,

1997), and *A Diplomatic History of Postwar Japan* (Yūhikaku, 1999). Professor Iokibe has been a visiting scholar at Harvard University and the London School of Economics. Prior to Kobe University, he was an associate professor at Hiroshima University.

KURUSU Kaoru is associate professor at the Osaka School of International Public Policy, Osaka University. She received her MA from Tokyo University and PhD from Osaka University. Her current research interests include human security policies in East Asia and theories of international relations. She has published a number of articles on human security and European security regimes.

OBA Mie is associate professor in International Relations at Tokyo University of Science. She received her BA at International Christian University, and her MA and PhD at the University of Tokyo. Her publications, both in English and Japanese, focus mainly on the development of regionalism in Asia. Her book entitled *Ajia Taiheiyō Chiiki Keisei no Dōtei: Nichi-go no aidentitii mosaku to chiikishugi (The Creation of the Asia Pacific Region: A History of the Search for Self-inclusive Regions by Australian and Japanese Policy-makers and Scholars)* received the Masayoshi Ohira Memorial Prize and the Okita Saburo Award for Policy Studies in 2004. Her current research interests include the formation of the Asia Pacific Council (ASPAC) in the 1960s and the role of the United States in the development of multilateral institutions in the Asia–Pacific Region since the 1990s.

Caroline ROSE is senior lecturer in Japanese Studies and currently head of the Department of East Asian Studies at the University of Leeds. She received her BA and PhD at Leeds and has studied at Fudan University in Shanghai and Tsukuba University in Japan. Her specialism is contemporary Sino-Japanese relations, with particular reference to the history problem and reconciliation. She has published two monographs on Sino-Japanese relations and articles on Japanese history education, Chinese and Japanese nationalism, and Sino-Japanese relations in the East Asian context. Her current research focus is on reconciliation in North East Asia, the Yasukuni Shrine problem in Sino-Japanese relations, and Japanese diplomatic history of the First World War and the inter-war period.

SHIBAYAMA Futoshi is professor at the Faculty of Policy Studies, Aichi Gakuin University. He received his PhD in history from Yale University. He currently focuses on US–Japan Relations in the 1940s and the 1950s, Japanese intellectual history in the 20th century and Anglo-American military relations in the early Cold War period. His publications include 'US Strategic Debates over the Defense of Japan: Lessons for the Twenty-first Century' in *The Journal of American-East Asian Relations*, Vol. 9, Nos. 1 and 2, and other articles in the fields of military history and strategic studies.

TOMARU Junko was associate professor in the Faculty of Foreign Studies, Sophia University from 2002 to 2007 and is now professor in the School of

Political Science and Economics at Waseda University. Her field is post-war international history and international migration in the Asia–Pacific region, with a current focus on British and Japanese policies towards South-East Asia from the late 1940s to the 1960s. She received her BA and MA from the University of Tokyo, and her MLitt and DPhil degrees from the University of Oxford. Her publications include *The Postwar Rapprochement of Malaya and Japan, 1945–61* (Macmillan, 2000, awarded the Masayoshi Ohira Memorial Prize in 2001), and 'Formation and Transformation of British Cultural Policies in South-East Asia, 1942–1960' in *International Relations* (Japan Association of International Relations), vol. 146 (November 2006).

John SWENSON-WRIGHT is the Fuji Bank University Lecturer in Modern Japanese Studies and a fellow of Darwin College, Cambridge. A graduate of Oxford University and the Nitze School of Advanced International Studies (SAIS), Johns Hopkins University, in Washington, DC, he has a D.Phil. in International Relations from St. Antony's College, Oxford. His early research focused on early Cold War US–Japan foreign and security relations and was published as *Unequal Allies? United States Security and Alliance Policy Towards Japan, 1945–1960* by Stanford University Press in March 2005. His current interest focuses on contemporary political and security interests in North-East Asia, with particular reference to Japan and the Korean peninsula. In addition to his work at Cambridge, he is an Associate Fellow at Chatham House, where he convenes a research and discussion group on contemporary Korea.

John WESTE held lectureships in Japanese Studies at the University of Durham (1995–2004) and Leeds (2004–06). He studied in Japan at the University of Tsukuba and obtained his PhD from Cambridge. His publications cover areas including post-war Japanese rearmament and Anglo-Japanese relations.

Preface

This book is an analysis of Japanese diplomacy in the 1950s from a multilateral perspective, based on multiarchival research, by historians and political scientists working both in Japan and in the UK. The research for this joint project began with a series of seminars at Kobe University and the establishment of a research group to share findings with visiting scholars from abroad. The group developed a particular focus on Japanese diplomacy in the 1950s, a topic which, we considered, still lacked the academic attention and analysis it deserved. The project was generously funded by the Japan Society for the Promotion of Science (Grant-in-Aid for Scientific Research) and the Toshiba Foundation, which enabled us to hold three most inspiring and fruitful UK–Japan joint workshops between April 2001 and March 2004.

Until recently, studies of post-war Japanese diplomacy have tended to concentrate on Japan's bilateral relations with a particular country, especially the US, and to a lesser extent, the UK, the People's Republic of China, the Soviet Union, Korea and Indonesia, and so on. Only recently has scholarship begun to take a comparative stance on various bilateral relations and to treat post-war Japan in triangular or multilateral relations concerning particular issues such as the occupation of Japan, South-East Asian development and international associations such as the General Agreement on Tariffs and Trade (GATT) and the Bandung Conference. In addition, the opening of the hitherto confidential postwar archival documents after the lapse of the 30-year rule and the end of the Cold War has encouraged scholars to consult wider primary sources including those showing a multilateral perspective. These documents enable scholars to have a much more balanced view of the international background. Collaborative research is increasingly in vogue, enjoying the support of funding from research councils and national funding bodies. This has enabled scholars to share different perspectives through joint research projects. One recent contribution in this field is the five-volume series on the *History of Anglo-Japanese Relations, 1600–2000*, published both in English and Japanese with contributions by British, Australian and Japanese academics. Though the period covered is much narrower, this book can also take pride in having multinational contributors – five Japanese, one Ghanaian, two British, one

Australian, and one American – all having a command of at least two languages and having read archival documents from two or more countries.

We were very pleased to be able to continue with the project despite some changes in the membership and the movements of members between universities. These movements were due in part to somewhat disappointing developments, in the form of the closures of the Centre for Japanese Studies at Stirling University and the Department of East Asian Studies at Durham University. In any country, the scaling down of research on foreign countries in universities means a narrowing of the path to the understanding of international relations for a long time to come. It was especially sad, and ironic, to see the scaling down of Japanese Studies in Britain, at the very time that British Studies, especially the history of the British Empire and British diplomacy, was attracting so much academic interest in Japan and when calls for joint research were increasing. Therefore, this book is also a record of our perseverance and unshaken enthusiasm for joint study, despite the tide of contraction of Japanese Studies in the UK.

Professor Iokibe Makoto

Acknowledgements

The editors would like to thank all the contributors and those who attended the workshops and seminars since the inception of the project for their devotion and support throughout. We should like to express our particular gratitude to Professor Iokibe Makoto, President of the National Defense Academy and Emeritus Professor of Modern Japanese Political and Diplomatic History in the Graduate School of Law and Politics at Kobe University, for his thoughtful guidance, academic advice, and warm encouragement throughout the research project and the preparation of this book. In addition, our thanks go to Professor Tomaru Junko for her unstinting efforts throughout the project in maintaining communication between the UK-based and Japan-based members of the group, and in ensuring that we all kept to schedule. Linking our two academic communities in this way took both time and considerable patience, for which both of the UK-based editors are grateful. We would like to thank Professor Minohara Toshihiro at Kobe University for his valuable support throughout the project in maintaining a kind of roving secretariat with Professor Tomaru, and we are also indebted to Dr Hattori Satoshi for his assistance in the initial two years. Dr Kweku Ampiah, formerly of Stirling University and now at Leeds University, was kind enough to organize and host the first joint workshop at Stirling, and Dr John Swenson-Wright generously hosted the workshop at Cambridge with the help of Ms. Zoe Conway-Morris. Dr Ampiah deserves special thanks from all the joint project members for carrying out main contact role on the UK side for the first two years.

The contributors are most grateful to the Japan Society for the Promotion of Science for the Grant-in-Aid for Scientific Research, and the Toshiba Foundation for covering the research trips of some of the UK contributors. The research upon which much of this book is based would not have been possible without the support and forbearance of staff who assisted the contributors in their search for primary and secondary source material at various archives and libraries in the UK, US, Japan and other countries. We are also grateful to the accounting secretaries of Kobe University and Sophia University as the receiving bodies of the Grant-in-Aid for Scientific Research. We would also like to thank our editor at Routledge, Mr Peter Sowden, for his patience and forbearance.

Caroline Rose and John Weste

Note on style

Japanese and Chinese personal names appear in the conventional way with the surname first (for example, Kishi Nobusuke, Mao Zedong). In the case of Asian scholars who have published in English, however, the surname is given last according to Western convention. Chinese personal names are given in pinyin with the exception of those that remain more familiar in Wade Giles (for example, Chiang Kai-shek instead of Jiang Jieshi). Macrons are used to indicate long vowel sounds in Japanese, except when referring to familiar place names that are widely used in English (such as Tokyo).

Abbreviations and terms

ABCC	Atomic Bomb Casualty Commission
AEC	Atomic Energy Commission
Chōsen Sōren	Zainichi Chōsenjin Sōrengōkai, General Association of Korean Residents in Japan
CIA	Central Intelligence Agency
CINCFE	Commander-in-Chief, Far East Command
CITPC	China International Trade Promotion Committee
COS	(United Kingdom) Chiefs of Staff Committee
CRO	(United Kingdom) Commonwealth Relations Office
DS	(United States) Department of State
ECAFE	Economic Commission of Asia and the Far East
ECOSOC	(UN) Economic and Social Council
ECSC	Economic Coal and Steel Community
EEC	Economic Commission for Europe
EPA	Economic Planning Agency
FAO	(UN) Food and Agriculture Organization
FEC	Far East(ern) Command
FO	(United Kingdom) Foreign Office
GA	General Assembly
Gensuikyō	Japan Council against Atomic and Hydrogen Bombs
GHQ	General Headquarters
HMG	Her Majesty's Government
ICJ	International Court of Justice
ILO	International Labour Organization
IMF	International Monetary Fund
IOA	(United States) International Organizations Affairs Office
JCEIA	Japan China Export Import Association
JCP	Japan Communist Party
JCS	(United States) Joint Chiefs of Staff
JCTPDL	Japan China Trade Promotion Dietmen's League
JITPA	Japan International Trade Promotion Association

JLC(om)	Japan Logistical Command
JPS	(United Kingdom) Joint Planning Staff
JSP	Japan Socialist Party
JSPOG	Joint Strategic Plans and Operation Group
JSM	(United Kingdom) Joint Staff Mission
KMT	Kuomintang
LDP	Liberal Democratic Party
MITI	Ministry of International Trade and Industry
MoFA	(Japan) Ministry of Foreign Affairs
NATO	North Atlantic Treaty Organization
NPR(J)	National Police Reserve of Japan
OCB	Operations Co-ordinating Body
PPS	(United States) Policy Planning Staff
PRC	People's Republic of China
PSB	Psychological Strategy Board
RoC	Republic of China
SC	(United Nations) Security Council
SCAP	Supreme Commander of the Allied Powers
SDF	Self-Defence Forces
SEATO	South-East Asian Treaty Organization
UN	United Nations
UNESCO	UN Education, Science and Culture Organization
USIA	United States Information Agency
WHO	World Health Organization

Introduction

Caroline Rose and Tomaru Junko

The academic literature on post-war Japanese diplomacy has tended to overlook Japan's role in regional and global relations during the period between the end of the Allied occupation in 1952 and the start of Japan's rapid economic growth in the 1960s, generally presenting Japan as a passive actor of little relevance or importance. However, in terms of international relations, the 1950s were crucial as a transitional period in various ways: this decade saw the completion of post-war settlement schemes, the onset of the Cold War in East Asia with the establishment of the People's Republic of China (PRC) in 1949 and the Korean War in 1950, and extreme anti-communism of Western élites as symbolized by the domino theory and McCarthyism. The period also witnessed the acceleration of decolonization and the growth of Third World solidarity, the increase in the number of international actors in the form of non-governmental, regional and international organizations, and the rapid expansion of transnational movement of people, goods, and money. In other words, the 1950s can be defined as the period when global history and national history became ever closer and diplomacy became more entwined both with global trends and domestic issues.

In the face of such sweeping change, Japan did not sit passively by. On the contrary, as the chapters in the book reveal, there was a vitality to Japan's own visions of, and attempts at, rehabilitation and reintegration into the evolving regional and global structures. While Japan did not always figure as highly as its politicians and policy makers might have liked in the foreign policy considerations of other nation states (often being sidelined by others for their own strategic reasons), many countries did attach a great deal of importance to rebuilding relations with Japan throughout this period of readjustment and transformation.

This book, therefore, is an effort not only to shed light on Japan in the 1950s but also to place Japanese diplomacy in the wider multilateral context of post-war international relations and to analyse it from various perspectives and levels – namely, the political, economic, security aspects, as well as domestic, regional, and international levels. Our focus is on the process of Japan's attempts to rehabilitate itself and reintegrate into regional and international affairs, and the degree of success to which Japan attained what we identify as Tokyo's three main policy objectives. The first objective was Japan's return to Asia, much of which Japan had invaded or occupied during the Second World War. The second was Japan's (re-) entry into the global community and evolving international organizations. The third was to attain economic and military security through economic reconstruction, alliance formation, and rearmament. In order to achieve these objectives, the Japanese governments of the 1950s had to make various interrelated policy decisions, such as approaches to the US, the USSR, two Chinas, South-East Asian countries, the UK, the UN and other international or regional associations.

The contributors to this book consider Japan's approach towards the above three policy objectives from two core perspectives, namely international and regional conditions and domestic constraints. First, we explore how other nations and groups responded to Japanese initiatives and to what extent they supported or blocked Japanese efforts. As Japan attempted to return to the global community, pledging to be a member of Asia and a bridge between the East and the West, Japanese diplomatic initiatives often faced opposition from some Asian countries and the UK, who were wary of a resurgence of pre-war Japanese expansionism. The extent to which the external actors' own rivalries and interests produced differing responses to Japan is, therefore, a recurring theme throughout the book. Second, in terms of Japan's domestic environment, the contributors also consider which sections of Japanese society can be identified as supporting or opposing particular diplomatic policies, and the ways in which external diplomatic issues were sometimes utilized as a tool to promote or obscure domestic concerns.

The chapters in the book reveal the various ways in which change at national, regional, and international levels impacted upon Japan's foreign policy-making actors, but also how Japanese diplomatic behaviour impacted upon bilateral, regional and international developments. The 1950s was a decade of immense change for Japan, and it is worth rehearsing the major developments to provide a context for the chapters that follow.

Japan shifted in the 1950s from a state under occupation to an independent state keen to forge a (semi-) autonomous foreign policy, with a programme of economic rehabilitation under way and growing trade and investment links within the region and beyond. Political and social change was a key feature of the 1950s in Japan. Fissures soon emerged between the political left and right, creating a cleavage that was to last until well into the 1980s, and which split opinion on some of the key foreign policy concerns of the time, not least Japan's security. Two camps had already emerged by the late 1940s. On the one hand, the conservative camp favoured a pro-US, pro-UK stance for Japan – what was then called in Japan a 'partial peace' – while, on the other hand, the socialist camp favoured permanent neutrality and a 'comprehensive peace'.[1]

This domestic cleavage emerged against the backdrop of emerging Cold War politics in Asia. This was marked by the 1949 communist revolution in China, and the outbreak of the Korean War in June 1950, two events which, in US opinion, confirmed the importance of fully incorporating and retaining Japan as the key East Asian member of the Western, democratic camp. To this end, a peace treaty, which could be presented to the Japanese as balanced, non-punitive and a symbol of Japan's common interests with the free world was important. The signing of the 1951 San Francisco Peace Treaty, and the simultaneous signing of the US–Japan Security Treaty brought Tokyo very firmly into alignment with the capitalist world. Nonetheless, the Japanese government in the early 1950s was keen to avoid being integrated in America's alliance system in East Asia in terms of military co-operation and displayed caution in subsequent talks with the US on rearmament. A slight thaw in Cold War tensions emerged with the death of Stalin in March 1953, the end of the Korean War in July 1953, the Geneva Conference of April 1954 and the French surrender and eventual withdrawal from Vietnam. These develop-ments removed, to a certain extent, the tension surrounding the rearmament issue between the US and Japanese governments. In addition, the Japanese government had to turn its attention, and budget, to economic recovery once the Korean War boom ended. Tension between the US and Japan did increase, however, in the af-termath of the Lucky Dragon Incident of March 1954 when a Japanese crew of 23 was exposed to radioactive fallout from an American hydrogen bomb test in the Bikini atoll. The incident triggered the anti-nuclear movement in Japan, building upon the popular anti-militarist norm that had evolved after the war.

Political power changed hands a number of times in Japan in the 1950s, though remaining within the firm grasp of the conservative parties: Prime Minister Yoshida Shigeru's Liberal Party was in power from 1948 to 1954, followed by Hatoyama Ichirō's Democratic Party from 1954 to 1956. Ishibashi Tanzan of the newly merged Liberal Democratic Party (LDP) was prime minister for a brief period from December 1956 to February 1957, before illness forced him to resign whereupon Kishi Nobusuke, also of the LDP, became prime minister from 1957 to 1960. The merger of the two conservative parties in 1955, which marked the beginning of stable LDP leadership of Japanese politics until 1993, by no means guaranteed agreement on matters of foreign policy. Indeed, the lack of intra-party unity on such issues as the nature and speed of rearmament, the general balance of relations between the West and Asia, the degree to which Japan should rely upon the US, and the form of Japan's Russia and China policies were hotly contested in the 1950s. Each prime minister held a slightly different stance on foreign policy matters, thereby bringing about shifts in the country's foreign policy direction. The positions of each prime minister differed for a number of reasons: their own backgrounds, beliefs, allegiances and loyalties; constraints imposed by domestic constituencies; and a rapidly changing international geopolitical environment of-fering greater or lesser opportunities for economic interaction and the chance for reintegration into international society.

Prime Minister Yoshida was one of those who favoured the partial peace that would take Japan into the Western camp, binding it closer to the US in political and security terms and, increasingly, as the decade progressed, in economic terms. It also entailed Japan's recognition of the Republic of China (Taipei) as the sole rep-resentative of China, thereby deferring the fulsome development of economic and political links with North-East Asia, now predominantly under communist con-trol. However, Yoshida's foreign policy is also notable for its attempts to develop trade and cultural relations with the People's Republic of China (PRC) despite the constraints imposed by the US, and trading restrictions under the Co-ordinating

Committee for Multilateral Export Controls (COCOM) rules. Though a staunch critic of communism, Yoshida did not fully share the concerns of some in the US about the menace of a Sino-Soviet alliance, foreseeing instead the possibility of a split between the two communist countries.[2] A key element of his foreign policy was an appreciation of the need for Japan to avoid isolation and become a member of international society.[3] To achieve this, Japan needed to focus on reconstruction and the pursuit of economic growth that would be enabled through an expansion of foreign trade, which in turn necessitated good external relations. Even though the US–Japan relationship remained central to Japan's foreign policy after 1952, Japanese prime ministers nonetheless sought, albeit cautiously, to develop or re-kindle relations with, for example, Great Britain, the PRC, and South-East Asia.[4]

Yoshida was succeeded in 1954 by Hatoyama Ichirō, who, despite his personal opposition to Yoshida's policies, nonetheless left the fundamentals of Yoshida's foreign policy intact. While he argued that Yoshida had ' "sold out" Japan's na-tional interests' to the US, he concurred that trade would be the mainstay for Japan's survival on the international stage and that participation in international society was essential. Whereas Yoshida had talked more of relations with the free world and participation on a global scale, Hatoyama enunciated the specific need for Japan to become a 'member of Asia'.[5] He also stressed the importance of independence and self-reliance for Japan, seeking to reduce what he perceived as Japan's over-dependence on the US. He sought further 'expansion' of Japan's foreign policy activity through trade (for example, with the PRC), and was keen to normalize relations with the Soviet Union. Normalization would, it was hoped, achieve the two aims of resolving the Siberian prisoner of war issue, and secur-ing the USSR's support for Japan's entry to the UN.[6] The Soviet–Japanese Joint Declaration of October 1956 signalled, for many, Japan's return to international society and enabled Japan to become a member of the United Nations.

Although the inability to resolve the territorial dispute over the Kurile islands prevented the conclusion of a peace treaty with the Soviet Union, Hatoyama had succeeded in departing from the partial peace of the Yoshida years. This was not without some political cost, and Hatoyama's actions were strongly opposed do-mestically, not least by former prime minister Yoshida himself and the anti-main-stream factions. The US also exerted pressure on the Hatoyama government in the form of Secretary of State John Foster Dulles' warning that should Japan sign a peace treaty with the Soviet Union, the US would continue to occupy Okinawa. Amongst Hatoyama's other foreign policy goals were his desire to normalize rela-tions with the PRC, and the aim to set in motion the revision of the Security Treaty with a view to gaining greater autonomy with respect to the US and the removal of US military bases.[7] Illness forced Hatoyama to resign in December 1956. Had Ishibashi Tanzan, Hatoyama's immediate successor, not been struck down by ill health himself within two months of taking up prime ministerial office, it is likely that he would have pursued diplomatic normalization with the PRC. This prospect became increasingly unlikely, however, once Kishi Nobusuke became prime min-ister in February 1957, despite the fact that he had pledged to continue Ishibashi's policies, and reappointed all of Ishibashi's ministers.[8]

One of Kishi's main foreign policy objectives, akin to that of Hatoyama, was the revision of the US–Japan Security Treaty, the aim of which was to achieve a more equal status with the US. Kishi also proposed three principles of foreign policy, namely a UN-centred diplomacy, co-operation with the free world, and the maintenance of Japan's position as a member of Asia.[9] With regard to the third principle, Kishi envisaged a need for Japan to improve its status in the region, to improve 'welfare in Asia through development co-operation',[10] and to develop the Japanese economy through reparations and technical and economic assistance programmes. To that end, Kishi was keen for Japan to strengthen its links with South-East Asia, not least as a means of advancing Japan's economic power and regional influence, but also as a possible means of gaining greater equality with the US by taking a leadership role in South-East Asian development.[11]

The re-establishment of bilateral relations with South-East Asian nations had begun in the early 1950s under the Yoshida government, with reparations payments and the conclusion of peace treaties with those countries that had not participated in the San Francisco Peace Treaty. Rebuilding relations with South-East Asia was not an easy task, given varying degrees of anti-Japanese sentiment hailing from wartime experiences. In addition, the Cold War structure impeded Japan's interaction with the communist states of the region. Nonetheless, Kishi's two tours of South-East Asia and the despatch of reparations negotiators resulted in agreements with Burma, the Philippines, Indonesia, Laos, Cambodia, and Vietnam in the 1950s.[12] By contrast, Kishi seemed less concerned with improving relations with other East Asian nations, notably the PRC. A staunch anti-communist known for his pro-Taiwan rather than pro-Beijing leanings, Kishi angered the PRC by making a visit to Taiwan soon after taking office and proclaiming his support for Chiang Kai-shek's return to the mainland. Relations with the PRC were to deteriorate still further during Kishi's time in office, only to improve after he was forced out of office in the wake of the security treaty revision. Similarly, Japan's relations with South Korea, despite the attempts of the US to bring about some form of political co-operation, were hampered in the 1950s by animosity on both sides and an inability to agree on such issues as compensation, territorial disputes, and the status of the South Korean government.

It was ironic that, despite Kishi's initial intentions and some improvement in Japan's status with regard to the US as the result of the revision of the US–Japan Security Treaty, the revision blurred the issue of prior consultation, left the question of Okinawa reversion unresolved for another decade, and ultimately wedded Japan even more closely to America's Far Eastern security strategy. Japanese public protest against the revision grew to such an extent that Kishi had to resign from his premiership just after the ratification of the revised treaty in 1960.[13]

In spite of numerous difficulties posed by the legacy of Japan's wartime actions and the impediments presented by the post-war bipolar system, Japanese foreign policy makers were keen to be incorporated into newly evolving regional structures in the 1950s. East Asian groups and organizations began to form in the early 1950s in order to strengthen ties across a broad spectrum including economic, political, cultural themes. For example, taking a cue from the Asian

Relations Conference of 1947 organized and hosted by India, Asian countries began to coalesce with Arab countries in the UN in the latter months of 1950 on regional matters such as the Korean War. Asian countries also began overwhelmingly to challenge the opinions of non-regional powers such as the UK in the Economic Commission for Asia and Far East (ECAFE) from 1951. India, Burma, and Indonesia also began to develop closer contacts with the PRC.[14] The gradual departure of the former colonial powers added momentum to these trends as the newly democratizing and independent states started to formulate domestic and foreign policies aimed at recovery and growth.

An alternative to the East–West split began to emerge in the form of the non-aligned movement led by India and made up of Asian and African countries which rejected the notion of leaning to one or other side. The first high point of this trend came in April 1955 with the Asian–African Conference held in Bandung, Indonesia, and hosted by five Asian countries. It was the very first international conference to be attended exclusively by the official representatives of the 29 countries in Asia and Africa, most of which were newly independent. The Bandung declaration confirmed the group's joint determination to end imperialism, to attain racial equality and to seek peaceful settlement of conflicts. The Japanese government considered the invitation to this conference as an ideal opportunity to gain acceptance back into Asia. However, in view of the American fear of communist influence and British apprehension of anti-colonial radicalism in the conference, Japan had to assume a rather low-profile role.[15]

Beyond the region, Japan was also aware of the need to reintegrate itself into international society. The first half of the 1950s saw the expansion of membership in international organizations, not least the UN. Japan sought a place in these bodies, for example by applying for membership to the International Monetary Fund (IMF) and the General Agreement on Tariffs and Trade (GATT) in 1952. The US sponsored Japan's accession to such bodies, but such applications were not always readily accepted: the UK, for example, opposed Japan's application to GATT for fear of Japanese competition and out of a certain amount of antipathy relating to the war. It was not until 1955 that Japan gained entry. Similarly, Japan's acceptance into the UN was achieved only after lengthy negotiations and complicated politicking which often had little to do with Japan's qualities per se and much more to do with symbolic politics of allegiance and alliance during the Cold War.

By the end of the 1950s, Japan was actively pursuing three major objectives: economic and military security; a return to Asia; and re-entry to the global community. This book considers these broad objectives in more detail by focusing on specific issues and events.

Organization of the book

The book is divided into three parts, each containing three chapters: Part I looks at Japan in the eyes of the Anglo-American powers; Part II at Japanese efforts to gain membership of newly forming regional and international organizations; and Part III considers the role of domestic factors in Japanese foreign policy.

In Chapter 1, Shibayama Futoshi reveals that, although attaching little importance to Japan itself, the US and the UK initially had very different views of where Japan fitted into definitions of the *casus belli* for a counter-nuclear assault. By early 1952, reflecting American predominance in East Asia and within the Anglo-American relationship, the UK came to agree with the US and accepted that an attack on Japan could constitute *casus belli*. John Weste's chapter (Chapter 2) shows Britain's uncertainties and internal rivalries as to the depth of post-war Japanese democracy and any future military role for Japan. The UK's willing acceptance that the US hold the determining external role in Japanese rearmament further emphasizes the relative decline of British influence in East Asia. In Chapter 3, Tomaru Junko traces the UK's changing view of Japan's role in South-East Asia and sees a wary convergence of Anglo-Japanese interests in South-East Asia from 1953, and on the UN membership issue after the Bandung Conference in 1955.

In Chapter 4, Kweku Ampiah considers Japan's participation in the Bandung Conference, focusing on American concerns about Japanese behaviour. The chapter also points to Japan's attempts to act independently of the US and to seize the opportunity the Conference offered to develop contacts with Asian countries. In Chapter 5, Oba Mie looks at the process of Japanese entry into the UN's Economic Commission for Asia and the Far East (ECAFE) in 1954 with particular reference to the developing notion of Asian identity, Japan's potential economic role in Asia, and the Asian response to Japanese participation. Chapter 6 by Kurusu Kaoru highlights the 'symbolic politics' surrounding the question of Japan's UN membership, a reflection of Cold War geopolitics. The chapter illustrates the ambivalence of other countries towards Japan's quest for membership in 1955, in contrast with Japan's own emphasis on the membership issue.

The three chapters in Part III highlight the role of domestic factors in Japanese foreign policy planning, and reveal the pluralistic nature of foreign policy making through case studies on the Lucky Dragon Incident, the return of Okinawa from the US to Japan, and Sino-Japanese relations. John Swenson-Wright's chapter (Chapter 7) focuses on the Lucky Dragon Incident as an example of the potential strains between the two alliance partners with America holding the senior position, and Japan the junior. He considers the extent to which American concerns over Japan's capacity to sustain a stable and reliable position within the alliance, as highlighted by a Russian defector and a domestic Japanese spy scandal, affected American views of Japan as a trustworthy partner. In Chapter 8, Robert Eldridge analyses Japanese foreign policy formation with regard to the revision of the US–Japan security treaty and Okinawa factor, arguing that policy making was hindered by party politics and politicians' personal rivalries, in addition to competing pressures from the bureaucracy, press, and public opinion. These factors contributed to Okinawa not being included in the revised treaty area, probably causing the delay in Okinawa's eventual return to Japanese administration. In Chapter 9, Caroline Rose examines Japanese policy planning towards the PRC and highlights the level of interest within certain sectors in Japan in maintaining links with its neighbour despite the rupture in 1958. She explores the use of informal diplomacy, arguing that this was an important means of keeping the channels of communication between the two countries open, but that differences of opinion within the LDP on its China policy hampered attempts to return the PRC–Japan relationship to some semblance of normality.

Some recurring themes emerge from this study of Japan's foreign policy in the 1950s. A number of the authors note the importance with which Japanese, and at times US, officials viewed the need for Japan to restore its status in the region as soon as possible. This can be seen in the efforts made by Japanese officials to secure the country's involvement in ECAFE in the early 1950s (Chapter 5), or in the US perception of the need for Japan to attend the Bandung Conference to prevent its isolation from Asian countries (Chapter 4). At the same time, the US and indeed other countries displayed a certain amount of residual distrust in Japan's foreign policy choices. Some in the US were concerned about neutralist tendencies in Japan, and the disturbing potential for Japan to forge closer links with the communist bloc. Tomaru (Chapter 3) and Weste (Chapter 2) note that the UK recognized Japan's growing importance in the 1950s, but harboured some suspicions of Japan's intentions. The conscious attempts to move towards an independent foreign policy is noted in a number of chapters, for example Ampiah (Chapter 4), Kurusu (Chapter 6) and Rose (Chapter 9). These chapters illustrate, for example, the fact that Japanese officials were not always able to rely on the United States to represent Japan's interests in the region and internationally, or that Japanese policy simply differed from that of the US and Japanese interests might be better served by not adhering to the US line. As a result, Japanese policy makers sought a more independent path. Finally, the chapters that focus on the domestic context of Japanese foreign policy (Chapters 7–9) show that its formation was subject to the pressures of competing views and influences, demonstrating the democratic and pluralist nature of the policy-making process, but at the same time often limiting the extent to which policy makers could act effectively. Never monolithic, Japanese foreign policy and diplomatic ventures of the 1950s yet again confirm what we are now understanding to be the complexities involved in any state coming to terms, reluctantly and otherwise, with changing international, regional and domestic conditions.

Notes

1 Togo Kazuhiko, *Japan's Foreign Policy 1945–2003*, Leiden: Brill, 2003, p. 49; Hosoya Chihiro, *San Furanshisuko kōwa e no michi*, Tokyo: Chūō Kōronsha, 1984, pp. 258–65.
2 Togo, *Japan's Foreign Policy*, p.119; Kōsaka Masataka, *Saishō Yoshida Shigeru*, Tokyo: Chūō Kōronsha, 1968, pp. 61–62.
3 B. Edstrom, *Japan's Evolving Foreign Policy Doctrine: From Yoshida to Miyazawa*, Basingstoke: Macmillan, 1999, p.13.
4 Edstrom, *Evolving Foreign Policy*, p. 22-3; J.W. Dower, *Empire and Aftermath: Yoshida Shigeru and the Japanese Experience, 1878–1954*, Cambridge, MA: Harvard University Press, 1979, Chapter 12; Kōsaka, *Saishō Yoshida Shigeru*, pp. 80, 117.
5 Edstrom, *Evolving Foreign Policy*, pp. 26–8.
6 Iokibe Makoto, *Sengo Nihon gaikōshi*, Tokyo: Yūhikaku Aruma, 1999, pp. 79–80.
7 Iokibe, *Gaikōshi*, p. 85. For US–Japan relations during the Yoshida and Hatoyama ad-

ministrations see also Michael Schaller, *Altered States: The United States and Japan since the Occupation*, New York: Oxford University Press, 1997; and Ishii Osamu, *Reisen to Nichibei kankei: Pātonashippu no keisei*, Tokyo: Japan Times, 1989.
8 Edstrom, *Evolving Foreign Policy*, p. 35.
9 Iokibe, *Gaikōshi*, p. 88.
10 Togo, *Japan's Foreign Policy*, p. 197.
11 Iokibe, *Gaikōshi*, p. 92. For details on post-war Japan–Asia relations from 1952 see L. Olson, *Japan in Postwar Asia*, New York: Praeger, 1970.
12 South Vietnam had signed and ratified the San Francisco Peace Treaty but also received reparations from Japan. 'Semi-reparations' were agreed with Thailand, Malaysia, and Singapore during the 1960s.
13 For details on the revision, see Sakamoto Kazuya, *Nichibei Dōmei no Kizuna: Anpo kaitei to sōgōsei no mosaku*, Tokyo: Yūhikaku, 2000, Chapter 4; and R. Buckley, *US-Japan Alliance Diplomacy, 1945–1990*, Cambridge: Cambridge University Press, 1992, pp. 69–98.
14 Okakura Koshirō, *Bandon kaigi to 50 nendai no Ajia*, Tokyo: Daitō Bunka University Tōyō Kenkyūjo, 1986, pp. 25–33.
15 Miyagi Taizō, *Bandon kaigi to Nihon no Ajia fukki: Amerika to Ajia no Hazama de*, Tokyo: Sōshisha, 2001; K. Ampiah, 'Japan at the Bandung Conference', *Japan Forum*, 7–1, 1995, pp. 15–24; Okakura, *Bandon Kaigi*.

Part I

Japan, Anglo-American rivalry, and indifference

1 The US, Britain, Japan, and the issue of *casus belli* 1951–2

Could a Soviet attack on Japan justify starting a third world war?

Shibayama Futoshi

To what extent did the United States commit itself to the defence of Japan by the September 1951 US–Japan Security Treaty? This has been a longstanding and contentious issue amongst Japanese, but newly declassified British documents provide us with new and reliable materials to help address this question. On 13 September 1951, the chairman of the US Joint Chiefs of Staff (JCS), General Omar N. Bradley, informed the new chief of the British Joint Staff Mission (JSM), Air Chief Marshal Sir William Elliot, that the United States was determined to defend Japan even at the risk of starting a third world war with atomic weapons. This statement was made only five days after the US and Japan signed the Security Treaty in San Francisco.

> Take the situation in Japan. Your paper [COS (51) 106-British document on *casus belli* of the third world war] does not discuss that. If the Soviet Union should jump on Japan we would be in a general war and we probably would recommend use of the A-bomb. Japan is as important to US strategically as the Soviet central position is to them.[1]

This confirmed Britain's great fear that the US believed a Soviet attack on Japan would be a *casus belli* for an all-out war, which would inevitably mean a Soviet atomic counter-bombardment of London.

At that time, the US military believed that the establishment of a powerful Japanese ground force was indispensable for deterring the Russians from commencing their amphibious attacks on Japan proper. Most American ground forces in East Asia were engaged in fierce fighting in the Korean War, which broke out in June 1950, and the Japanese archipelago was left highly vulnerable. This chapter charts the often heated Anglo-American discussions on the issues of *casus belli*, the related issue of Japanese rearmament and particularly the US view of the Japanese National Police Reserve (NPR). It also considers how the Japanese viewed the NPR.[2]

No stop line in Japan: COS (51) 106 and the British approach to a Soviet attack on Japan

In early January 1951, US forces in Korea were facing savage Chinese assaults, which threatened an American retreat from Korea. Simultaneously, the US was also concerned that their intelligence indicated a Soviet military build-up in East Asia, possibly for an attack on Japan. To the Americans, this attack would mean all-out war and the use of atomic bombs. However, between the US and Britain, there was an enormous difference in how each interpreted the term 'all-out war'. At a meeting of 24 January 1951 between the JCS and the State Department, despite the US struggle in Korea, the JCS claimed that 'in general, from a military point of view, time is on our side'.[3] Indeed, in the background to this statement was the fact that the US enjoyed a distinct military advantage: by late 1950, it already possessed over 500 atomic bombs and at least 264 bombers to deliver them.[4] Furthermore, the US had already established a network of forward bases surrounding the Soviet Union, while Russia held no forward bases with which to threaten the US. There was no immediate and massive Soviet atomic threat to the continental United States and the Americans expected that US industrial power could easily overwhelm that of Russia, particularly after a US nuclear strike. To the British, this ultimate American victory would mean nothing if a Soviet atomic and/or conventional air attack from its European bases devastated the British Isles. This difference in understanding, and possible consequences of an all-out war led to a divergence in Anglo-American policy on how to respond to a Soviet attack on Japan.

The UK Chiefs of Staff Committee (COS), in a 27 February 1951 report did not include a Soviet attack on Japan in the list of 'circumstances which at present seem to justify the launching of full-scale atomic war'.[5] It considered that Soviet aggression against West Germany, Austria (including Vienna) and Turkey would become a *casus belli*, while an attack on Greece would become so only 'if the situation cannot be restored by any other means'.[6] An attack on Berlin was equally a possible cause for war.[7] In the case of a possible escalation of the Korean War to a general East Asian war, the British military feared that an American knee-jerk response would be to launch a global war against Russia. They intended to contain any American panic by delineating the so-called 'stop line', that is the geographic line of *casus belli*, Russian violation of which would prompt both the US and UK to agree to all-out war. To the British, no East Asian concern should ever be deemed a justifiable *casus belli* given that it would expose Western Europe, and more specifically Great Britain, to a catastrophic Russian attack. The COS concluded that, first, a US nuclear assault could never deliver a knock-out blow to Russia and, second, that the Soviets, despite the US strike, would overwhelm continental Western Europe and 'inflict very serious damage on the United Kingdom'.[8]

Prior to the COS report, the British military had already intended to approve Japanese rearmament, primarily for Japan's own internal security, but also to repel, in conjunction with US forces, a Soviet invasion. It was still far from a *casus belli*.

In a report of 4 December 1950, the Joint Planning Staff (JPS) recommended that 'Japan should be permitted forces of a size suitable to carry out her obligations for internal security and defence' and that Japanese armed forces should consist of 'naval vessels up to frigates, excluding submarines', and balanced air forces, except for strategic bombers.[9] With China's entry into the Korean War and the subsequent full-scale UN retreat, the JPS claimed that these events further underlined 'the necessity for Japanese rearmament in the near future', and that, related to the conclusion of a peace treaty, 'some arrangement' should be made 'to ensure that US forces do not actually leave Japan until sufficient Japanese forces are available to ensure the security of Japan in the event of Russian aggression'.[10] On 11 December 1950, COS, on the basis of the JPS report, in turn proposed a US–Japan bilateral defence pact and the formation of balanced Japanese armed forces (but lacking large naval vessels and strategic bombers).[11] COS departed from the 1949 JPS report, which had not condoned air and sea forces for Japan.[12]

In February 1951, COS believed that the Soviets would not dare to attack Japan due to America's strategic command of Japan's air and sea lanes. However, the British worried about the American belief in a monolithic Sino-Soviet relationship and the subsequent notion that any threat of an atomic bombing on Russia would force the Chinese to cease any military attack on neighbouring countries. The British firmly believed that the People's Republic of China was not a mere satellite of the Soviet Union, and that any atomic threat to Russia would be utterly useless in controlling the Chinese. Thus, COS concluded that atomic warfare in East Asia was militarily meaningless and politically disastrous, and recommended that the British government should discuss the 'stop line' with the US as soon as possible.[13] At a 6 March Staff Conference on COS (51)106, Prime Minister Clement R. Attlee underlined that the British government never intended to 'hand over to America the decision to use the atomic weapon or to issue an ultimatum'.[14] Two weeks later, the British ambassador in Washington, Sir Oliver Franks, suggested to the Staff Conference that the British government should present COS (51)106 to the US and involve Secretary of State Dean Acheson, Secretary of Defense George C. Marshall, and hopefully US President Harry S. Truman's adviser, W. Averrell Harriman, in the discussions. Attlee directed Franks to make 'this preliminary approach to the Americans' as soon as possible.[15]

The US military concern: a Soviet attack on Japan and its global meaning

Since late 1950, the US military had become concerned about a possible Soviet invasion of Japan. On 19 December 1951, Marshall spoke of Japan's vulnerability to a Soviet attack.[16] In turn, Douglas MacArthur requested that Washington send four National Guard divisions, then in training, to Japan. Concerned about 'the increased Soviet activity reported in the Maritime Provinces' and 'reports of a build-up of Soviet and unrepatriated Japanese forces in Sakhalin', MacArthur, on 7 January 1951, ordered augmented 'reconnaissance of the vulnerable North and West approaches to Hokkaido'.[17] In a 9 January teletype conference, the Far

East Command (FEC) warned the Department of Army of the possibility that the Soviets might invade Japan under the cover of 'a puppet Japanese Gov[ernmen]t in exile' and its Japanese forces, while, in fact, leaving 'actual assault and combat op[eratio]ns to Soviet line div[ision]s'.[18] At a 15 January meeting with Chief of Staff of US Air Force, General Hoyt B. Vandenberg, and Chief of Staff of the US Army, General John Lawton Collins, MacArthur claimed 'with some emotion, that his command should not be held responsible for the defense of Japan while required to hold in Korea'. He then suggested confronting this possible Soviet threat with a combination of 'four light Japanese divisions' and two, possibly four, American National Guard divisions, though their deployment in Japan was not yet decided.[19]

In a 30 January 1951 memorandum, MacArthur requested that JCS equip the NPR to the level of a *de facto* army with heavy equipment including medium tanks and heavy artillery.[20] Collins also supported MacArthur's recommendation, since JCS had already approved the Joint Outline War Plan 'REAPER' (7 December 1950), which assumed the outbreak of general war in 1954, and included a force of 10 Japanese divisions 'as a goal'.[21] Moreover, the US Army estimated that in 1951, Japanese divisions together with US forces would hold Japan against Soviet attacks, while North Atlantic Treaty Organization (NATO) forces would not hold out in Europe. The US Army was concerned about the possible psychological shock of simultaneously losing both continental Western Europe and Japan at the beginning of an all-out war. Collins recommended that JCS should refer this issue to the Secretary of Defense for further discussion with the Secretary of State and the President.[22] Even before the JCS decision, he recommended that the Department of Army, owing to the military urgency, should send heavy equipment to the NPR under the name of the 'Special Far East Command Reserve', but that it should be withheld from the Japanese for the time being.[23]

On 5 February 1951, the JCS approved Collins' proposal. On 15 February, Marshall asked Acheson's approval for a draft letter to Truman:

> The Joint Chiefs of Staff consider, and I strongly agree, that the gravity of the current threat to the security of Japan makes it urgent to ship immediately to General MacArthur the equipment which he has requested. According to the Joint Chiefs of Staff, this threat is expected to become particularly acute by early May. This threat consists of a Soviet capability to mount amphibious and air borne attacks on Japan, the present absence of ground forces to defend Japan, and the improved weather conditions expected in late April and May in the area.[24]

The US military now presented Japanese rearmament as a preparation against a direct Soviet threat to Japan.

In a 23 February 1951 memo, Brigadier General Ridgely Gaither warned the chief of G-3,[25] Major General Maxwell Taylor, that the Soviet threat to Japan could topple not only the US defence of Japan, but also the entire American global strategic planning.[26] He complained that the severe shortage of US ground forces in Japan guarding against direct and indirect Soviet threats sharply increased Japan's vulnerability. He estimated that, by mid-April, the Soviet Union could employ as many as 'ten divisions in amphibious operations against Japan, supported by one airborne division and large air force units'.[27] According to his perspective, the Soviets, by starting a war in East Asia, could divide the US and its NATO allies, force the US to withdraw from Korea and to terminate its naval protection of Formosa. Furthermore, he warned that this development would impede American military deployment in Europe and force the US to persuade its NATO allies to use A-bombs as compensation for the lack of conventional troops:

> Assuming that Russia is well aware of our troop dispositions, and our intent to rearm Japan to some degree, its present defenseless picture might well be the deciding factor as she weighs the timing of open war. By a stroke against Hokkaido she could:

> a   Engage US in the Far East with an excellent chance that our NATO Allies might not become involved.
> b   Cause our immediate withdrawal from Korea.
> c   So engage our Naval Forces as to uncover Formosa to an attack by the Chinese Communist forces.
> d   Seriously compromise our European deployment:

> > 1   With the 8th Army in serious danger, we would certainly have to deploy all available combat-ready forces to insure its extrication.
> > 2   With the prospect of a major war in Asia, we would have to reinforce Okinawa and Alaska.
> > 3   With Europe still quiet we would be faced with the problem of persuading reluctant NATO allies to authorize opening of Atomic warfare from allied bases.[28]

In order to avoid this fate, Gaither recommended a rapid build-up of ground troops in Japan by despatching two National Guard divisions and shipping heavy equipment to the NPR. Despite this evaluation, on 1 March 1951, the State Department demanded the postponement of furnishing the Japanese with heavy equipment until the successful conclusion of a peace treaty. On 2 April, Marshall yielded to the State Department proposal.[29]

The Japanese government's views on rearmament and the Soviet threat to Japan

Differing from the US military leaders, Japan's prime minister, Yoshida Shigeru, never believed that the Soviets would attempt any direct attack on Japan. On 13 January 1951, Yoshida stated that with the

> situation objectively viewed, both blocs will never go to an all-out war. [The] present confrontation will eternally continue, though, from time to time, there

will be ups and downs, during which [Japan] should not be tricked by psychological warfare claiming, 'War will break out soon.' I think that the Soviet Union will never invade Japan.[30]

He made this statement to a retired diplomat, Hotta Masaaki, who had expressed concern over a potential Soviet invasion of Hokkaido at a meeting of Yoshida's military advisors on 26 December 1950. Hotta believed that any Soviet invasion would take the form of guerrilla-style warfare, and 'not real military action', possibly with the 'Red Japanese' returning from the Soviet Union.[31] (The Japanese government believed that the detained Japanese POWs were being brainwashed to become Soviet agents or warriors for Communism.) Yoshida never changed his stance, even at the famous Yoshida–Dulles Conference during January–February 1951 on the Japanese peace settlement. At a 31 January meeting, Yoshida told John F. Dulles, US ambassador responsible for the Japanese peace settlement, that there was no 'immediate danger' in East Asia. He went on to ask where Dulles thought the immediate danger would emerge, stating that he believed it would be Europe. He added that without clarification of this point it would be hard to formulate any concrete security policies.[32] However, Yoshida admitted his unfamiliarity with present global military conditions, and requested further information from Dulles.[33]

There was also evidence that the Japanese government expected a British initiative to end the Korean conflict. On 5 October 1950, Yoshida stated that he deplored that Britain had come 'down in the world', but Japanese diplomats still believed Britain to be a master of diplomacy.[34] On 10 January 1951, the American consulate in Sapporo, Richard B. Finn, indicated to his Japanese counterpart that the US would, in a 'matter of time', withdraw its troops from Korea and even more vigorously encourage Japan's rearmament.[35] Faced with this depressing prospect, the Japanese diplomat expressed his hope that the 'big power in Western Europe', Britain, would succeed in its diplomatic efforts to prevent any further military escalation. Finn pointed out British military weaknesses, arguing that British diplomacy was thereby weakened, and claimed that only the US could take responsibility for maintaining world peace.[36]

Yoshida believed that the Japanese government should prepare to guard less against external than against internal threats, notably the Japanese Communist Party (JCP) and the Chōsen Sōren (Zainichi Chōsenjin Sōrengōkai, the General Association of Korean Residents in Japan). At a 19 January 1951 meeting, Yoshida's military advisers met to settle the size of Japan's security forces. Former Rear Admiral Tomioka Sadatoshi presented his assumptions for the case of internal disturbances: 15 per cent of Japanese communists and Chōsen Sōren would be lightly armed and active insurgents, while a limited number of troops sent by a foreign power might also be expected to participate.[37] He estimated that the Japanese government had to establish a ground security force of 120,000 men to protect against domestic insurgents only, or 150,000 if to also ward off insurgents aided by enemy troops.[38] Tomioka was at first reluctant to present figures for a coastal security force on the basis of domestic security concerns only, because he intended to acquire governmental acceptance of as large a coastal security force as possible. However, Hotta forced Tomioka to present a figure by reiterating the Japanese government's frame of reference, that is: 'if war [with the Soviet Union] breaks out, America should take care of all. What number is the minimum for a coastal security force, only for the guarantee of internal security?'[39] Tomioka presented a figure of 80,000 tons of naval vessels, with the largest ships being destroyers of 1,500 tons.[40]

However, Yoshida's military advisers also argued for the need to create armed forces capable of meeting external security needs while simultaneously respecting Yoshida's basic stance. At this same 19 January meeting, former Lieutenant General Kawabe Torashirō pointed out that internal disturbances and a war might occur simultaneously. He stressed the need to prepare for external security, either with or without US or UN assistance.[41] However, Hotta countered Kawabe's opinion arguing that 'either America or the UN would defend Japan'.[42] Former General Shimomura Tadashi agreed to limit the remit of future Japanese ground forces to guard against the JCP and Chōsen Sōren, but he also indicated that Japan should plant the 'seeds of military preparedness for defence against an external threat'.[43] He acknowledged that Japan should expect the US to cover areas where Japan was unable to defend its national territory, but he calculated that an absolute minimum of ground forces for internal security should number 200,000, consisting of 150,000 troops and 50,000 officers and cadres.[44] Those who attended accepted this number in addition to 80,000 tons of vessels for the coastal security force.[45] They also agreed to a small number of aircraft as a part of ground and coastal defence forces. Kawabe claimed that in terms of air defence, American power was inadequate, and that Japanese participation was essential. He called for the nurturing of an air corps as the 'seed of a future air force'. Shimomura went as far as to suggest 2,000 aeroplanes, but Tomioka admonished him saying that this number would be difficult to realize.[46] Setting aside the matter of air power, the Japanese government used the conclusions of the 19 January meeting to prepare for the Dulles–Yoshida conference.[47]

Yoshida was prepared to accept informal rearmament to promote the conclusion of a peace treaty and to avoid any constitutional amendment.[48] At a 3 February 1951 meeting, he notified the Americans of his wish to establish informal armed forces under the name of a police force. According to Japanese minutes of meetings over 6–7 February, MacArthur and Dulles accepted Yoshida's approach, although the proposed size of ground forces was at first merely 50,000, consisting entirely of officers and cadres.[49] In fact, both FEC and the Pentagon accepted the notion of informal rearmament, but they could not afford to accept Yoshida's vision aimed at slowly developing the army from an officer corps of 50,000 to a 200,000-strong ground force, due to the ongoing military emergency.

MacArthur immediately assigned the NPR to the mission of assuring internal security. On 1 March 1951, the FEC circulated 'Operation Order No. 1 Emergency Alert Plan', aimed at suppressing any Japanese communist insurgency, 'insidious propaganda, strikes, or open conflict' and countering limited Soviet military action.[50] By this order, the FEC could mobilize 'the metropolitan Tokyo

Police, the National Rural Police and the National Reserve Police'.[51] At the same time, the FEC intended to regard the NPR as an indispensable force in the event of a Soviet attack on Japan. As early as 3 April 1951, the FEC integrated NPR forces into an emergency war plan to counter massive Soviet intervention into the Korean conflict and a direct attack on Japan. This plan considered the withdrawal of UN forces from Korea to Japan in order to concentrate them for the defence of Japan. However, before the arrival of these troops in Japan, FEC expected the NPR to provide 'ground defense of assigned sector'; that is, southern and northern Japan.[52] However, immediately prior to President Truman recalling MacArthur, General Matthew B. Ridgway and MacArthur agreed that Soviet military intentions were still 'entirely defensive'.[53]

Anglo-American negotiations on *casus belli*

The American response to British requests for talks on *casus belli* was quite slow. In May 1951, the British indicated to the Americans their desire to hold discussions on COS (51)106. On 4 May 1951, the director of the US Policy Planning Staff (PPS), Paul Nitze, H. Freeman Matthews of the State Department, and Chief of Air Staff, Royal Air Force, Sir John Slessor discussed COS (51)106. Nitze pointed out that the British document did not include Japan in the list of *casus belli*. Slessor suggested that the British would 'give further consideration to this problem'.[54] On 12 May, Franks and Sir Roger Makins of the Foreign Office requested that the US should commence its examination of the report. Franks initially provided Acheson with a copy and, then, Slessor, Elliot, Nitze, and Sir Christopher Steel of the British Embassy held a luncheon discussion on its contents. Meanwhile, Elliot expressed the British hope that the JCS, 'after having studied the paper, would produce a comparable paper setting out the American view'.[55]

In fact, the Americans had already considered the *casus belli* issue. In early April 1951 Carlton Savage of the PPS had already prepared a paper, 'Circumstances Under Which the United States Would Be at War with the Soviet Union: use of Atomic Weapons'.[56] Departing from the British position, he focused upon whether or not the Soviets intended to start a general war, rather than whether or not the Americans should use atomic bombs. He recommended that the US should start an all-out war only in the case of the Soviets attacking US territory, NATO countries, Berlin, Vienna, Greece, and Japan. However, in the case of a Russian attack on Japan or a large-scale intervention in the Korean War, he still suggested that the US should attempt to localize the conflict as much as possible. Only if this were not possible should the US enter into all-out war.[57]

Furthermore, Savage claimed that the US should not necessarily rely on Anglo-American co-operation on the issues of *casus belli* and the use of atomic bombs:

> In discussions with the British we must make no commitments restricting the freedom of the United States to use atomic weapons whenever we consider their use necessary. In turn, we can expect no British commitment, beyond

that contained in the Atlantic Treaty, to go to war with US against the Soviet Union in future contingencies.[58]

In short, he suggested that, beyond the provisions of the Atlantic Treaty, the US and the UK should enjoy military freedom of action, and both countries could disagree on Far Eastern issues.

The US military was also concerned about the uneasy relationship developing between the US and the UK, particularly with regards to Far Eastern issues. The biggest disagreements lay in the assessment of the PRC's loyalty to the Soviet Union and in the significance of Far Eastern issues to the Western strategic position in general. The US military disagreed with what it held to be the overly optimistic British view that the PRC was not a faithful and obedient ally of the Soviet Union, and was concerned about the possibility that the US would have to fight on the Chinese mainland without British assistance. Moreover, it feared that NATO countries would not fight Soviet 'volunteers' over what was for them an 'insignificant' Far Eastern issue.[59] In other words, the Joint Strategic Survey Committee (JSSC) could not imagine that NATO countries would risk World War Three, meaning the utter devastation of Western Europe, for the defence of East Asian nations. The best countermeasure was to preserve the American free hand in military operations in the Far East without causing any political and military strain on US relations with the UN, NATO and Great Britain. This also meant that the US should establish Far Eastern military command arrangements in which it could freely use Japan and other island nations in the Pacific for military operations, while minimizing any British and NATO political intervention.[60]

In this context, the JSSC claimed that, as a minimum, the US should be able to use Japanese bases for any exigency in the Far East, with or without UN aegis. It expected that, even under a military alliance with Japan, 'the maximum arrangements should envisage not only rights similar to those in the treaty concerning military bases in the Philippines but also a treaty of alliance with Japan'.[61] However, this alliance was not to be at the same level as NATO, but rather one like the Pacific Pact, which Dulles was then advocating.[62] In practice, this meant that the US would not share war plans and military organization with Japan and could still dominate this military alliance. On 20 April 1951, the JCS approved this remarkable report, authorized Collins to inform the assistant secretary of the army, Earl D. Johnsonn, of its contents, and forwarded a memorandum to Marshall in which they claimed that the revised addendum of the US–Japan Security Treaty did not still satisfy the JCS.[63]

For the British, the US reaction to the issues of *casus belli* and the use of atomic bombs was still irritatingly slow. On 19 July, Franks informed Acheson of how much importance the British attached to this issue and criticized the fact that 'some of the Military in the Pentagon, particularly the [US] Air Force, were anxious to evade so far as possible political limitations on their power to strike'. He stressed that this issue was so highly political in nature that it should 'not be dealt with on a purely military basis'. Acheson answered that Franks' 'intuition about part of the Pentagon was not wrong', and he agreed that this issue was 'ultimately political'. He then acknowledged the significance of holding Anglo-American military talks before any politico-military talks.[64] On 31 July, Makins informed Franks that holding military talks first conflicted with an agreement amongst the cabinet-level ministers of attending to this issue 'as a politico-military matter', but Attlee approved Acheson's idea of 'preliminary talks at the Military level'.[65]

Japanese rearmament and Ridgway's fear of a Soviet attack on Japan

At a 4 July 1951 command conference, Ridgway changed his evaluation of Soviet intentions from 'defensive' to aggressive: he 'felt the time may have come for this command [FEC] to take some additional measures in preparation for possible Soviet hostilities.'[66] He became particularly nervous about 'the fact the Soviets were stocking POL [petroleum]', and he directed his 'commanders to give this considerable thought and discuss it with him at their next meeting'. He also reported his interview with Yoshida on 3 July, in which, after explaining 'Soviet capabilities', he urged the Japanese government to start 'their civil air defense preparations' and to promote 'co-ordination between police reserve [NPR] and our [American] field commanders'. He believed that the co-ordination would 'be vitally necessary if police reserve units are to be used effectively'.[67] On 25 July, Ridgway directed his subordinates to make thorough preparations for a Soviet attack, and was particularly worried about the timings of the Korean armistice talks and the Japanese peace conference.[68]

In a 2 August cable, Ridgway now suggested to Washington that the Soviets might engage in a general war concentrating on East Asia while adopting a posture of active defence in Europe. He warned that the Soviets might 'avoid hostilities in Europe if practicable, but if forced . . . [would] conduct an active defense in such manner as to seek to avoid invoking North Atlantic Treaty obligations'.[69] This notion derived from the Far East Command's war games CINCFE Operations Plan 4–51, which took place in June 1951. Ridgway also estimated that, even if the NATO allies simultaneously entered into war with the US, Russia could employ its 'entire offensive effort as now deployed in the Far East, to rapidly augment it from the West, and to maintain, if not increase, that augmented potential during the crucial initial phase of the war'.[70] This notion was quite different from US war plans since 1946, which had assumed an initial Soviet advance into Western Europe and the Middle East. This possible Soviet strategy could readily force the UK into the most difficult dilemma; that is, either electing not to participate in the war at the cost of Anglo-American special relations or making an immediate British entrance into armed conflict in the knowledge of near certain Soviet nuclear strikes against London. On this basis, Ridgway indicated to Washington that the Soviets could split the Western allies.[71]

Concerned about this possibility, Ridgway begged Washington for more air and naval reinforcement to secure the movement of US–Japan ground troops to, and around, the archipelago. He intended to secure 'prior to such an attack, sufficient [air and naval] forces, so that even with an initial heavy loss in both aircraft and in shipping, there will remain a sufficient minimum to insure beyond any reasonable doubt, my ability to redeploy my ground forces throughout the theatre as I must do to defend the Japanese Main Islands against an all-out attack'.[72] In short, Ridgway considered that by maintaining command of Japanese air space and sea lanes he could secure sufficient ground forces to defend Japan.

As a result of the war games held over 1–3 August, FEC acknowledged that plans 'should be provided for operational control of JNPR [NPR] units by [American] JLC [Japan Logistical Command] and XVI Corps'.[73] In revising CINCFE Operations Plan 4–51, the Joint Strategic Plans and Operations Group (JSPOG) asked G-3 (Operations) of the FEC to prepare a 'NPRJ Annex' relating to 'the proposed revised FEC General War Plan'.[74] G-3 acknowledged the significance of using the NPR in view of the limited US ground forces available in East Asia. This was a significant change in assigned missions for the NPRJ from fixed to mobile defence as an indispensable part of combined US–Japan forces.

> Because of the limited forces available to CINCFE for the defense of Japan, it is considered highly desirable to utilize to the maximum the potential of the NPRJ. It would be further desirable to distribute to CG [Commanding General] JLCOM, CG XVI Corps and Chief, CAS (A) [Civil Affairs Section, Administrative] an approved basic plan for the utilization of the NPRJ to facilitate and expedite the preparation of preliminary supporting plans.[75]

However, G-3 recommended that this proposed NPR Annex should be considered 'a separate plan in itself' from 'the revised FEC General Emergency War Plan' for approval.[76] In a 20 August letter to General Headquarters (GHQ), SCAP, the US Army XVI Corps Headquarters (responsible for the defence of Hokkaido and Northern Japan), stressed that 'the defense of Hokkaido will depend largely on the employment of JNPR units to delay an invasion which may be effected by the enemy in the Wakkanai and/or Nemuro areas'.[77] Further, it underlined that GHQ should design NPR training to provide them with 'adequate personnel to employ demolitions to the maximum to include destruction of ports, tunnels, bridges and key defiles'.[78] GHQ replied that 'by 1 December 1951 engineer battalions and infantry pioneer platoons will be capable of executing demolition projects under emergency conditions'.[79] By that time, FEC had come to consider the situation as being explosive, and it directed its subordinate commanding officers to consider 'the fact that the enemy potentially has the capability of launching surprise atomic attacks in the Far East Command', and the possibility that 'the enemy may at any time implement this capability'.[80]

In a 3 September 1951 report for JSPOG, G-2 calculated that the Soviet Union now possessed a 'theoretical maximum of 15 [atomic] bombs for use in the Far East at present', but also recommended that the Americans should double the number 'for defensive planning purposes'.[81] It argued that the Soviet leadership would select 'atomic bomb targets in the Far East' to achieve 'maximum physical destruction of American military power' and not for 'destroying Japanese nascent economy, for example, or in attacking her people'.[82] As for the most likely target, G-2 was particularly concerned about Russia's 'first-punch sneak attack like that of Pearl Harbor' against Kadena Air Force Base in Okinawa, where 'two of the three B-29 groups in FEC' were present, consisting of '2/3 of the long-range air power initially available'.[83] The second target was thought to be Tachikawa Air Base on the grounds that it was the only major air depot in FEC, with Yokota Air Base coming up in third position.

G-2 considered that the Soviet Union would not 'employ atomic bombs on troops in the early stages of a general war, or against US forces, as now disposed in the Far East'. However, it also warned that the destruction of one or two US divisions in Korea or Japan with simultaneous atomic attacks on key targets in Japan might cause the immediate collapse of Far East forces if faced with a determined ground attack. Moreover, it also warned that an air burst centred over Tokyo's government and administrative districts would eliminate both US occupation administrative machinery and Japanese government agencies and, if coordinated with an attack on Honshu, could 'instantly deprive the Japanese people of both the Emperor, the Diet, and the American Occupation authorities'.[84]

On 12 September, FEC integrated the NPR into its war plans against the Soviet Union, without notifying the Japanese government. 'Neither details of this Annex nor the fact that CINCFE plans envisage the use of the NPRJ [Japan] in the event of an emergency will be disclosed to any Japanese national without prior specific approval in each instance by CINCFE.'[85] According to this plan, the Japanese government was to be directed to release the NPR 'to CINCFE, through SCAP', and 'NPRJ units will be attached as follows: (1) To CG XVI Corps: All NPRJ units in the 1st and 2d Region Areas'; '(2) To CG JLCOM: All NPRJ units in the 3d and 4th Region Areas'.[86] Even after ratification of the Peace Treaty, this plan assumed that the Japanese government would allow the US government to direct NPR units, according to 'Para 1, Chapter IV, "Collective Defense Measures" of the [US–Japan] Administrative Agreement'.[87] In a 13 September cable on post-treaty relations between FEC, the Japanese government, and the US diplomatic mission, Ridgway informed JCS that the establishment of US–Japan combined forces would be the only way to cope with the Soviet threat for some time to come.[88] On 15 September, this plan for integration was distributed to CG, JLCOM and CG, XVI Corps.[89] In a 21 September cable, Ridgway informed Washington that FEC was finishing the revision of Operation Plan CINCFE No. 4–51.[90]

Behind the San Francisco peace conference: Anglo-American talks on a Soviet attack on Japan and *casus belli*

In early August 1951, the Americans were determined to force the British to accept the idea that a Soviet attack on Japan or large-scale intervention in the Korean War were reasonable *casus belli* for all-out war. At a 6 August State–Defense–JCS meeting, Acheson proclaimed that 'the British needed education on how serious to our national interests an attack by the Russians on Korea and Japan would be'.[91] However, the Americans approved only the first part of a 3 August document, entitled 'United States Position on Considerations Under Which the United States Will Accept War and on Atomic Warfare'. According to the first part of the document, the US would enter into general war if the Soviets attacked the Continental US (including Alaska, and Canada); NATO territory; UN forces in Korea; US overseas possessions and/or bases (including Japan); US occupation forces in Western Germany (including Berlin); the US Occupation Zone of Austria (including Vienna); Trieste; and/or Japan. Though remote in possibility, the US also included the Republic of the Philippines, members of the Organization of American States, Australia, and New Zealand.[92]

At this meeting, the Americans did not approve the second and third parts of the report, which dealt with the issue of using atomic bombs, even in a limited war or conflict. At the 6 August meeting, Deputy Secretary of Defense Robert A. Lovett underlined the possibility of war with the Soviets and using A-bombs without anticipating an escalation to a general war; and Acheson agreed.[93] In the third part of the report, the Americans criticized British notions of a 'stop line' highly dependent on geographic considerations, while ignoring 'the nature of the attack' and 'the apparent firmness of purpose of the attacker'.[94] Furthermore, the second and third parts discussed the possibility that the US might have to fight the Russians alone while America's allies maintained neutrality. The third part even stated that 'British and other European bases are not absolutely essential to a United States strategic air offensive'.[95]

The Americans did not use these parts of the report in their discussions with the British, but this episode illustrated the American ambivalence towards the British. Ironically, NSC-114/1 (8 August 1951) warned that the Soviets intended to 'exploit all opportunities to split the Western Allies, particularly the United States and the United Kingdom', especially on the matter of 'German and Japanese rearmament' and 'the establishment of American bases overseas', while they conducted 'a specious peace campaign designed to exploit both fear of a new general war and reluctance to make the sacrifices necessary to redress the balance of power'.[96]

Meanwhile, the British could no longer wait for an American reply. In a 24 August cable, COS directed JSM to make 'a last attempt to have COS (51)106 discussed in Washington', while they also stated that JCS 'should know that we are getting extremely impatient at the endless stonewalling in Washington on this subject'.[97] In a 28 August letter, Franks reported that Acheson admitted that 'the Americans have not behaved well on this subject' and he suggested holding preliminary military talks between JCS and Elliot, hopefully with Chief of Imperial General Staff Sir William 'Slim or Slessor'.[98]

In late August, the Air Defence Committee warned COS that 'in the foreseeable future the Soviet Air Force using the atomic bombs' could inflict 'mortal damage on the UK' and they recommended that the British should take 'some offensive action' to reduce 'this threat by a factor of the order of 50%' at the very beginning of the war. Even in the new version of Anglo-American–Canadian emergency war plan, 'Plan Cinderella', JPS glumly assumed that in the event of a Soviet air attack, 'in the worst case[,] the United Kingdom could expect to operate as little more than a main base', which could provide 'little man-power and no material support' for 'overseas theatres'.[99]

To avoid this outcome, the Air Defence Committee suggested that there was 'a reasonable chance of effecting the object [neutralizing Soviet air bases] by the use of 50 atom bombs and a force of 200 B.9 and 60 Canberra intruder aircraft'. They recommended that the COS should discuss this issue with JCS and requested them to give 'high priority' to this task 'in relation to other N.A.T.O. air offensive projects'.[100] According to a 11 September telegram, the new British Foreign Secretary Herbert Morrison, then in Washington, informed Acheson that the 'subject was of vital political importance because use of the atomic weapon by the Americans might well draw down annihilating retaliation on the UK' and 'it would be intolerable that this should be risked without our first having been informed and consulted'.[101] However, Acheson stressed that, in the case of using non-British bases for atomic warfare, it 'was politically impossible for him [the President] to admit that he had accepted any limitation on American freedom to use their most powerful weapon'.[102] Listening to Acheson's argument, Morrison stated that 'as a matter of commonsense the United States government obviously would not resort to general war without consulting other Allies' and that the 'real point at issue therefore was in what circumstances we might have to resort to general war'.[103] In this context, he believed that the military conference between the JCS and Elliot on COS (51)106 was highly significant.

At this meeting, Acheson informed Morrison that Japanese rearmament was designed to deter a Soviet attack on Japan and not to send any Japanese forces to Korea:

> Mr. Acheson said he wished to assure the Secretary of State [Morrison] that the United States had no intention of employing Japanese troops in Korea. The Joint Chiefs of Staff recognised that the formation, training and equipment of three or four Japanese divisions would take a considerable time. The United States could not yet spare all the necessary equipment and weapons. The proposal was to expand the existing Japanese police reserve and intensify its training giving it modern weapons as they become available. The Joint Chiefs of Staff were concerned lest Japan should be left defenceless if it became necessary to transfer to Korea the two National Guard divisions now employed on internal security duties in Japan. In that event, the Russians might decide to try an airborne landing on Hokkaido from bases in Shakhalin or the Kurile Islands. This was a danger against which it was considered important to take every precaution.[104]

The British were thus forcibly made aware of the American understanding of the role of Japanese ground forces in regulating *casus belli* and the use of atomic bombs.[105]

At a 13 September Anglo-American military conference, JCS refused to commit to any prior consultation with the British on the use of atomic bombs in retaliation against a possible Soviet attack on Japan or Korea, though not so in the case of commencing general war. Immediately after Elliot explained the gist of COS (51)106, Bradley pointed out that this document failed to include the case of Soviet attack on Japan, and, as cited above, he stressed the US resolve to defend Japan even by starting another world war with A-bombs. Surprisingly enough, Elliot, though not evident in COS (51)106, expressed his willingness to accept Bradley's views. He then requested the Americans to commit to prior discussions before using atomic bombs in the Far East. Much colder than Bradley, Collins declared: 'but if the Soviets attack Japan we would go to war even alone and we would use the A-bomb. No UK bases would be involved.'[106]

Elliot warned that American freedom in using atomic bombs in the Far East would invite tremendous political difficulty in Britain, and only prior Anglo-American 'discussion' could overcome this. He stressed that the US 'must realise that we are a better ally than the others' and there were 'bases in the UK'. Bradley countered as follows: 'admitting you are our best ally, where do we stop?' Elliot responded that he was 'only suggesting you start with us'. Collins then ridiculed the British political system, which, in his view, would politicize the consultations by providing explanations to 'your politicos'. Shocked by this comment, Elliot now warned, 'if your answer is "no" the consequences might be unpleasant'. Intimidated, Collins then replied that the American freehand was limited to 'operations in the Far East'. Elliot still insisted that the US should consult with the British even on Far Eastern issues. Bradley stated that the US would consult on the 'matter of general war', but the JCS could not commit to any consultation on the use of the A-bomb in the Far East. Meanwhile, Bradley openly questioned 'the practicability' of the British notion of 'stop line'.[107]

After these preliminary military talks, there was 'a politico-military meeting' attended by Franks and Elliot as well as Bradley, Nitze, and Matthews. However, there was no British breakthrough in undermining the American stronghold on no prior consultation on the use of atomic bombs in the Far East. More troubling still, Bradley informed Elliot that Ridgway took a more serious view than the JCS of 'the possibility of [a] Russian attack on Japan' and he stressed that 'if the Soviet Union attacked US forces in Japan, the Americans would be at war with the Soviet Union and it would not be a local situation'.[108]

At the time, Ridgway was more concerned about Japan's vulnerability to Soviet attack than any imminent danger to US troops fighting in Korea.[109] In a 15 September cable to Ridgway, the JCS expressed their concern 'about [the] lack of reserves available [to the] Eighth Army in [the] event [of an] all-out Communist attack now apparently imminent enemy capability'.[110] They suggested that Ridgway move one division to Korea out of the two divisions and one regiment deployed in Japan, while allowing a veteran division in Korea to return to Japan, if at all possible. However, in a 18 September cable, Ridgway stated, 'I do not REPEAT not share your concern for the security of [the] Eighth Army'.[111] His major concern was the Soviet reaction to the peace treaty and Japanese rearmament. For that reason he opposed the deployment and underlined the significance of buying time until a Soviet offensive against Japan would become difficult due to the severe winters of northern Japan, which by '15 November, the probability of such an effort would be of a low order'. Ridgway then requested the JCS to send one F-86 wing and one B-26 wing as reinforcements.[112] In a 19 October cable, he informed Commanding Generals, XVI Corps and JLCOM of his new directive: 'be prepared, when directed by SCAP, to assume control of NPRJ forces as directed in Annex F (NPRJ) to Far East Command General Emergency War Plan'.[113]

The British acceptance of the stop line, Japan

Under the COS directive, the JPS reviewed the Anglo-American talks of September 1951, and 'revised' COS (51)106. The new report recommended that the British should insist that, even in the case of Russian direct attack on Japan or large-scale intervention in Korea, the Anglo-American side should now contain this to a 'local action'.[114] However, though in handwriting, obviously added after the formulation of this report, Japan was nonetheless included in the second category of stop lines which would trigger a general war. Japan thus became the only stop line in the Far East. The report categorized 'the circumstances which at present seem to justify the eventual resort to general war, including full scale atomic attack into two categories of stop lines: the first, aggression against West Germany, Austria (excluding Vienna), and Turkey; the second referred to a situation which could not be 'restored by any other means' and was applicable to Greece, Yugoslavia, Japan [added in handwriting], and 'possibly' Berlin.[115] The JPS also insisted that the British should disagree with the American argument of limiting the scope of discussions 'to deal solely with the circumstances in which general war might arise' and that the British should attempt to include 'full consideration of the nature and effect of atomic warfare'.[116]

In a 13 December report, COS became more willing to adopt the American view. They added that 'we feel that there is much force in the American contention' that 'a Soviet attack on Japan, or an attack by major Soviet military units against U.N. forces in Korea, would almost inevitably lead to general war'.[117] Moreover, the COS report this time printed 'Japan', rather than leaving it in handwriting as in the previous piece. On 5 February 1952, the British informed the Americans of their agreement with the US view on the outbreak of general war as triggered by a Soviet attack on Japan. At the Anglo-American political–military meeting, Elliot proclaimed: 'as regards Korea and Japan, we recognised that Russian attack on US forces in Korea or Japan, which resulted in war between Russia and the US, would automatically involve us'. At the same time, the British reiterated their notion of a 'stop line'.[118]

However, by late February, the Americans revised their view, arguing that a Soviet attack on Japan was a distant possibility. At a meeting on 29 February 1952, Nitze and John Allison of the State Department informed the Canadians that 'the US. Government was now inclined to regard the possibility of an attack on Japan as a more remote contingency than it had been six months ago'.[119]

Conclusion

The extent to which the US committed itself to the defence of Japan under the US–Japan Security Treaty has been a longstanding issue amongst the Japanese. In view of the Anglo-American controversy over whether a Soviet attack against Japan constituted *casus belli* for a third world war, when the Treaty was concluded it was clear that the US intended to defend Japan at the risk of world war, including nuclear strikes. Moreover, the US forced the UK to accept the strategic notion that a Soviet attack on Japan was sufficient *casus belli*. This symbolized how the US was able to apply pressure to the UK to force the acceptance of Japanese integration into an Anglo-American global defence system. In this way, the US forcefully linked the defence of Japan with that of Western Europe. Interestingly, the Japanese neither were aware of this process, nor were they informed, even though this was the most significant premise in Japan's post-war defence posture. In April 1952, the US and the UK discussed the timing and style of a Soviet ultimatum and the British came to categorize Japan as one of the five territories for which an ultimatum from the Anglo-American powers in the case of a Soviet attack would prompt general war. These included: '(a) All N.A.T.O. territories (other than those mentioned separately); (b) Western Germany; (c) Allied Zones of Austria; (d) Yugoslavia; (e) Japan'.[120] Japan was the only Asian territory in this category. Moreover, the British intended to integrate the Canadians into this Anglo-American arrangement on *casus belli*. At a 13 May 1952 meeting, COS discussed with 'Makins the desirability of our taking the Canadians into our confidence concerning "STOPLINE" question' and they requested Makins to obtain Franks' views on how to process the discussions 'with the Canadians'.[121]

The US view was that the NPR constituted a partial deterrent against a Soviet attack on Japan, and it also integrated the NPR into combined US–Japan forces. Britain never blocked this process. Without any awareness of the harsh Anglo-American exchanges on *casus belli* in the context of Japan, the Japanese government considered that the NPR was mainly for internal security. They did not realize that the NPR would be expected to serve as a deterrent against a Soviet attack on Japan, in other words, a deterrent against a third world war.

Notes

1   National Archives, Kew, London (hereafter NA Kew), DEFE 20/1, 'Summary of Note Recorded by the Secretary and Deputy Secretary, Joint Chiefs of Staff at United States–United Kingdom Military Conference, Held in Room 2C-923, the Pentagon on Thursday, 13 September, 1951, at 10.00.'
2   The NPR was established by order of the Supreme Commander of the Allied Powers (SCAP), General Douglas MacArthur in June 1950. Recruitment was set at 75,000 men with the initial objective being Japan's internal security in the light of the US occupation army's departure for the Korean frontline. However, as Cold War tensions heightened, noticeably when China intervened in the conflict in November 1950, the US began to promote the development of the NPR along military lines, to the approximate level of US light divisions, though lacking in medium tanks and heavy artillery. Shibayama Futoshi, 'Chōsen Sensō no bunmyaku ni okeru Bei'Ei ni totte no

Nihon saigunbi no imi henka, 1950.6–1952.8', *Dōshisha Amerika kenkyū* 37, 2001, pp. 37–78.

3   US Department of State, *Foreign Relations of the United States, 1951* (hereafter *FRUS, 1951*), vol. I, Washington, DC: US Department of State, 1977, p. 35.

4   M. P. Leffler, *A Preponderance of Power: National Security, the Truman Administration, and the Cold War*, Stanford: Stanford University Press, 1992, pp. 369–70.

5   NA Kew, DEFE 20/2, COS (51)106, 27 February 1951.

6   Ibid.

7   Ibid.

8   Ibid.

9   NA Kew, CO 537/5640, JPS (50)148 (Final), 4 December 1950. See also FO 371/83889, JPS (50)148(S) (Preliminary Draft), 29 November 1950; JPS (50)148(S) (Draft) Limited Circulation, 1 December 1950.

10   NA Kew, CO 537/5640, JPS (50) 148 (Final), 4 December 1950.

11   NA Kew, DEFE 5/26, COS (50) 516, 11 December 1950.

12   NA Kew, DEFE 4/27, JPS (49) 163 (Final), 20 December 1949.

13   NA Kew, DEFE 20/2, COS (51) 106, 27 February 1951.

14   NA Kew, DEFE 20/1, COS (51) 42, Mtg, 6 March 1951.

15   Ibid.; NA Kew, DEFE 20/1, COS (51) 50, Mtg, 20 March 1951.

16   B. I. Kaufman, *The Korean War*, New York: Knopf, 1986, pp. 117–18.

17   National Archives, Washington, DC (hereafter NA Washington DC), RG 554, Box 352, 'GHQ, UNC, FEC, SCAP, G-3 Section Portion of the COMMAND REPORT for the Month of January 1951' (hereafter G-3 Command Report); Records of GHQ, FEC, SCAP and UNC, Military History Section, Command & Staff Section Report, 1947–1952, TS, 1951 (hereafter MHS, RG 554). Memo for JCS (19 January 1951) CCS 381 Far East (11–28–50) Sec. 2, RG 218.

18   NA Washington DC, MHS, RG 554, Box 352, DATT 4210 (January 9, 1951) in 'G-3 Command Report, January 1951'. Russia had detained over 370,000 Japanese POWs since the end of the Pacific War.

19   NA Washington DC, RG 218, CCS 381 Far East (11–28–50), Sec 2, Memo for JCS, 19 January 1951.

20   NA Washington DC, RG 319, G-3 091 Japan TS Sec. I-B, JCS-1380/97, 30 January 1951.

21   Ibid; NA Washington DC, RG 319, G-3 091 Japan TS Sec. I-B, G-3 to C/S, 20 January 1950.

22   NA Washington DC, RG 319, G-3 091 Japan TS Sec. I-B, JCS-1380/97, 30 January 1950.

23   Ibid.

24   NA Washington DC, RG 319, G-3 091, Japan TS Sec. I-B, JCS-1380/100, 19 February 1951.

25   G-3, contained within the US Army General Staff, is responsible for planning and operations.

26   NA Washington DC, RG 319, G-3 091, Japan TS Sec. I-B, Gaither to Taylor, 'Current Unresolved Problems Relative to the Security of Japan', 23 February 1951.

27   Ibid.

28   Ibid.

29   NA Washington DC, Gaither to Taylor, G-3 091 Japan TS sec. I-B, RG 319 'Current Unresolved Problems Relative to the Security of Japan', 23 February 1951; *FRUS, 1951*, vol. VI, pp. 888–95, 898–900.

30   Ministry of Foreign Affairs, *Nihon gaikō bunsho: heiwa jōyaku no teiketsu ni kansuru chōso* (hereafter *Nihon gaikō*), vol. I, nos. 1–3, Tokyo 2002, pp. 559, 601.

31   *Nihon gaikō*, vol. I, nos. 1–3, p. 601.

32   *Nihon gaikō*, vol. II, nos. 4–5, pp. 37–8.

33   Ibid. p. 38.

34 *Nihon gaikō*, vol. I, nos. 1–3, p. 681.
35 Diplomatic Record Office, Tokyo (hereafter DRO), 'Saigunbi mondai ni kansuru zairyō: Beigawa kanpensuji no ikkō hōkoku no ken', 18 January 1951.
36 Ibid.
37 *Nihon gaikō*, vol. I, nos. 1–3, p. 829.
38 Ibid.
39 Ibid., p. 830.
40 Ibid.
41 Ibid., p. 831.
42 Ibid.
43 Ibid.
44 Ibid., p. 832.
45 Ibid., p. 833.
46 Ibid., p. 832.
47 Ibid., pp. 831–33; *Nihon gaikō*, vol. II, nos. 4–5, pp. 184, 192.
48 Not only Yoshida, but also the American military considered constitutional amendment necessary to establish Japanese armed forces, in view of Article Nine of the 1946 Constitution. However, due to the urgent military situation in East Asia, they could not afford the time it would take to amend the Constitution and had to embark upon informal rearmament. On Yoshida's views, see *Nihon gaikō*, vol. II, nos. 4–5, pp. 172–74.
49 *Nihon gaikō*, vol. II, nos. 4–5, p. 173, pp. 88–90.
50 Douglas MacArthur Memorial Archives, Norfolk VA, RG 6, Series III, Box 100, 'Operation Order No. 1', 1 March 1951.
51 Ibid.
52 Douglas MacArthur Memorial Archives, Norfolk VA, RG 6, Series III, 'Operation Plan: CINCFE No. 4–51', 3 April 1951.
53 NA Washington DC, MHS, RG 554, Box 348, 'Memo for record: Command Conference, Chief of Staff Conference Room, 1600, 3 July 1951', 4 July 1951, attached to 'Staff Section Report, Office of the Commander-In-Chief and Office of the Chief of Staff, July 1951'(hereafter Staff Section Report.)
54 *FRUS, 1951*, vol. I, p. 826.
55 NA Kew, DEFE 20/1, COS (51) 311 'Record of Conversation' attached to 'Copy of a letter dated 18th May, 1951 from Sir Oliver Franks to Sir Roger Makins', 28 May 1951.
56 *FRUS, 1951*, vol. I, pp. 814–20.
57 Ibid.
58 Ibid., p. 820.
59 NA Washington DC, RG 319, G-3 091 Japan TS, Sec. I-D, JCS-2180/14, 19 April 1951.
60 Ibid.
61 Ibid.
62 Dulles proposed a Pacific Pact to secure the region that would include US, Japan, the Philippines, Australia, New Zealand, and possibly Indonesia. The British came to view this proposal as a plot to integrate Australia and New Zealand into the defence of Japan. See NA Kew, PREM 8/1404, Washington to Foreign Office, 129, 12 January 1951.
63 NA Washington DC, RG 319, G-3 091 Japan TS, Sec. I-D, JCS-2180/14, 19 April 1951.
64 NA Kew, DEFE 20/1, Makins to Franks, 31 July 1951.
65 NA Kew, DEFE20/1, Franks to Makins, 31 July 1951.
66 NA Washington DC, RG 554, MHS Box 348, 'Memo for Record', 26 July 1951; 'Memo for Record', 30 July 1951 in 'Staff Section Report, July 1951'.
67 Ibid.

68 NA Washington DC, MHS, RG 554, Box 348, 'Memo for record: Command Conference, Chief of Staff Conference Room, 1600, 3 July 1951', 4 July 1951; 'Memo for record' (26 July 1951); 'Memo for record' (30 July 1951) in 'Staff Section Report, July 1951'.

69 NA Washington DC, MHS, Box 353, C 68161, 2 August 1951 in 'G-3 Command Report, August 1951'.

70 Ibid.

71 Ibid.

72 NA Washington DC, RG 554, MHS, Box 353, 'Part I' and C8171, 2 August 1951 in 'G-3 Command Report, August 1951'.

73 NA Washington DC, RG 554, MHS, Box 354, 'Staff Section Report, August 1951'.

74 Ibid. In fact, in a July 29 memo for record, GHQ's G-3, referring to the NPRJ expansion, acknowledged the possibility that 'SCAP could direct the change [of the Japanese constitution] at any time prior to the ratification of the peace treaty.' However, it believed that such a SCAP initiative 'conceivably could result in the fall of the present [Japanese] Government and irreparable damage to peace treaty negotiations.' RG 554, MHS, Box 354, 'Memo for Record', 29 July 1951.

75 NA Washington DC, RG 554, MHS, Box 354, 'Memo for Record', 29 July 1951.

76 Ibid.

77 NA Washington DC, RG 554, MHS, Box 354, Laskowski to Chief, Civil Affairs Section, GHQ, 20 August 1951; RG 554, MHS, Box 354.

78 Ibid.

79 NA Washington DC, RG 554, MHS, Box 354, O'Brien to CG, XVI Corps, 'Demolition Training of JNPR Units' in 'G-3 Command Report, September 1951' undated.

80 NA Washington DC, RG 554, MHS, Box 354, Warden to CG Eighth Army, CG XVI Corps, CG JLCOM and others, 1 September 1951.

81 NA Washington DC, RG 554, Box 29, Records of GHQ, FEC, SCAP and UNC, Assist. C/S G-2, Intelligence Reports 1950–1951, G-2 to JSPOG 'Estimate on Soviet Use of Atomic Weapons Against the Far East Command', 3 September 1951. On this number, G-2 explained that, based on the 'existing data', the Soviet Union was considered to possess 'not more than 75 atomic bombs, as of 1 Sept 1951'. Though based on 'admittedly fragmentary data', G-2 estimated that the Soviets could produce atomic bombs 'at a rate of 4 to 5 monthly' and could accelerate the pace to 'an average rate of 7 per month during 1952'. G-2 assumed that the Soviets would use a 'priority ratio of 5–3–2 for targets in the US, Western Europe and the Far East. Ibid.

82 Ibid.

83 Ibid.

84 Ibid.

85 NA Washington DC, RG 554, MHS, Box 354, 'Annex F', attached to Warden to CG XVI Corps and CG JLC, 'Annex F' 15 September 1951 in 'G-3 Command Report, September 1951'.

86 Ibid.

87 Ibid. This plan quoted a proposed provision: '1. In the event of hostilities or when in the opinion of either party hostilities are threatened in the Japan area, and all Japanese organizations, excepting local police, having military potential, shall, at the option of the United States, be placed under the unified command of a Supreme Commander designated by the US Government after consultation with the Japanese Government'. Ibid.

88 NA Washington DC, RG 554, MHS, Box 354, C50742, 13 September 1951.

89 NA Washington DC, RG 554, MHS, Box 354, Warden to CG XVI Corps and CG JLCOM, 'Annex F', 15 September 1951.

90 NA Washington DC, RG 554, MHS, Box 354, C51294, 1 September 1951 in 'G-3 Command Report, September 1951'.

91 *FRUS, 1951*, vol. I, p. 878.

92 Ibid., pp. 866–67.
93 Ibid., p. 879.
94 Ibid., p. 874.
95 Ibid., p. 873.
96 Ibid., p. 130.
97 NA Kew, DEFE 20/1, COS (W) 92, 24 August 1951.
98 NA Kew, DEFE 20/1, Franks to Strang, 28 August 1951.
99 NA Kew, DEFE 4/46, JPS (51) 75 (Final), 24 August 1951. By this plan, Japan was expected to ally itself with the Anglo-American side, and, more significantly, Japan was expected to be the only non-Caucasian ally. DEFE 4/46, Annex II to JPS (51) 75 (Final), 24 August 1951.
100 NA Kew, DEFE 20/1, COS (51) 501 and AD (51) 91, 31 August 1951.
101 NA Kew, DEFE 20/2, Foreign Secretary to Prime Minister, 2899, 11 September 1951. On American records of this meeting, see *FRUS*, 1951, vol. I, pp. 88–83.
102 NA Kew, DEFE 20/2, Foreign Secretary to Prime Minister, 2899, 11 September 1951.
103 Ibid.
104 NA Kew, FO371/92064, 'United State–United Kingdom Talks at Washington: Far East', (draft), 11 September 1951.
105 Ibid.
106 NA Kew, DEFE20/1, 'Summary of Note Recorded by the Secretary and Deputy Secretary, Joint Chiefs of Staff at United States–United Kingdom Military Conference', 13 September 1951.
107 Ibid.
108 NA Kew, DEFE 20/2, 2964, 'Foreign Secretary to Prime Minister' 13 September 1951); ELL 195 29 October 1951); *FRUS, 1951*, vol. I, pp. 886–87, 889.
109 NA Washington DC, RG 554, MHS, Box 354, C 50152, 3 September 1951.
110 NA Washington DC, RG 554, MHS, Box 354, JCS 81533, 15 September 1951.
111 NA Washington DC, RG 554, MHS, Box 354, C 51095, 18 September 1951.
112 Ibid.
113 NA Washington DC, RG 554, MHS, Box 354, CX 53306, 'G-3 Command Report', 19 October 1951.
114 NA Kew, DEFE 20/1, JPS (51)29 (Final), 30 November 1951.
115 Ibid.
116 Ibid.
117 NA Kew, DEFE 20/2, COS (51)741, 13 December 1951.
118 NA Kew, DEFE 20/2, Untitled (UK record of meeting held with Mr H. Freeman, State, 5th February 1952).
119 NA Kew, DEFE 20/2, 'Annex A', attached to the letter from Marten to Makins, 28 March 1952.
120 NA Kew, DEFE 20/2, 'Appendix' to JPS (52)46, (Final), 25 April 1952. See also, DEFE 20/2, 'Appendix' to JPS (52)46 (Revised Final), 4 July 1952; 'Appendix' to COS (52)371, 16 July 1952.
121 NA Kew, DEFE 20/2, Ewbank to COS, 11 June 1952.

2 Great Britain and Japanese rearmament, 1945–60

John Weste

Introduction

The intention of this paper is to place Japanese rearmament in the context of British assumptions of a global role in the late 1940s and 1950s, as cast by Churchill's notion of the Three Circles. In hindsight, relative British decline and the consequent reduction of interest and influence in East Asia is as clear as American preponderance. However, the United Kingdom did not intend to be a faint taste of the bygone in the new American-led world order. British interest in US–Japanese rearmament planning testifies to this: it was an important concern to London in terms of its global strategy; that is, the crucial British links with the Commonwealth, Japan, and the United States. Moreover, some deft manoeuvring could obtain for the UK a niche, however tiny, in Japan's military planning and strategic overview, and thus provide Japan with a small, yet to the UK a helpful, alternative to the United States in military matters. Hitherto, scholarly work has emphasized the American role in Japan's reacquisition of a military capacity, yet to neglect the interests and actions of the UK in this area needlessly curtails our understanding of the global context of Japanese rearmament. That Britain did not attain the levels of influence it desired does not mask the importance of the attempt.

With the surrender of Japan in August 1945, the US-led occupation began to implement its two basic goals of Japanese demilitarization and democratization. Although both were long-term objectives covering a range of themes including the social, economic, and psychological, immediate and tangible progress on demilitarization was demonstrated in several key areas. Namely, the Imperial Army and Navy were abolished and veterans were demobilized, military armaments and equipment were destroyed, and the manufacture of weaponry was banned. Article Nine of the American-inspired 1946 Constitution seemingly guaranteed the future of a pacifist and disarmed Japan by stating that 'land, sea, and air forces, as well as other war potential, will never be maintained'.[1] Neither was disarmament vehemently resented by the Japanese people: the Imperial Army and Navy were utterly discredited by defeat; moreover, the atomic bombs dropped on Hiroshima and Nagasaki, and a pervasive war weariness, had profoundly weakened the popular faith in military solutions to national problems. Nonetheless, the occupation of

Japan was not conducted in a vacuum, and international events also impacted upon the course of policy.

The Cold War, in East Asia symbolised by the 1949 communist victory in the Chinese civil war, and the June 1950 outbreak of war in the Korean peninsula, worked upon and rapidly evaporated American intentions to disarm Japan. Washington's pressure on Tokyo to rearm increased and, while by no means satisfied with the progress and scale of rearmament, the US nonetheless ended the occupation in 1952 well assured that the process was in place. In July 1950, the Japanese were ordered to form the 75,000-strong National Police Reserve (NPR). Any ambiguities as to the latter body's status were clarified with the August 1952 formation of the National Security Force, which was in turn replaced in May 1954 with the Self-Defence Force (SDF).[2] By the mid-1950s, Japan had emerged as the key US military ally in East Asia, was the recipient of US military aid through the Mutual Security Assistance programme, and had begun developing, naturally closely linked with the United States, a modern military force.

The American involvement in post-war Japanese rearmament has attracted a great deal of scholarly attention.[3] This is entirely understandable: the US had become a global superpower, it led the occupation of Japan and replaced Great Britain as the leading Western power in Asia and the Pacific. Further, it also held both the financial and military capacity to promote Japanese rearmament in ways far beyond the other Western allies. Nonetheless, holding a dominant position does not equate to possessing the sole interest. A rearmed Japan was of core global concern, whether it be viewed positively, with suspicion, or with outright hostility and fear. America's allies, let alone its enemies, fell into all of the above categories and were adamant that their own national concerns be considered in US proposals for Japanese rearmament. Central among these allies was Great Britain.

While weakened by the Second World War and clearly no longer in the same league as the United States or the Soviet Union, the United Kingdom was still one of the world's more powerful nations. It ended the conflict with a formidable military capacity and with much of the empire recaptured and intact. That anti-colonialism and relative British decline would render this empire increasingly incoherent and less relevant to the economic and military security of the home islands was not at all clear in the late 1940s and early 1950s. Further, the British élite had absolutely no intention of accepting second-class status for themselves in global affairs. Indeed, as Winston Churchill explained to the Conservative Party conference in 1948, and sought to demonstrate more concretely in 1951 when he returned to power, Britain lay at the heart, the 'very point of junction', of three interlocking circles: Great Britain and the Empire; the English-speaking dominions, Great Britain and the United States; and, finally, a United Europe. Only Britain, Churchill, grandiloquently proclaimed, could claim a place in each.[4] Each circle would work to reinforce the other and thus permit Britain a global role as a counter balance to the US and the USSR. The difficult issue of Japanese rearmament would, therefore, have to be faced in the context of the close alliance with the United States, the English-speaking Commonwealth, especially Australia and New Zealand, and, finally, with Japan itself.

Whatever the Churchillian rhetoric, the British connection with Japan's post-war recovery is an important one and, whether this relationship was mediated through the 1945–52 occupation, through South-East Asia, or through direct economic links, Anglo-Japanese relations were more important and active than the focus hitherto on the US–Japanese nexus might suggest.[5] A study of Japanese rearmament, especially in the sense of external pressure on the process of Japanese remilitarization, needs to be placed in this broader context, too. Aside from providing an additional external perspective, an examination of the UK interest in Japanese rearmament also sheds light on at least two core themes, which coloured this relationship over the 1950s, if not for considerably longer.

First, it is significant just how quickly, after the Pacific War, the British metropolitan elite recognised that Japan remained an important nation. Japan mattered to Britain politically, economically and, through rearmament, also militarily. By 1952, with the occupation over, Japan was once again a sovereign state and would need to be accepted and understood as such. However, this acceptance posed many conundrums. Obviously, it impacted upon relations with the Commonwealth: fear of a resurgent Japanese militarism and historically well-founded doubts as to Britain's military commitment saw Australia and New Zealand sign the ANZUS Treaty exclusively with the United States in 1952, much to British international humiliation. Close ties with the US were also crucial to Britain, yet did not always sit comfortably with what London often regarded as rather unhealthily intimate bonds between Washington and Tokyo. Finally, if one were to accept Japanese importance as a fact, then it also brought the troubling obligation to treat Japan appropriately. If, for example, Japan were both a sovereign and a significant nation, then why adamantly deny Japan admission to GATT, even against strong American pressure to the contrary?

The second theme is centred on the simple fact that importance bears little or no relationship to affection, respect or trust between neither people nor nations. Decades of economic friction, particularly in textiles, and the bitter memories of war powerfully conditioned British views of Japan. Speaking for a nation, in 1952 the Foreign Secretary, Anthony Eden, acknowledged that Japan counted 'for a great deal and will count for more', but was certain to add, perhaps even with some understatement, that the Japanese 'were not easy to like'.[6] To be precise, the Japanese could not be trusted. For a start, one could assume they would cheat at trade. The diaries of the chairman of the Cotton Board, Sir Raymond Streat, consistently emphasise industry's fears in this regard.[7] Equally, the Japanese were politically suspect. Could they be trusted to remain democratic and allied with the West? Malcolm MacDonald, the British Commissioner-General to South-East Asia in 1948–55, was one of many to suspect not: the Japanese were, by their dictatorially authoritarian nature, inherently susceptible to authoritarian rule.[8] Finally, and crucially, could Japan be trusted with an enlarged military establishment? Or would militarist elements re-emerge, overthrow shallow democratic institutions and once again pose a military threat, and this time with the added twist of revenge and, even worse, yet again threaten to fulfil the Kaiser's vision of the 'Yellow Peril' but now in alliance with Chinese communism?

Defeat in war might well have tempered Japanese ambition and dampened the perceived illiberal and baser aspects of Japanese society, but few were utterly convinced the change was necessarily permanent. Nonetheless, 'Japan existed and would exist, with all its talents and its terrifyingly large population',[9] and rearmament was a crucial area in which Britain would be faced with reconciling these two antagonistic themes domestically, within the Commonwealth, with the United States, and, of course, with Japan itself. However, logically, before rearmament must come disarmament.

Demilitarizing Japan

Surely this task should have been one of more pleasurable aspects of defeating and occupying Japan, or at least it should have afforded some relief. Instead, it proved to be an exceedingly wearisome and frustrating activity. Not only did it provide a yet further arena for the squabbles of the Cold War, but also provided an early insight to the difficulties to be overcome if Britain were to successfully jump the hoops of Churchill's future Three Circles.

In March 1946, the US Department of State forwarded Britain a draft treaty on Japanese disarmament and demilitarization, the preamble of which made clear that 'the total disarmament and de-militarization of Japan will be enforced as long as the peace and security of the world may require'.[10] To that end, all Japanese armed forces, including land, sea, air, paramilitary and special police, were to be abolished, and the manufacture or import of military equipment would be prevented. This Treaty, which was envisaged to last for 25 years after the end of the occupation, would be enforced through a system of quadripartite inspection, that is by the UK, USSR, US, and China.[11]

The British response was wary. Commonwealth considerations figured highly in the minds of both civil and military figures: the Dominions, especially Australia and New Zealand, given they were 'even more vitally concerned than we ourselves, and are participating in the occupation of Japan', had to be consulted first.[12] The chiefs of staff went so far as to suggest that the principally concerned Dominions should be joint signatories to the Treaty in light of their majority contribution to Commonwealth occupational forces in Japan.[13] Others feared the political ramifications, and insisted that the draft Treaty be kept top secret as the Australian response to its existence 'would undoubtedly be a violent' one.[14] The notion of Dominions being joint signatories was completely ignored by the US, leaving Britain hoping the Russians would reject the Treaty out of hand. While not immediately forthcoming, a pugilistic Australian response had only been delayed, as was made clear one year later when consideration of the disposal of the Japanese fleet came to the fore.

Initial plans for what remained of the Imperial Navy were apparently finally settled by the US in early 1947 when it proposed that vessels were to be categorized and then equally distributed between the UK, US, USSR and China. Australia was adamant that the disposal of the Japanese fleet was for a peace conference to discuss. The Australian Embassy in Washington was instructed to protest to the State Department that 'on any matter affecting the future of the Pacific, Australia should participate directly with other nations concerned.'[15] In other words, Australia was demanding equal treatment and its own share of the Japanese fleet. The Soviet Union had also launched its own protest, namely at the suspension of vessel allocation in October 1947, leaving 104 ships still unallocated. The Americans argued the remaining ships were necessary for occupation duties (and this was not entirely unreasonable: minesweeping, for example, was a major post-war operation in Japanese coastal waters). Nonetheless, the Soviets maintained that this delay broke the previous agreement on equal allocation.

Perhaps to mollify at least Dominion outrage, Britain further proposed to reallocate a portion of its share to interested Dominion governments and, reflecting the European dimension, yet a further portion to France and the Netherlands. As the Dominion Office argued, Australia, the Netherlands and France each held a better claim on the basis of their contribution to the naval war against Japan than either China or the USSR. Such generosity was made easier by the realistic assessment that the UK did not need any of the Japanese ships.[16] Canberra responded vigorously, stating that 'we cannot agree to the giving to the Netherlands a share of the Japanese fleet' and neither can 'we . . . see that there is any real moral obligation to make a share to the Netherlands for their part in the war against Japan which was minimal in character.' Highlighting differing internal Commonwealth security concerns, the Australian government went on to add that

> moreover . . . the Netherlands is using every means in its power . . . to bring the Republic of Indonesia to a point of submission . . . In doing so, the Netherlands are threatening the peace of this area . . . their action is inimical to the interests of Australia and we cannot be party to any arrangements such as you suggest.[17]

In effect, disarming Japan saw the United States ignoring British requests that the Dominions be joint signatories to the quadripartite inspection system, Australian demands that the allocation of Imperial Navy remnants be held over to a peace conference, and the Russian insistence on the immediate allocation of warships. Equally, it also saw Australia make a limited challenge to the US on matters it considered important to its standing as regional Pacific power and, further, contest with the UK over continental European relations perceived as being in conflict with the security concerns of an important Commonwealth nation. Little wonder the Dominion Office resignedly commented that 'if we had our way, these ships would all be on the bottom of the sea.'[18] Instead, it was the notion of a permanently disarmed Japan which was to rest with the fishes.

Rearming Japan

The Cold War in East Asia impacted directly upon US planning for Japanese military security. Tensions between the capitalist and communist camps were exacerbated by the 1949 formation of the People's Republic of China and resultant Kuomintang retreat to Taiwan, and the June 1950 outbreak of war between North and South Korea. Washington proved itself willing to override opposition from wartime allies, Asian victims of Japanese military aggression, and domestic Japanese interests in order to promote large-scale rearmament. Of course, it is important not to assume that the Japanese were simply passive and waiting to satisfy American demands: Tokyo's world view and interests did not always match Washington's. The debate over the desirability of rearmament, and its pace and direction, was an intense one and the cause of much conflict between politicians, bureaucracy, business and even members of the defunct Imperial forces domestically and also diplomatically with the US. The United States never attained the level of rearmament in Japan it hoped for.

Japanese rearmament can be traced with the following chronological markers: the 1950 National Police Reserve was succeeded in 1952 by the National Security Force and then, in 1954, by the Self-Defence Force, in which form the modern Japanese military exists to this day. Each development bore the mark of strong external American pressure, whether diplomatic, political or economic. By 1953, Vice-President Richard Nixon felt sufficiently secure to announce during a visit to Japan that Article Nine had been 'an honest mistake'.[19] Further, virtually since the start of the occupation, sections of the US military had also formed clandestine links with pro-rearmament Japanese, and not necessarily with the knowledge or approval of the Japanese government or official US agencies in Japan.[20] All of the above developments were of interest to the British and, of course, to a great many others as well.

An American-sponsored rearmament of Japan affected Britain in at least three areas, each of which matched one of Churchill's Circles. First, in terms of Anglo-US relations: what did the Americans have in mind, and where (if anywhere) would Britain fit in? Second, Commonwealth relations also figured: how would the diverse membership of the Commonwealth respond and would they individually support or reject a rearmed Japan? Third, there was also the matter of Japan. Limited rearmament could perhaps provide Britain with an opportunity to create a role for itself as partial mediator between the US and Japan (and other powers) and thus water down an overly thick relationship.[21] Britain might yet be able to help guide the process and recover some lost influence. Moreover, the fact also had to be considered that a rearmed Japan could potentially provide a lucrative market for weapons exports.[22]

Finally, in 1950, with President Truman's appointment of John Foster Dulles as his special envoy to Japan, concrete Anglo-American negotiations, which culminated in the 1952 San Francisco Peace Treaty with Japan, commenced.[23] British minds, in the UK Liaison Mission[24] in Japan, in the various government offices in London, and in the UK Embassy, Washington, now focused directly on the matter of Japanese rearmament and military relations. Although Britain eventually co-sponsored the Treaty with the US and sought, mostly unsuccessfully, to modify American terms, the main negotiating points between the two powers centred on commercial concerns, the status of China in a peace settlement, and post-war regional security treaties.[25] While it was clear that the US intended to make its own defence arrangements with Japan through the US–Japan Security Treaty, the actual military arrangements and obligations on Japan were less clear.[26] Adding to this confusion, Her Majesty's Government (HMG) representatives everywhere suspected that the US was deliberately and unjustifiably withholding information on its designs for Japanese rearmament to the great detriment of a mature understanding of Japanese security amongst the Western allies and public opinion. This was believed to be all the more dangerous given that the Peace Treaty itself set no limits on rearmament which, as the British Embassy in Tokyo quickly pointed out, was also known to public opinion.[27]

Remote control: HMG on Japanese rearmament

There were two main government bodies whose debates fed into the formation of government policy. First, there was the British military establishment, which culminated in the Joint Chiefs of Staff, and, second, the Foreign and Commonwealth Office, with its Japan specialists, and also its specialists in Japan, namely the Liaison Mission (and later, Embassy) staff. In preparation for eventual peace treaty negotiations (the British had hoped as early as Spring 1947 that the US would convene an international conference to discuss peace with Japan), it was the Chiefs of Staff Committee which first prepared a detailed analysis on a Japanese peace treaty and rearmament. Interestingly, their conclusions were not at all far removed from Dulles' own propositions the following year. This report was prepared without first seeking to clarify US and Commonwealth views.[28]

In general terms, the Chiefs of Staff recognised American preponderance in the East Asian region generally and that US interests in the peace treaty would be predominant, but Commonwealth defence interests, namely Australia's and New Zealand's, were also acknowledged. Consequently, Japanese rearmament would best be viewed from an Allied rather than a purely British perspective. A further consideration was how, most effectively, could one curtail, as one must, Japanese military activity, and here the Chiefs concluded that a bilateral defence treaty between Japan and the US would constitute the most efficacious means. Finally, the impact that acquiescence in Japanese rearmament would have on the separate peace treaty with Germany was also considered.

In order to reach these conclusions, a resurgent Japanese military was analysed from several perspectives and top of the list was Japan's potential as an aggressor nation. The conclusion rapidly reached was that in isolation Japan formed a risible military threat: the almost total lack of natural resources ensured this fact. Any Japanese military successes enjoyed in the recent conflict depended upon a now denied capacity to exploit the raw materials of Asian conquests. However, there was no idle assumption that Japan would find isolation so splendid as others had done, hence the worry that 'should she become party to any combination of powers in the Far East, such as is now represented by the Communist bloc, she might develop sufficient strength to threaten territories throughout the Pacific and the Far East.'[29] Equally, though, the value of what could be denied to the enemy should also be appraised and, certainly, Japan held great value to the

West: Okinawa was the main US strategic airbase in the East Asia, for example. The Chiefs, incidentally, were not alone in reaching similar conclusions. Malcolm MacDonald also held that the fall of Japan to communism would be an 'untenable blow to our security in the Pacific' in light of Japan's 'strategic land area . . . the potential industrial power of this populous nation and . . . its energetic, efficient and aggressive military capacities.'[30]

Indeed, it was the last which remained the major concern, and Japan, no matter how strategically valuable, would need some tendons nicked in this regard. A peace treaty, therefore, should prevent any nation from exploiting Japan's potential in a manner hostile to the Commonwealth, eliminate any possibility of Japan once again becoming an aggressor, and allow the Western democracies essential military rights in times of war. Three potential solutions existed: (i) to keep Japan permanently disarmed and demilitarised; (ii) to permit limited Japanese rearmament; and (iii) to arrange a US–Japan bilateral treaty.[31]

The first two were rejected almost out of hand. The first was both politically and militarily undesirable; keeping Japan disarmed for all time would require an indefinite occupation, which was unrealistic as the Allies were unprepared to pay for it, and would alienate the Japanese. The second was seen as but one step to uncontrolled Japanese rearmament, as, once the occupation forces left, Japan would be dangerously free (the example cited was Germany after the Treaty of Versailles) to pursue its own objectives. The clear choice was a US–Japan bilateral treaty: it would provide for Japanese internal security, guard against an external aggressor, and leave Japan with an imbalanced military force and a minimal military industry. Such a treaty should also be signed concurrently with the peace treaty to ensure there was no vacuum after the withdrawal of occupation forces. In military terms, Japan would supply bases and ground troops (approximately 200,000 men) leaving the US responsible for the maritime and aeronautical spheres.[32] The US as the senior partner, and supplying Japan with materiel where necessary, was the best means of control available.

These policy recommendations were not without costs and required some basic rethinking of previous assumptions. Neither can one imagine that they were of great comfort to politicians mindful of the negative public reaction to UK compliance in Japanese rearmament. A key concern was economic, particularly ship building. A sound economy was essential if Japan were to resist communist temptations, and this required an expanded mercantile marine. Previous tonnage and speed restrictions should all be virtually removed and a valuable industrial addition to the Western democracies realized. Potential damage to the UK economy was recognized but dismissed: UK attempts to limit Japan would have considerable unnamed repercussions and in any case would be ignored by the US. Formal means of control over Japanese rearmament must also be foregone as an international inspectorate would now only arouse resentment. Communist participation, such as originally envisioned in the 1946 quadripartite system, was simply unacceptable.[33]

The Foreign Office was also being kept abreast of developments through the Liaison Mission in Tokyo. Its head, Sir Alvary Gascoigne,[34] prepared a lengthy report in September 1950 motivated by the strained international relations in East Asia and the need for a peace treaty with Japan. Again, Gascoigne repeated the view that the Allies must immediately take measures to 'retain Japan, the key to North Western Pacific and the main East Asian goal of Russian imperialism, within our sphere of influence'.[35] In this context Japan would either rearm and defend itself, or it would not and thus leave the democratic nations to shoulder the burden. There were only two choices and further delay in ascertaining which it would be was unacceptable.

The basic question, from the viewpoint of UK interests and the experience of the 1930s and 1940s, was whether a rearmed Japan was good or bad for the UK. The answer was, on balance, that a rearmed Japan would be preferable. While this basic conclusion mirrored that of the Chiefs of Staff, Gascoigne leapt far beyond them (and the Japanese government) in terms of strategic planning for the new Japanese military. A purely defensive Japanese military was not enough: the new Japanese army should also have an offensive capacity for, with World War III in the offing, it would be necessary in taking the fight to communism in continental Asia.[36] This was a startling suggestion and well beyond what was politically conceivable for the British government. Gascoigne considered, and then immediately rejected, concerns about the ramifications of such a suggestion on Japanese democratic development. Again, reflecting the basic Foreign Office view of the transitory nature of the Allied occupation, the 1946 Constitution, the supposedly cherished fountainhead of post-war democracy, 'will, in my opinion, be in any case emasculated after the peace, and one of the first modifications which is likely to be made to it will be the complete deletion of Article 9.'[37] By this analysis, the peace treaty would less celebrate the success of democratic reform than mark its virtual irrelevance.

Ironically, were they but aware of it, Japanese politicians and civil servants would have found in Gascoigne's statement a knowing confirmation of their own suspicions. During the Korean War, when pressed by Colonel Frank Kowalski[38] as to why Japan would not heighten its rearmament pace despite American help, an official replied that Japan would, but not until 1955 when the war would be over. Pressed further, the official explained:

> Should Japan have 300,000 ground troops [as Dulles was demanding], a strong argument would be made that we don't need that many to defend Japan from attack and the United Nations, under your influence, would ask us to cooperate by sending at least a hundred thousand to Korea. Once these troops are despatched, there is no telling when they will be withdrawn.[39]

Either ignorant of or unimpressed by these very real Japanese government concerns, Gascoigne went on to consider the reverse, namely, how to prevent the Japanese and their offensive army from independently despatching 100,000 troops to Korea.[40] His conclusion, and one that came to be repeated regularly, was that this should be done by means of 'remote control'. The button would be pressed the moment the Japanese military exceeded in size some informal, unwritten and yet pre-determined number. The form this 'button' would take was British and American control over Japan's supply of raw materials.[41]

Gascoigne's review was no small stimulus throughout the British government. Malcolm MacDonald queried the Foreign Office (FO) as to whether the topic should be discussed more broadly by British governors and representatives in South-East Asia. The FO itself cabled its thoughts on Gascoigne's report to the Washington Embassy to stress the need for a fuller British investigation to present to the Americans in case they unilaterally went ahead, rearmed Japan and presented HMG with a *fait accompli*. In November 1950, the Foreign Secretary, Ernest Bevin, called for a discussion paper, which would be initially based upon the chiefs of staff reviewing their earlier 1949 document. At this point, the FO's main concern appears to have been the negative publicity Japan's tentative steps towards rearmament would attract and for the Americans to have the need 'for extreme discretion about what has already been done impressed upon them'.[42]

The Joint Planning Staff submitted its draft report on 1 December 1950. It basically revisited its 1949 parent, but, reflecting heightened Cold War tensions, it now specifically identified Japan as the main East Asian goal of Russian imperialism and China as a powerful agent of international communism. A potential Japanese threat was again gauged and again found to be limited, at least in the short term. However, a long-term risk was identified in Japan's desire to expand, either economically or territorially, which Allied planners would need to accommodate in order to retain Japan for the West: 'This economic fact will inevitably provide for a motive for Japanese military aggression unless suitable political and economic measures are taken to allow for it.'[43] That Japan would be a significant power with understandably commensurate ambitions is clearly acknowledged. The pre-eminence of the US was restated as was the need for a bilateral US–Japan security treaty. A regional defence pact was discounted as militarily desirable but politically impossible for fear that Asian powers would see it as an example of US and UK imperialism.[44] This time Commonwealth views were taken note of, but were not necessarily addressed. For example, New Zealand's belief that Allied supervisory mechanisms in Japan were essential to enforce rearmament prohibitions was condemned as impracticable and unacceptable. In summary, Japanese rearmament was desirable and could be best achieved through a non-restrictive US–Japan bilateral defence pact signed after the peace treaty. There would be no restrictive clauses or control machinery. The long-term military objective would be a regional pact though it was also judged to be politically impossible in the short term. Japan should be encouraged to develop balanced land forces and asked to voluntarily refrain from acquiring strategic bombers, surface naval vessels larger than frigates, and submarines. In line with Gascoigne, the Chiefs of Staff also held that any excessive rearmament or distasteful Japanese military adventurism could be limited by restricting the materials needed to fuel the economy; that is, by pressing the remote control.[45]

As US–UK peace treaty negotiations continued over 1950–1951, Bevin upheld the Foreign Office and Chiefs of Staff line that America should retain its forces in Japan and conclude a separate bilateral security treaty. Such a treaty would free

Britain from the financial and logistical difficulties of co-guaranteeing Japanese security, while also providing some assurance to British territories and Commonwealth partners in South-East Asia and the Pacific.[46] However, over late 1951 and 1952, as the Peace Treaty came closer to implementation and calls for gradual Japanese rearmament more obviously expressed, HMG representatives in Japan, such as Sir Esler Dening, pressed for a common and more detailed view to be formed on Japan's rearmament and military security. To that end, in January 1952 he had the three service chiefs in Tokyo prepare a brief report to which he attached his own summary. Such reports became a regular part of his activities and were, for the most part, sent to the Foreign Secretary, Anthony Eden.

In general terms, Dening observed a potential for rearmament in that much of Japan's heavy industry had survived the Second World War and could be readily adapted for armaments manufacture; further, a large pool of skilled labour also existed. Nonetheless, he held even moderate independent rearmament to be completely beyond Japan's capacity for simple economic reasons. His sympathies seemed to lie with the Japanese Prime minister, Yoshida Shigeru, in that while some form of rearmament was not unwarranted, it must rely absolutely upon US large-scale support in order to avoid harming the economy. This perspective was absolutely consistent with Britain's political and foreign policy principles, and was thus a 'natural policy for the Government to adopt and it is difficult to see how it could adopt any other.'[47] Dening was equally clear, however, that economic constraints did not equal a long-term deprecatory Japanese input into its own military security, as,

> if Japan has no burden of rearmament whatsoever, her capacity to compete in the economic field with the products of United Kingdom will be proportionately greater. And since countries which seek to preserve their neutrality . . . are not absolved from the need to provide for defence forces, it would seem unreasonable that Japan should escape entirely from such obligations.[48]

Between these two concerns, Dening also spotted an opportunity for the UK to involve itself in US–Japan military relations. Astutely, he foresaw the considerable conflict between the latter two nations over Japan's economic ability to support rearmament and counselled that the US should make a very close study (as, indeed, it was) of Japan's capacity 'if acute differences are not to arise'.[49] Failing that, Britain could at last offer 'counsel [which] may perhaps be welcome.'[50] This highly desirable role made a definite UK conclusion as to the present and future scale of Japanese rearmament essential.

Further reports emphasising this point followed in succession. In late March, the Liaison Mission again warned of the need to focus on Japan's rearmament. The contrast between HMG's stance on German and Japanese rearmament was emphasized, with Tokyo-based officials warning that even with a united and near-sovereign Japan 'with us German rearmament is almost an obsession while Japanese rearmament we have left entirely to the Americans'.[51] That this failure to pay proper heed could come at the cost of the British economy was emphasised: 'the expenditure by Japan on rearmament has a vital bearing upon her capacity to compete with us in the economic field'.[52] The Mission could only conclude that although the UK regarded German rearmament as 'vital to the defence of Western Europe and our islands', it did not hold Japanese rearmament as essential to the 'defence of the free world, though the Americans do.'[53] This was perhaps not strictly true. For example, Malcolm MacDonald, the Commissioner-General of the United Kingdom in South-East Asia 1948–55, regularly made clear his strong belief that a continued Japanese alliance with the Western democracies was essential to resisting communism; admittedly, he also emphasised Japan's contribution as more economic than military. Even so, the importance of a viable Japanese economy was stressed at the highest levels of government, and again from a very early date. In 1948, the Foreign Secretary, Ernest Bevin, emphasised the undesirability of leaving 'ninety millions of people . . . in a cesspool of poverty'.[54] In Bevin's mind, economic security was a pre-condition to Japanese stability in the global community.[55] Even so, as epitomized by the 1957 Sandy White Paper, London's gradual turn from imperial possessions to Western Europe as the base of UK military security was clear.

The Liaison Mission also sought to assess the domestic Japanese response to rearmament. It was clear that strong public opposition existed on the part of 'the majority of the potential cannon-fodder ie the young' but that the longevity of such resistance could not be assumed. Indicative of the fundamental British doubt that defeat and occupation had made any deep impact upon Japan, Mission officials judged that resistance to rearmament would be based 'on purely materialistic and not moral objections . . . because the Japanese is not by nature religious and moral considerations do not weigh much in either the conduct of government or business'.[56] In essence, Japanese rearmament was probable and Britain would simply have to come to terms with it. The question lay over the speed and scale, but even here the Japanese ability to resist US pressure was recognized, in that, if Japan rearmed, 'the Japanese people will swallow rearmament to the extent that it is considered good for them by their rulers, but not necessarily to the extent considered good for them by the Americans.'[57]

Dening also attempted to explain the domestic Japanese situation to the Foreign Office. In his view, Article Nine and related constitutional problems could be circumvented, but public opinion was the core difficulty. Rearmament was inevitable, whereas the public, motivated by a fear of a revival of pre-war militarism, sought to shun reality. The Prime minister, Yoshida Shigeru, was held to embody this spirit by following a popular line against a policy which he must later face. Election campaigning during September 1952 only made this more obvious with rivals such as Hatoyama Ichirō lambasting Yoshida for being weak-kneed, hypocritical and unpatriotic. Such attention made it impossible to rearm quietly whilst pretending not to, and led to the October 1952 general election being fought partly on the rearmament issue. Dening regarded it a genuine error on the part of the Western Allies for the domestic Japanese debate to have rushed so far ahead of any co-ordinated external view on rearmament. The culprit was also clear: the

United States had failed to take Britain into its confidence and the views of the Pacific Commonwealth nations into account, with the result that Japanese public suspicion of US motives would remain as long as Japanese rearmament remained an American-only concern.[58]

'We do not know how clear US thinking is on this question':[59] Anglo-American relations and Japanese rearmament

Military security was hardly the first instance in which British officials found themselves ignored by their US counterparts: the Foreign Office had earlier noticed an American reluctance to share its economic policies for Japan, for example.[60] Such precedents, however, were of little consolation to Dening. It must be made clear that his concerns lay not in the notion of a rearmed Japan nor of American sponsorship of the process, but rather that an opportunity to act in concert, and obtain international and domestic Japanese understanding and support for rearmament, was being wasted. If Japan were to be expected to maintain military forces as part of any East Asian collective security arrangement, then 'her co-operation will be better secured if this view is put to her collectively than if one power continues at present to make all the running.'[61] The American failure 'to discuss with us freely and frankly the problem of Japanese rearmament and the outlook for the future' had left the UK 'at a disadvantage'. Emphasizing his concerns, Dening further contacted the Foreign Office to stress that a great advantage lay in 'a frank exchange of views between the US and ourselves' and that 'this can only be brought about in Washington; at present there is no disposition on the part of the Americans here to discuss the future with us.'[62]

The Foreign Office proved to be quite alive to such views, and in mid-February 1952 apprised Sir Oliver Franks, ambassador to the US, of the situation. The Chiefs of Staff were also consulted and concluded there was no military justification for pressing for an exchange of views with the US. Unsatisfied, the FO believed that the economic and political considerations were such that the matter should be brought up directly with the US Department of State. John Pilcher, of the FO's Japan and Pacific Department, ascertained that there was much force in Dening's view that

> public opinion in this and other Allied countries may be unprepared for the degree of rearmament which the United States government consider essential. Little can be done to correct this situation, unless the United States government are prepared to take us into their confidence.[63]

Franks was requested to sound out the Department of State on the need to prepare public opinion in the UK and the Commonwealth, and to request a broad outline on US plans for Japanese rearmament, especially with regards to speed and size.

Franks moved rapidly and within a fortnight cabled back to confirm that a member of the Embassy staff had approached John Allison, the assistant secretary of state for Far Eastern Affairs.[64] Allison was sympathetic and agreed that Japanese rearmament would have political ramifications in Japan and abroad. Clearly, there was also division within the US, as the Department of Defense was ill-disposed to accept this point and believed it to be a US concern only. Allison also agreed that it was desirable that HMG be informed of US plans, but that such aspirations were little more than a velleity given the lack of official US government agreement on both the size and the speed of Japanese rearmament. The most information he could offer was that a committee was being prepared to decide these very matters, which would then be subject to joint US–Japan discussions in Tokyo. As a long-term plan, he also spoke of a single overall Pacific pact agreement perhaps including the US, Japan, Philippines, New Zealand and Australia. Japan would participate in joint discussion of the allocation of defence resources in this area so as not to feel discriminated against.[65] This committee appeared to be rigged for silent running, at least as far as Britain was concerned.

Some nine months later in November 1952, the Foreign Office was again approaching Franks to enquire why the US was not taking the UK into its confidence on Japanese rearmament. He was specifically asked if this perceived American reticence was based upon any fears that HMG would be obstructive (and was immediately assured it would not be).[66] Again, Franks was quick to assure Eden that he was unaware of any particular reason for the Washington to ignore London on this issue. Instead, he considered it more a reflection of internal US discord between State and Defense leading to an American approach best characterized as piecemeal rather than comprehensive and long term. On fears that London might be seen as confrontational, Franks was explicit.

> The point that Her Majesty's Government can only assist in educating public opinion to accept the necessary measure of Japanese rearmament if they are kept fully informed of its intended scale and speed has been put forcefully to the State Department on more than one occasion.[67]

Almost immediately after this telegram, the Washington Embassy was able to inform London that papers containing new recommendations on Japanese rearmament were circulating in the Department of State. Bob McClurkin, deputy director of the Office of North East Asian Affairs, confirmed as much but stressed that the Secretary of State had not approved the document. Informally, however, he confirmed US objectives to strengthen Japanese air power (approximately 600 combat aircraft of all types, but no long-range bombers) and ground forces of some 325,000 men. Naval forces were envisaged as remaining as a coastal defence force.[68]

However, it was not until April 1953 that UK, Australian, New Zealand and Canadian representatives were summoned to the Department of State to be fully informed of US plans. Representatives were not given any documentation to carry away with them and were allowed only to take notes. The broad framework rested on several basic assumptions: Japanese forces would be purely defensive in size and character; the US would provide all of the initial equipment and so would hold considerable control over the speed and scale of Japanese rearmament; that the Japanese economy could not withstand large-scale rearmament; that the US had no intention of withdrawing its troops from Japan; and that it intended to form combined command arrangements with Japan to operate in the event of hostilities involving Japan. More specifically, the US envisaged a ground force of 325,000 men and confirmed that covering three years up to June 1953, $500 million (enough to equip six divisions or 180,000 men) would be made over to Japan. Maritime forces would consist mainly of minesweepers (approximately 40), 18 frigates, 50 landing craft and sundry auxiliary vessels. The construction of aircraft carriers or other capital ships was not contemplated. Air strength was set at 225 interceptors, 75 all-weather interceptors, 150 fighter bombers, 54 shufti planes and 96 transport aircraft.[69]

Aftermath: 'we have no need to fear'[70]

Final American disclosure obviously required a UK response. The Chiefs of Staff met in May 1953 and, in essence, agreed that Washington's proposals were acceptable. Land force strength of 325,000 clearly exceeded the previous assumptions of 200,000 men, but again American safeguards and the massive increase in Chinese armed forces nullified any undue concern. In effect, Japan was left with a minimal defensive capacity but could make useful contributions to any Allied war effort; in no way could Tokyo balance the growing power of Beijing. This latter point was stated approvingly. There was clearly no desire on the part of the Chiefs that Japan indeed be encouraged to provide such a counter-balance despite the undoubted strict military attraction of such a proposal. Here they were possibly at odds with the Prime minister, Winston Churchill, who commented instead that 'this might well be the only effective manner of balancing the growing power of Communist China in the next decade.'[71] Regardless, here, at least, the Japanese government was at one with the chiefs of staff, though perhaps for different reasons.

Commonwealth views were also requested. Australia forwarded its March 1953 Australian Defence Committee report and added that the US proposals did not alter the conclusions. Appreciation for the opportunity to comment on such an important subject was also recorded. Basically, the Australians were in concord with the British: Japan would develop only a defensive force under US guidance, which was, again, acceptable. The key difference were Australian misgivings that the Peace Treaty did not contain limitations on Japanese rearmament, for example, the development of a strategic bomber force. Even so, Canberra, with one eye on Japanese reliance on the US for military equipment and funding, and the second on ANZUS, had no choice other than to accept a reality formed of good faith in John Foster Dulles' spoken promise that: 'we would have to take the United States on trust in respect of the scale of Japanese rearmament . . . but we need have no fear'[72].

US disclosure to Britain (and, in effect, to the rest of the world) held one final implication for the UK and that was the need for some housekeeping. Popular widespread domestic opposition to Japanese rearmament was something both Whitehall and Westminster were painfully cognizant of. There appears to have been a genuine concern that exaggerated reports would lead to unhelpful press coverage and questions in the House. Further, any failure to squash criticism ran the risk of arousing US suspicion of the British attitude, which would only aggravate Anglo-American policy differences in East Asia.[73] The solution was to prepare a simple statement to be trotted out whenever HMG's views were asked. The agreed text read that it was 'inevitable that Japan should assume a greater share of the responsibility for her own defence' and that, in the opinion of HMG, 'it is in the interest of the free world that Japan should have the forces to the extent required to defend her own territory.'[74]

Meanwhile, Dening continued to provide regular reports from Tokyo on the speed and nature of Japanese rearmament. UK service representatives in Japan also regularly observed Japanese troops, spoke with their officers and so forth. In January 1955, the Foreign Office Research Department produced what seems to be one of the final consolidated 'thought pieces' on Japanese rearmament for the 1950s. Initially, this report is quite mundane and repeats the basic mantra: Japan should have the means to defend its territory but these should not be of a size or nature to permit aggression. Indeed, it was posited that under the current Japanese government, 'the main concern of Western policy will be to ensure that Japan fully undertakes her responsibilities for defence, rather than that she oversteps them.'[75] The main interest, however, is that ten years after Allied victory and three after the end of the occupation, the FO experts blatantly still held little faith in the seaworthiness of Japanese democracy. The memorandum then continues to consider, without evidence of likelihood, that, should the post-war principle of civilian supremacy over the military fall, there was a considerable danger that Japan would return to the 1930s. In other words, Japan would rearm to a level far beyond that necessary for self defence and once again call for racial independence, with demands for assured markets providing the political impetus. The population was large enough to supply both large armed forces and an industrial base. The Anglo-American remote control was still in play, but batteries have a shelf life and the old fear of a hellish marriage of Japanese technical aptitude with Chinese raw materials voiced itself again. A sharp eye would have to be paid to watch for signs of Japanese militarism and any attempt on the part of Tokyo to reduce its dependency on the West for raw materials.[76]

From Tokyo, Dening attempted to contradict such speculation. He affirmed that all sections of Japan with any influence on the government opposed large-scale rearmament. Further, rearmament lacked popular support (he held that American pressure in its favour ensured this) and that veterans had specific targets such as welfare so were not a danger. Japan had learnt something from defeat and occupation, which should be, however cynically, recognized.

> Japanese ministers are interested exclusively in material benefits for their own country and themselves. They may be said to be working for the less spectacular aims of pre-war Japanese policy, but with a far healthier respect both for the feelings of the Japanese people, and for the reactions of world opinion than the politicians of the 'thirties some of whom are to be found among them.[77]

Of course, he was not hopelessly sanguine either, and realized that civilian dominance would have to be worked at and not lazily assumed. The debate over the National Defence Council emphasised the need to establish the principle of civilian supremacy; equally, the 1960 Security Treaty crisis showed how the close military relationship with the United States was not without potential threats to Japanese parliamentary democracy.[78] While there were undoubtedly some unscrupulous Japanese politicians, 'as long as Japanese democracy is vigilant, and parliament, the press, trade unions and other institutions have time to establish themselves, the danger will be small.'[79]

The FO Research Department subsequently redrafted its memorandum. Some of the more extreme language was recast and Britain would work at reducing to a minimum any Japanese irritation from close association with the West. One example of reducing such irritation was encouraging Japan to defend itself rather than rely solely on the US, as this would inevitably cause friction between the two. Pointedly, British denial of Japanese entry to GATT did not come under this category as it was rather an example of unavoidable discrimination, which should either be hidden or 'made palatable' through compensatory policies.[80] Britain should use its influence (what this 'influence' might be was never defined) to promote in Japan a greater understanding of the outside world so as to enlighten the Japanese of the benefits of close association with the West and to tactfully encourage the Japanese to preserve the democratic features of their constitution to ensure political control over the military. Finally, the FO did not entirely surrender its fears of a communist-led North East Asian power bloc and observed that historical links between the region and the Japanese economy could well draw them together.[81] Whatever these latter concessions, the point is clear nonetheless that despite concerns of exaggerated red-top reports on Japanese rearmament, HMG could look closer to home than Fleet Street to find those who would excite prejudice without cause.

Conclusion

Ultimately, Britain failed to gain a position of any measurable influence over either Japan's rearmament or America's external guidance over the process. While the attempt indicates a determination to retain a world role, it does not necessarily reflect the thoughtless and conditioned response of a flagging imperial power determined to retain a finger in every pie. The British Chiefs of Staff, for example, sought to cast Japanese rearmament as an allied and not a purely British concern; further, they suggested a bilateral US–Japan defence treaty as a means to guarantee long-term American control over the development of any post-war Japanese military force. Nonetheless, although willing to support American dominance, the UK had not bargained on being so thoroughly relegated to the backbenches. The eventual fate of the colonial empire in South-East Asia was still not entirely clear and key Commonwealth ties, particularly with Australia and New Zealand, meant Japanese rearmament was not always a distant and relatively meaningless process. The constant refusal of American authorities, both in Japan and in the continental US, to involve and inform Britain of Washington's intentions was frustrating to the extreme. The United Kingdom found such practices not only humiliating, but also a destructive measure which limited the capacities of the two powers to act in concert in promoting common free world interests. Clearly, at times the United States, and in this case particularly the Department of Defense, were either suspicious of British intentions, indifferent to Britain's role as an ally, keen to independently exploit perceived American core interests, or a mixture of them all.

However, Britain's interest in Japanese rearmament during the 1950s should not be so readily slapped aside. Japan's post-war global re-emergence did not simply reflect monolithic US–Soviet Cold War tussles. America's allies likewise believed their views on Japan, and rearmament (being particularly sensitive), should matter, and they were happy to voice them. Potentially these concerns could, as in the case of Australia, cut across and set at odds crucial relationships with the United States and the British Commonwealth. The study of British attitudes regarding Japanese rearmament and the US–Japan alliance provides one further aspect from which to consider London's attempt to retain a global position and interests in the post-war world, which matched its own political and military assumptions. From Tokyo's perspective, there was perhaps some worth in making a limited challenge to American dominance of the rearmament of Japan, but from Britain's, this very process again emphasized the difficulties the UK faced in trying to retain a high level of global influence in the post-war world. Churchill's Three Circles posited Britain as residing in the point of juncture, the very centre of global affairs. As Japan redeveloped its security forces, this position entailed aligning relations with the Commonwealth, the United States and with Japan, and convincing all three that simply speaking with each other and bypassing London was undesirable. Long-term failure in this area is clear: Japanese rearmament again proved that in the long run it was impossible for Britain to square the junction of any number of its circles. It is also possible to observe, however, an awareness of relative weakness, a definite recognition that Britain alone could no longer take an independent role in East Asia, and acceptance of American predominance, at least in East Asia. In this sense, Japanese rearmament in the 1950s represented a further opportunity for Britain to attempt to occupy the hinterland between the impossibility of global pre-eminence and of an unthinkable irrelevance in the American- and the Soviet-led post-war world order.

Notes

1 In full, Article Nine reads:

> Aspiring sincerely to an international peace based on justice and order, the Japanese people forever renounce war as a sovereign right of the nation and the threat or use of force as a means of settling international disputes.
>   In order to accomplish the aim of the preceding paragraph, land, sea, and air forces, as well as other war potential, will never be maintained. The right of belligerency of the state will not be recognised.

2 The SDF, in which form the Japanese military remains today, consists of three branches: the maritime, air and ground self-defence forces; it comes under the control of the Defence Agency, in effect a *de facto* ministry of defence.

3 See, for example, J. Dower, *Empire and Aftermath: Yoshida Shigeru and the Japanese Experience, 1878–1954*, Cambridge, MA: Harvard UP, 1979, pp. 369–470; J. Welfield, *An Empire in Eclipse: Japan in the Postwar American System*, London: Athlone Press, 1988.

4 W. Churchill, *Europe Unite: Speeches 1947 and 1948*, London: Cassell, 1950, pp. 417–18. On Churchill's 'Three Circles' concept, see J. Frankel, *British Foreign Policy 1945–73*, London: Oxford University Press, 1983, pp. 68–77.

5 On Britain and the occupation of Japan, see R. Buckley, *Occupation Diplomacy: Britain, the United States and Japan 1945–52* Cambridge: Cambridge University Press, 1982; P. Lowe, *Containing the Cold War in East Asia*, Manchester: Manchester University Press, 1997. On South-East Asia, see J. Tomaru, *The Postwar Rapprochment of Malay and Japan, 1945–61: The Roles of Britain and Japan in South-East Asia*, Basingstoke: Macmillan, 2000. On economic matters, see N. Yokoi, *Japanese Postwar Economic Recovery and Anglo-Japanese Relations 1948–62*, London and New York: RoutledgeCurzon: 2003; J. Weste 'Facing the Unavoidable – Great Britain, the Sterling Area and Japan: Economic and Trading Relations, 1950–60' in J. Hunter and S. Sugiyama (eds) *The History of Anglo-Japanese Relations, 1600–2000*, vol. 4, *Economic and Business Relations*, Basingstoke: Palgrave, 2002, pp. 283–313.

6 Malcolm MacDonald Papers, Palace Green Library, University of Durham (hereafter MMP), 22/10/24 Anthony Eden to Malcolm MacDonald, untitled, 23 May 1952.

7 See M. Dupree, (ed.) *Lancashire and Whitehall: the Diary of Sir Raymond Streat*, vol. 2, 1937–57 Manchester: Manchester University Press, 1987.

8 MMP 33/2/84 MacDonald to Anthony Eden, Foreign Secretary, 'Note on Japan', 26 July 1952. Apparently, it was this same authoritarian nature that unfortunately left the Japanese psyche as exposed to post-war communism as it was to pre-war militarism.

9 Dupree, *Lancashire and Whitehall*, p. 737.

10 National Archives, Kew (hereafter NA Kew), FO 371/54280 'Draft Treaty on the Disarmament and Demilitarization of Japan', 1 March 1946, p. 1.

11 Ibid., pp. 3–4.

12 NA Kew, FO 371/54280 'American Draft Treaty on Japanese Disarmament', 19 March 1946, p. 1.

13 NA Kew, FO 371/54280 Chiefs of Staff Committee Joint Planning Staff 'Future Treatment of Japan' 14 April 1946, p. 2.

14 NA Kew, FO 371/54280 Personal and Top Secret – From Sir Orme Sargent to General Ismay, untitled, 27 March 1946, p. 1. On Anglo–Australian policy making for Japan, see Buckley *Occupation Diplomacy*, pp. 142–54.

15 NA Kew, DO 35/2458 To the Australian Embassy, untitled, Washington, 7 May 1947, p. 2.

16 NA Kew, DO 35/2458 GCB Dobbs to HJ Oram, Treasury, untitled, 9 June 1947, p. 1.

17 NA Kew, DO 35/2458 Australian Government to Commonwealth Relations Office, untitled telegram, 5 April 1948.

18 NA Kew, DO 35/2458 GCB Dobbs to HJ Oram, Treasury, untitled, 9 June 1947, p. 2.

19 As quoted in S. and M. Harries, *Sheathing the Sword: The Demilitarisation of Japan*, London: Hamish Hamilton, 1987, p. 213.

20 On such developments, see Welfield *Empire*, pp. 65–70; J. Weste, 'Staging a comeback' in *Japan Forum* 11 (2) 1999:165–78.

21 R. Buckley 'Anglo-Japanese Relations, 1952–1960' in W. Cohen and A. Iriye (eds) *The Great Powers in East Asia 1953–1960*, New York: Columbia University Press, 1990, p. 172.

22 On British attempts to develop a weapons export market in Japan, see J. Weste, 'Facing the Unavoidable', pp. 297–9.
23 See R. Buckley, 'Joining the Club: The Japanese Question and Anglo-American Peace Diplomacy, 1950–1951' in *Modern Asian Studies*, 19(2), 1985, pp. 299–319.
24 As an occupied nation Japan was not accorded the right to host foreign embassies; instead Britain retained its presence through the United Kingdom Liaison Mission.
25 Buckley, *Occupation Diplomacy*, pp. 173–9.
26 The US–Japan Security Treaty was signed simultaneously with the Peace Treaty at San Francisco in September 1951 (Welfield, *Empire*, pp. 25–6). In negotiations with the British prior to the Peace Treaty, John Foster Dulles, President Truman's special envoy on Japan, advised that the Security Treaty would be defensive in nature, the first step towards a wider co-operative security arrangement in Asia, that the US would retain base rights in Japan and provide aeronautical and maritime security leaving Japan to focus on developing ground forces. See R. Buckley, 'Joining the Club' in *Modern Asian Studies*, 19(2), 1985, pp. 312–3.
27 NA Kew, FO 371/99470 Dening, untitled, 14 January 1952, p. 1.
28 NA Kew, FO 371/83887 Chiefs of Staff Committee, 'Japanese Peace Treaty – Defence Aspects', 23 December 1949, pp. 1–7.
29 Ibid., p. 2.
30 MMP 33/2/85–7, MacDonald to Anthony Eden, 'Note on Japan', 26 July 1952.
31 NA Kew, FO 371/83887 Chiefs of Staff Committee, 'Japanese Peace Treaty – Defence Aspects', 23 December 1949, p. 7.
32 Ibid., pp. 3–4. In the 1960s, Genda Minoru (planner of the Pearl Harbor operation, and the first post-war chief of the Air Self-Defence Force) stated that 'the greater part of the American forces stationed in Japan . . . are offensive in character . . . the main objectives of Japan's air defence network is to protect American's retaliatory power, to guard the bases from which American retaliatory power will take off' (Welfield, *Empire*, p. 111).
33 NA Kew, FO 371/83887 Chiefs of Staff Committee, 'Japanese Peace Treaty – Defence Aspects', 23 December 1949, pp. 4–5.
34 On Gascoigne, see P. Lowe 'Sir Alvary Gascoigne in Japan, 1946–1951' in I. Nish (ed), *Britain and Japan: Biographical Portraits*, Kent: Japan Library, 1994, pp. 279–94.
35 NA Kew, FO 371/83889/1194 Gascoigne to FO, 'The Problem of Japanese Rearmament', 18 September 1950, p. 1.
36 Ibid., p. 2.
37 Ibid., p. 3.
38 Kowalski was the American army officer who oversaw the training of the National Police Reserve, 1950–52. On his experiences, see F. Kowalski, *Nihon Saigunbi*, Tokyo: Simul, 1969.
39 J. Dower, *Empire and Aftermath*, pp. 388–9.
40 And yet it must also be acknowledged that there were private Japanese groups, often enjoying American patronage, actively engaged in planning precisely how to do that. See J. Weste, 'Staging a comeback', pp.165–78.
41 NA Kew, FO 371/83889/1194 Gascoigne to FO, 'The Problem of Japanese Rearmament', 18 September 1950, p. 2.
42 NA Kew, FO 371/83889/1194, 'Japanese Rearmament', 15 November 1950, p. 2.
43 NA Kew, FO 371/83889/1194, 'Rearmament of Japan', 1 December 1950, p. 5.
44 Even then, when the South-East Asia Treaty Organisation (SEATO) was formed in September 1954 the only non-Anglo-Saxon powers (apart from the three protocol states of Indochina) to participate were Pakistan, the Philippines and Thailand.
45 Ibid., pp. 9–11.
46 Buckley, 'Joining the Club', pp. 303–04.
47 NA Kew, FO 371/99470 Dening, untitled, 14 January 1952, p. 2.

48 Ibid., p. 3.
49 Ibid., p. 3.
50 Ibid., p. 4.
51 NA Kew, FO 371/99470 UK Liaison Mission in Japan, untitled, 24 March 1952, p. 1.
52 Ibid., p. 1.
53 Ibid., p. 1.
54 G. Daniels, 'Britain's view of post-war Japan' in I. Nish (ed) *Anglo-Japanese Aliena-tion 1919–1952*, Cambridge: Cambridge University Press, 1982, p. 262.
55 Ibid., p. 258.
56 NA Kew, FO 371/99470 UK Liaison Mission in Japan, untitled, 24 March 1952, p. 2.
57 Ibid., p. 2.
58 NA Kew, FO 371/99470 Dening to Anthony Eden, untitled, 15 September 1952, p. 5.
59 NA Kew, FO 371/99470 Dening, untitled, 14 January 1952, p. 3.
60 Buckley, *Occupation Diplomacy*, pp. 164–5.
61 NA Kew, FO 371/99470 Dening to Anthony Eden, untitled, 15 September 1952, p. 5.
62 NA Kew, FO 371/99470 Dening to FO, untitled, 14 January 1952, p. 5.
63 NA Kew, FO 371/99470 Pilcher to Franks, untitled, 14 February 1952
64 Allison was later the US ambassador to Japan; see: J. Allison, *Ambassador from the Prairie or Allison Wonderland*, Tuttle, 1975.
65 NA Kew, FO 371/99470 Franks to Eden, untitled, 27 February 1952, pp. 1–3. Point-edly, such consideration was not extended to Britain when the ANZUS Treaty was being negotiated. Britain's only compensation gained was the right to veto any Com-monwealth pact that included Manila. Buckley, *Occupation*, pp. 178–9.
66 NA Kew, FO 371/99470, FO to Franks, untitled, 10 November 1952.
67 NA Kew, FO 371/99470 Franks to Eden, untitled, 20 November 1952, pp. 1–2.
68 NA Kew, FO 371/99470 F.S. Tomlinson (Washington Embassy) to Pilcher, untitled, 25 November, pp. 1–2.
69 NA Kew, DO 35/5805 'Japanese Rearmament – Summary of US Proposals', undated, July 1953, pp. 1–2.
70 NA Kew, DO 35/5805 'Japanese Re-Armament views of the [Australian] Defence Committee', 26 March 1953, p. 1.
71 NA Kew, FO 371/105394, 'Japanese Rearmament', p. 3.
72 NA Kew, DO 35/5805 'Japanese Re-Armament views of the [Australian] Defence Committee', 26 March 1953, p. 1.
73 NA Kew, FO 371/105394 'Japanese Rearmament', 19 October 1953, p. 4.
74 NA Kew, FO 371/105394, Japanese Rearmament', undated, December 1953, p. 1.
75 NA Kew, FO 371/115254 'Japanese Rearmament', 31 January 1955, p. 17.
76 Ibid., pp. 17–18.
77 NA Kew, FO 371/115254 Dening to MacMillan, untitled, 22 June 1955, p. 3.
78 A law to create the National Defence Council was passed in 1954, but it was not until 1956 that the Council was established. It was chaired by the Prime minister and com-prised the ministers of foreign affairs and finance, the directors general of the Defence Agency and the Economic Planning Agency, plus several other cabinet members. The chairman of the joint staff council could be invited to attend, but sat in a subordinate capacity and had no part in decision-making (Welfield, *Empire*, pp. 86–7).
79 NA Kew, FO 371/115254 Dening to MacMillan, untitled, 22 June 1955, p. 4.
80 NA Kew, FO 371/115254 untitled and undated revised version of the 31 January 1955 'Japanese Rearmament' memorandum, p. 2.
81 Ibid., pp. 5–6.

3 Japan in British Regional Policy towards South-East Asia, 1945–1960

Tomaru Junko

After the surrender of Japan in August 1945, the United Kingdom's policy objective in South-East Asia was to regain colonial control of the pre-war stronghold of Malaya and to recover lost influence throughout the region, with Singapore as the centre. Towards the beginning of the 1950s, Britain faced three major challenges in the region. The first was the political pressure of growing anti-colonial nationalism in the dependencies against British control and regional influence. The second was of both military and political nature: the spread of communist influence from the People's Republic of China (PRC), including communist insurrection in Malaya (that is, the Emergency).[1] The third was an economic challenge: namely, the financial difficulty of matching domestic spending needs with the worldwide 'obligations arising from our [British] Imperial Heritage.'[2] In terms of post-war reconstruction and guaranteeing the security of British dependencies, little was left to devote to South-East Asia. In the mid-1950s, with the impact of the 1955 Asian–African Conference and the 1956 Suez Crisis focusing international pressure on the abusive exercise of imperial influence, the UK decided to revise its South-East Asia policy. Throughout the 1950s, these policies were carefully redeveloped by the UK as a means to retain formal and informal influence against the debilitating challenges and pressures posed by decolonization and nationalism.

Meanwhile, Japan, the former aggressor in South-East Asia, also made efforts to resume contacts with the region and to gain acceptance in international society once more as a repentant nation. The 'reverse course'[3] of the Allied occupation policy encouraged Japan in this approach. Thus, while still under American tutelage, Japan sought rapprochement with British Malaya and other South East Asian countries, and attempted to join regional organizations under UK leadership, such as SEATO.

This chapter considers how and why the UK formed and revised its South-East Asian regional policy over the 1950s, and how Japan was positioned in this scheme. It thus sheds new light on Japan's place in the reorganization of British imperial policies. In addition, the non-military aspects of British policies towards South-East Asia, such as economic, cultural, and even psychological strategies, will also be considered. Certainly, to date little attention has been paid to these themes compared to the South-East Asia Treaty Organization (SEATO) and other such strategic arrangements.[4]

British regional policies and Japan: 1945 to 1954[5]

In March 1946, just before the restoration of British civil government in Malaya, Lord Killearn was appointed in Singapore as the Special Commissioner for the United Kingdom in South-East Asia. The post was created in order to exert British influence more effectively through the horizontal co-ordination of British policies in the region, not only amongst the dependencies, but also with non-British territories and independent states. Lord Killearn took charge of the area consisting of Ceylon, Burma, Malaya (including Singapore), Borneo, Thailand, Indochina, Indonesia, and Hong Kong. He was also instructed to maintain close contacts with India, Australia and New Zealand.[6] The post was reorganized in 1948 as the Commissioner-General for the UK in South-East Asia with the first and longest-serving Commissioner, Malcolm MacDonald.[7]

MacDonald and his successors continued to play an important role in shaping British policies towards South-East Asia through their correspondence with the Foreign and the Colonial Offices, and through chairing the annual conferences of the British head of missions under their jurisdiction [hereafter, Commissioner-General's Conference]. These annual conferences were frequently attended by British representatives from India, Pakistan, Japan, Australia, New Zealand, the Philippines, and high-ranking officials from the Foreign Office. In this sense, the British perception of 'South-East Asia' was broader and more flexible than the general definition of today.[8] It should also be observed that in the British official documents of the 1950s and 1960s, the word 'Far East' was often used interchangeably with the broader 'South-East Asia'.[9]

The UK attached importance to the horizontal co-ordination of policy at the regional level in order to tackle common problems in post-war South-East Asia, such as reconstruction, anti-colonialism, and the threat of communism, in order to dispel the growing suspicion of Asian people against a renewed British presence. British policy makers at the Foreign and Colonial Offices were especially concerned about this latter point, being painfully aware that Britain had lost the confidence of many Asians by leaving Malaya to the enemy in 1942, and that Japan had also enjoyed a certain success in planting Pan-Asianism amongst the local population.[10] These sentiments, it was felt, could easily fuel a nationalist resentment against Western colonial control. Therefore, the UK emphasized that the new 'regional policy' sought stability and economic development in South-East Asia through the promotion of horizontal co-ordination and co-operation in 'partnership' with local people. It was hoped they would notice its nature was completely opposed to the pre-war policies of paternalistic 'trusteeship' characterized by vertical metropolitan control of each dependencies as separate compartments.[11]

Moreover, from 1947, the Foreign Office pledged that Britain's role in South-East Asia was as a 'pioneer of regional co-operation' to gradually guide South-East Asians from the outside along the path of reconstruction and development towards future autonomous political, economic, and military co-operation.[12] This new UK role can be regarded as a means to justify and retain British influence in the region without provoking anti-colonial nationalism, and to make future intra-regional co-operation favourable to Britain's continued presence.

Throughout the 1950s, British Foreign and Colonial officials, both in White-hall and in the region, often regarded South-East Asia as 'politically adolescent with teenage weaknesses' and 'easily offended, and as easily influenced for good'. The officials thus viewed Britain as the region's 'favourite uncle' whose duty was to patiently guide 'the strong new forces of nationalism into constructive channels and [to cope] with the hydra of communist penetration'.[13] In 1955, the then defence minister, Harold Macmillan, stated that Britain must help 'nourish the will of the peoples of South-East Asia to resist this [communist] menace'.[14] Though the tone still reveals the 'trusteeship' mentality of pre-war imperialism, Britain pursued this tactful 'regional' policy as a means of coming to terms with local anti-colonial nationalism, and to counter communist infiltration. By 1953, it was clear that the UK also valued the 'considerable stabilizing influence that India could exert in South-East Asia' and Delhi's neutralism as a counterpoise to Chinese communist influence. Britain thus expected India to supplement British influence and to take a leadership role in South-East Asia.[15] With the same objec-tive of taming Asian nationalism in mind, the Commonwealth was also valued as a link between Britain and the newly independent Asian nations.[16]

Meanwhile, to help guard South-East Asia against potential communist mili-tary and political threat, the UK became an inaugural member of SEATO. Ini-tially, London tried to interest more Asian Commonwealth countries in joining and expected that SEATO would promote non-military, especially economic, co-operation.[17] However, India and Ceylon became critical of SEATO, Malaya refused to join, and American enthusiasm for military containment outran British aims, leading the UK to eventually hold a rather ambivalent attitude to SEATO.[18] Even so, British efforts to maintain a major role in regional economic develop-ment continued through the Colombo Plan and the Economic Commission for Asia and the Far East (ECAFE). Nevertheless, aggravating financial difficulties and the increasing strain of SEATO commitments forced the UK to face a funda-mental question: how could a British role in South-East Asian economic develop-ment be sustained?

It was in this context of relative British decline and retreat from empire that Japan was held to be useful. In the early 1950s, there was strong opposition in the UK to any policy which might encourage the resumption of Japanese economic relations with South-East Asia, namely through trade, investment, the softening of immigration controls in British Malaya, and Japanese participation in interna-tional organizations such as the Colombo Plan and ECAFE.

Lancashire industrialists and the Board of Trade officials led the opposition, as they remembered severe export competition with Japan in pre-war Asia. Some British colonial officials were also apprehensive of a resumption of fifth-column activities by Japanese businessmen. However, amongst the British representatives in South-East Asia, a different opinion grew, which, in effect, sought to utilize Japan as an economic agent to help Britain shoulder its regional obligations.[19] For example, in September 1951, Commissioner-General MacDonald wrote to the Foreign Office that 'Japan could be useful' as a source of capital goods for economic development in both British and foreign territories in South-East Asia, while rearmament programmes prevented the UK and other European countries from providing such goods in sufficient quantity and time.[20] The Commissioner-General's conference later that year recommended that the Japanese 'return to South-East Asia should be viewed with friendly understanding', and even noted that 'Japanese technical ability, Japanese consumer and capital goods and Japanese influence might well prove to be a most important factor in the development and future stability of South-East Asia.'[21]

British local officials were also afraid that resisting Japan's approach to South-East Asia, given its strong American backing, would increase Anglo-American friction in the regional context.[22] Moreover, the then Head of the UK Liaison Mission in Tokyo, Esler Dening, and leading metropolitan officials feared that Britain's constant opposition to Japanese access to South-East Asia or international organizations would not only embitter Japan but also cause 'the irritation of Asiatic opinion'.[23] Although not as central to British considerations as the American plan of economically linking Japan and South-East Asia, the need to redirect Japanese trade away from China and communist influence was also considered by British officials, both in London and in South-East Asia.[24]

Opinions in favour of allowing a Japanese return to South-East Asia, and to regional and international organizations, gradually gained support in the metropolis. By the autumn of 1954, all major objections were overruled. The timing is attributable to several factors. First, the change from military to non-military means to stabilize Britain's key dependency, Malaya, as the Emergency gradually came under control and the pace of decolonization accelerated. Second, there was growing British concern with Asian opinion as the Colombo Powers began preparations for the first international conference of Asian and African countries. Finally, one must also consider Prime Minister Yoshida Shigeru's[25] revision of Japanese 'economic diplomacy' from 1953 to pay greater heed to local needs whilst simultaneously creating some distance for Japan from American policy objectives and thereby heading towards some co-ordination with British regional policy.[26]

As is well known, US–Japan relations experienced a crisis in 1954, mainly due to diplomatic and economic approaches to Japan by the USSR and the PRC, and to the Lucky Dragon Incident.[27] UK officials proudly noted that Japan attached more confidence in British than American policies towards Asia, and that Great Britain held the more advantageous position in terms of influencing Japan.[28] As a result, though never actually realized, the UK even considered the possibility of Japanese participation in SEATO. Aware of Japan's constitutional and political difficulties in entering into military arrangements, the Foreign Office anticipated that Japan's association with SEATO would be more an economic one.[29]

As the gatekeeper to South-East Asia thus softened its attitude, Japan was able to rapidly expand trade and joint ventures with Malaya and other South-East Asian countries (Figure 3.1), while still struggling to settle reparation issues so as to achieve political rapprochement.[30] Japan also made vigorous efforts to prove its

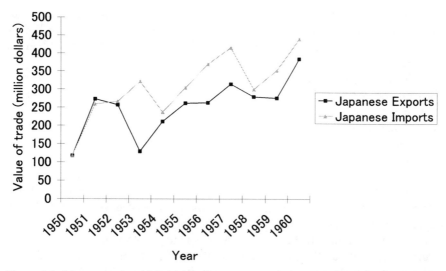

Figure 3.1 Japanese trade with British South-East Asia, 1950–60. Here, 'British South-East Asia' stands for British dependencies and former colonies now independent in the broader 'South-East Asia', namely India, Pakistan, Ceylon, Burma, Malaya, Singapore, and British North Borneo. Source: Japanese Ministry of Trade and Industry (1953), Tsūshō Hakusho (1953: 14–15; 1958: 556–67; 1961: 680–1).

value as a new member in international organizations by hosting ECAFE's annual session in Tokyo in 1955 and by sending various technical experts to South-East Asia under the Colombo Plan.

The revision of regional policies and Japan's position: 1955 onwards

Britain's new look for Asia

During 1955 and 1956, the UK faced two major challenges to its continued global influence, namely the Asian–African Conference and the Suez Crisis. The Asian–African Conference was held in Bandung, Indonesia, in April 1955, with government representatives from 29 countries in Asia, the Middle East, and Africa.[31] The organizers were the so-called Colombo Powers: India, Pakistan, Ceylon, Burma, and Indonesia, four of which were former British colonies. Britain feared that the Conference would become a forum for the Colombo Powers to agitate African countries and for PRC propaganda against Western colonial policies. The UK was also apprehensive that the Conference would disrupt relations with the new Commonwealth members, and would lead to a permanent Afro-Asian organization overlapping with existing regional organizations in which Britain held interests, namely the Colombo Plan, ECAFE, and SEATO.[32] The eventual tone of the joint communiqué, however, was neither so radically anti-colonial nor as anti-British as the UK had feared. Nonetheless, the Conference certainly enhanced Afro-Asian solidarity in world affairs and, according to UK observers, revealed the limitations of SEATO and the possible expansion of the Colombo Powers' influence, especially India's neutralism with its anti-Western inclinations.[33]

In May 1955, just after the Bandung Conference, the post of the Commissioner-General was redefined to include a co-ordinating role for SEATO and to keep a close eye on tensions in Indochina. Prime Minister Anthony Eden also decided to directly appoint the Commissioner-General in future. Certainly, criticism had been growing in the metropolis suggesting that MacDonald was too 'Asian-minded' and insufficiently active in directing a co-ordinated anti-communist front and conveying London's views to the local elite. As a result, MacDonald was transferred to India as high commissioner in May 1955 and Robert Scott, the Foreign Office advocate of reform, assumed the post of Commissioner-General.[34] This change represented the strengthening of vertical metropolitan control over South-East Asia, most likely due to the fear that MacDonald-style horizontal regional co-ordination might be utilized by the Colombo Powers to promote regional anti-colonialism or wider Afro-Asian activities prejudicial to British influence.

The Conference also boosted the influence of the Afro-Asian Group in the United Nations.[35] In fact, from September 1955, the Afro-Asian Group began to have periodical meetings in the UN and increased its numerical strength thanks to the collective admissions of 11 new Afro-Asian members in 1955 and 1956. As a counterpoise to this trend, Britain planned to organize a 'European group' in the UN.[36]

The Anglo-French invasion of the Suez Canal zone in early November 1956, and the subsequent withdrawal later in the year, dealt a severe blow to British international prestige and status. Most damagingly, international criticism and pressure, led by the US and exercised through UN resolutions, revealed Britain's inability to act independently on the international stage. The Minister of State for Foreign Affairs, Lord Reading,[37] also observed that the Suez Crisis had 'at least temporarily shaken our [British] position in South-East Asia' and recommended that something to be done to 'firmly reassert ourselves'.[38] A resident British journalist in Singapore reported to Eden that there had been 'a sense of Asian unity' since the Bandung Conference and that, in terms of Suez, 'much more harm' had 'been done to British prestige out here by the variety of subsequent excuses and explanations for the attack on Egypt than by the attack itself'.[39]

In December 1956, just as the British troops were withdrawing from Suez, the annual Commissioner-General's Conference in Singapore discussed the impact of the Crisis on the British position in Asia and how best to limit the damage. Attendees viewed the state of affairs with alarm and agreed there was 'an urgent need for a new look' for some shift in emphasis and increased efforts in the British regional policy.[40] The Conference concluded that the

> most significant reaction in Asia will prove to be that typified by Japan, where Anglo-French action was condemned not because it was attempted but be-

cause it is held to have failed, and where the inference has been drawn that Britain is no longer a first class power. [41]

It was also noted that Suez had shown that Britain 'cannot hope to "go it alone" in Asia'. In addition, the 'new China' and the Afro-Asian 'bloc' were considered as constituting major threats to British influence. This image of 'new China' was most likely derived from Zhou Enlai's success in demonstrating a moderate attitude at Bandung, and from his various other discussions with Asian leaders. It was also agreed that:

> The Afro-Asian 'bloc' could be very dangerous if it succeeds in plaiting together communism, anti-colonialism, and Moslem feeling. It should be our aim to prevent this happening and to lose no chance of pulling the strands apart.[42]

In fact, most of the Conference proposals were based on ideas expressed since April 1956 by the then Commissioner-General, Robert Scott.[43] Therefore, the New Look was not only a response to the Suez Crisis, but also intended to meet the post-Bandung situation in South-East Asia. This New Look policy can be summarized in five points. The first was to drop the Anglo-American spheres of influence concept by which Britain had left Japan, Korea, Formosa, and the Philippines to the US control with minimal consultation of London's views. Instead, British officials now wished to extend SEATO-type consultation and co-operation with America, Australia and New Zealand more widely in Asia. Suez had at least taught the lesson of the pitfalls of an international policy put into place without first obtaining the support and understanding of nations with a stake in the region.

Second, the New Look also called for closer consultation with India on South-East Asia policy. This feature reflected an element of pre-Bandung continuity. Equally, Britain must also have felt a particular necessity for such consultation given India's major role in the Bandung Conference and the Afro-Asian Group in the UN, in addition to Delhi's open condemnation of British policy and action in Suez. India even threatened to leave the Commonwealth if Britain went to war over Suez.[44] In this respect, MacDonald's transfer to India in May 1955, given his experience as a secret liaison between his father, former Prime minister Ramsay MacDonald, and Gandhi during the round-table conference in 1931,[45] can be interpreted as British attention towards the closer links between India and South-East Asia.

The third point was to promote co-operation between the smaller nations of South-East Asia with some scope for a regional organization to promote economic partnership, similar to that of the Organization of European Economic Co-operation, with possible Australian participation.[46] The fourth point was to emphasize non-military aid, such as administrative and technical training, to non-British and non-Commonwealth territories in South-East Asia. The third and fourth points also represented a degree of continuity from pre-Bandung policies, but with more importance now attached to promoting British guidance in non-British and Commonwealth territories.

The fifth point was that British publicity should concentrate more on presenting current policy and promoting trade than on countering communism. British representatives in South-East Asia wished to obtain the maximum publicity value from aid and to portray Britain as 'a bustling, up-to-date, enterprising country, with less emphasis on the land of beautiful cathedrals and ancient monuments'.[47] To this end, they proposed trade fairs, exhibitions, English-language teaching, and diplomacy through the personal exchanges of visits between important figures. Evidently, Britain had observed the success of Moscow and Beijing's 'cultural offensive' in Asia, as typified by the activities of Bulganin and Zhou Enlai, in addition to offers of aid. To help this publicity campaign, British officials requested more funding for the British Council. Though noting the overriding importance of financial concerns in view of the grave financial difficulties at home, regional officials suggested cuts to defence expenditures rather than economies in civil expenditure.

As a whole, despite some pre-1955 continuities, the New Look also had some innovative aspects. In particular, it gave greater consideration to the wider region with more emphasis on non-British and non-Commonwealth countries such as the Philippines and Japan, and sought to involve countries bordering the South-East Asia region, namely Australia, New Zealand, and India, to support British regional policies. Furthermore, it focused on a cultural and psychological approach to South-East Asia in order to promote an understanding of British policies. Some of these proposals were also in line with London's inter-departmental committee on East Asia recommendations to the Cabinet in July 1956: an emphasis on non-military policies, technical aid through the Colombo Plan, and on British Council activities in non-SEATO countries including India and Japan.[48]

Many of the New Look proposals were approved in London and implemented soon after. Personal visits were quickly promoted and, for example, in October 1957, the former Secretary of State for foreign affairs, Lord Reading, attended the Colombo Plan Consultative Meeting in Saigon and paid goodwill visits to Burma, Cambodia, Laos, and Thailand.[49] Moreover, in January 1958, Harold Macmillan toured India, Pakistan, Ceylon, New Zealand, and Australia, and attended the Commissioner-General's Conference. This was the first time that a prime minister had attended the Commissioner-General's Conference.[50]

On cultural policies, Anglo-Asian university collaboration was promoted, as was an exhibition of Asian art commencing with a display of Japanese antiquities planned from Autumn 1955. Moreover, the Cabinet Committee of July 1958 recommended an extended programme of English education in Africa, India and South-East Asia.[51] In the same year, the Commonwealth Scholarships Programme was established to invite Commonwealth students to study in Britain.[52] The emphasis on English education in the developing, rather than developed, nations, and on enhancing cultural and educational contacts with India and South-East Asia through the British Council, was in line with the Drogheda Committee recommendations, which were themselves hotly debated and finally enforced by the

Foreign Secretary, Anthony Eden, in November 1954.[53] As a result, from around 1956, government grants to, and the expenditure of, the British Council began to increase more rapidly (Figure 3.2).

The UK adopted the New Look policy not only directly towards South-East Asia, but also in relation to its actions in the United Nations. The British fear of an increased anti-colonial influence promoted by the Afro-Asian Group in the UN became a reality through the Suez Crisis, as demonstrated by the Group's full-scale condemnation of British action and the successful proposal and carrying of a General Assembly Resolution demanding withdrawal.[54] In addition, as the *New Statesman* observed in September 1956, hostility to the West was reinforced by the sense of Moslem brotherhood with Suez propelling Egypt forward as a leading anti-colonial nation and as the defender of Islam.[55]

This trend was what London had been dreading since the Bandung Conference. A member of the UK delegation to the UN reported that the Bandung group with its 'enormous voting power' had attained 'a remarkable degree of cohesion', which was 'powerfully stimulated' by the First Special Emergency Session on the Suez Crisis. Indeed, since the 11th General Assembly, just after the British military action, Britain had begun to send to the UN 'a lobbyist for the Afro-Asian delegations' instead of one for the Arab delegations, in order to monitor the Bandung group's behaviour and further influence it if opportunity arose. In New York, the 'lobbyist', formally appointed as a 'liaison officer', co-operated with Britain's UN Ambassador and liaison officer for the South Asian delegations appointed by the Commonwealth Relations Office to monitor and influence the Afro-Asian Group.[56] Moreover, from the 12th General Assembly onwards, the number of liaison officers increased from one to two.

Britain's UN delegation observed the Afro-Asian Group's behaviour in the UN, state by state, and made every effort to prevent joint action against British

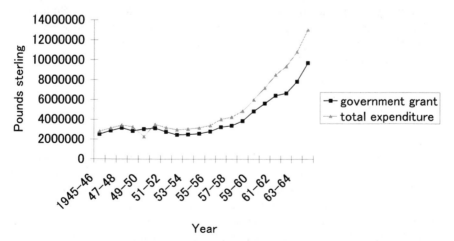

Figure 3.2 Income and expenditure of the British Council, 1945–65. Source: Frances Donaldson, *The British Council: the First Fifty Years*, Jonathan Cape: London, 1984, pp. 382–3, Appendix 5: Table of income and expenditure 1934–84.

interests. They also tried to exploit internal division through overtures to members friendly to Britain, such as Thailand, Pakistan, Malaya and Turkey.[57] Darwin has analysed that one of the four doctrines of British diplomacy after the Suez Crisis was to avoid isolation in the UN and to maintain the legitimacy of British international action.[58] It is now clear that the focus of such a new policy in the UN was on the Afro-Asian Group, and especially its Asian members. It can also be said that the New Look enhanced the UK's multilateral approach to Asian countries as a group, which had begun before the Bandung Conference.

British new look policies: the Japanese context

How, then, did British decision makers place Japan in the New Look for Asia, especially vis-à-vis South-East Asia? It is noticeable that the UK began to expect Japan to adopt a political role in South-East Asia in addition to its hitherto economic role. Before and during the Bandung Conference, Britain refrained from openly giving advice to any of the participating countries to avoid being criticized for intervening and did not expect much from Japan's participation. However, the UK informally expressed the hope that Japan, and other friendly nations, would exercise a 'moderating influence' to prevent the Conference from becoming radically anti-colonial and from yielding to communist propaganda. Japan was eager to co-operate with the UK, as the Hatoyama administration[59] was openly seeking greater independence from American influence in terms of foreign policy and considered the Conference a great opportunity to be accepted back into Asia.[60]

In June 1956, an inter-departmental memorandum for the British Cabinet Policy Review Committee on Asian policy stated that:

> Our policy should be to promote stability and to help the small neighbouring countries, as well as our own territories, to improve their administration and security . . . In peacetime we thus have an important role to play in South-East Asia: in North-East Asia we must leave the main effort to the Americans, while not neglecting the opportunities that offer, especially in Japan, for maintaining our own influence.[61]

In addition, during the Commissioner-General's Conference in December 1956, the British Embassy in Japan submitted a brief warning about the possibility of a Japanese approach to the Afro-Asian Group in order to obtain Tokyo's own influence in world affairs and, more specifically, in South and South-East Asian markets.[62] In fact, by the end of July 1958, the British Foreign Office held that Japan, under the premiership of Kishi Nobusuke,[63] showed a firmer commitment to the Free World than had previous Japanese prime ministers and was steadily increasing its influence amongst the Afro-Asian countries. The Foreign Office thus expected to indirectly sustain the UK's leverage over Asian countries through Kishi.[64] It cannot be a mere coincidence that, from around 1955, the British government publicly advocated the benefits of locking Japan into the Western camp by accepting Tokyo's participation in international organizations, on a variety of public occasions including interviews by members of parliament, the Commonwealth Prime Ministers' Conference, and Prime Minister Harold Macmillan's meeting with the Japanese foreign minister, Fujiyama Aiichirō.[65] Undeniably, the Afro-Asian Group was a hidden factor behind Britain's Cold War strategy of accepting Japan into international organizations.

Kishi's grand tour in 1957 was the first post-war visit of a Japanese premier to South-East Asia, as well as to Commonwealth nations in South Asia, Australia and New Zealand. He worked vigorously for the settlement of reparations and for rapprochement with South-East Asia through economic assistance for local development. Kishi even proposed the South-East Asia Development Fund, with American financial support, though ultimately he proved unable to obtain support either from Asian countries or from the US and UK.[66] Britain must have also noted that, during Kishi's visit to newly independent Malaya and the de-colonizing Singapore, both the Malayan Prime minister, Tunku Abdul Rahman, and Singapore's Chief Minister, Lim Yew Hock, made speeches indicating their willingness to learn from Japan as an example of Asian development.[67] On Tunku's return visit to Japan in 1958, a British Embassy official in Tokyo reported to London that Malayan officials did not accept any offer of help from the British Embassy and complained with a degree of jealousy about 'the lack of any allusion, however oblique, to the fact of his country's being a member of the Commonwealth family' in Tunku's public speeches.[68] Moreover, even in the Philippines, which had probably the most intense anti-Japanese sentiment in South-East Asia, Kishi succeeded in softening the antagonistic tone of the local press by expressing 'heartfelt sorrow' about the wartime Japanese behaviour at a banquet speech.[69]

By observing such trends, the UK must have sensed the tendency of the newly independent nations of South-East Asia to look to Japan and away from Britain and the other former suzerains. Seeking to retain political influence indirectly through Japan was one logical British response. In fact, the 1961 Commissioner-General's Conference discussed the possibility of the external leadership of South-East Asia being exercised by India, China and Japan, but ultimately agreed that Japan was then still too distracted by economic development and relations with the US. However, three years later, a Foreign Office memorandum came to consider Japan a more promising regional leader than India given its economic and technical abilities, and potential long-term use to Britain.[70]

In the United Nations, too, British attention was drawn to Japan's role in relation to the growing influence of the Afro-Asian Group. Since the restoration of Japanese sovereignty in April 1952, Japan had made every effort to obtain membership of the UN as a shortcut for acceptance into international society (and had despatched an observer to the UN since November 1952). Participation in the Bandung Conference not only opened a new pathway back to Asia, but also was a step towards UN membership. The leader of the Japanese delegation to Bandung, Takasaki Tatsunosuke, was active in lobbying for Afro-Asian support for Japan's full UN membership.[71] After the last-minute exclusion from collective accession at the end of 1955, with the subsequent domestic outrage, the Japanese observer sought closer co-ordination with the Afro-Asian Group and obtained an invitation to the Group's meetings from June 1956.[72]

Over the Suez Crisis, too, the Japanese Ministry of Foreign Affairs aimed at 'implicitly showing how unnatural it is that Japan is not yet a member of the UN' by sending a representative to the Suez Canal Users' Association meetings and by supporting the referral of the Crisis to the UN.[73] At the same time, Japan showed an understanding attitude towards the UK, as requested by London. The Japanese government also advised against (and, further, declined to attend) a conference of Bandung participants, sponsored by the Colombo Powers, on the Suez Crisis, on that grounds that discussion outside the UN would reduce the effectiveness of the UN's own resolutions.[74]

Therefore, the most likely reason for British support for Japanese UN membership in December 1956 was not only to keep Japan in the Western camp, but also to secure at least mild pro-British sentiment in the UN. In fact, with Japanese membership almost certain before the formal vote, Lord Reading suggested to the Japanese ambassador in London that once accepted to the UN, Japan request the Afro-Asian countries to refrain from radicalism. He also implied that the UK considered Japan a suitable candidate for non-permanent membership of the Security Council.[75]

The British delegation to the UN also defined Japan as one of the 'non-conformists' in the Bandung group, along with Turkey and Pakistan.[76] Sir Pierson Dixon, the British ambassador to the UN, reported that the Japanese representatives' 'particularly friendly attitude' to his delegation was 'most encouraging' and he welcomed speeches made in New York by Japanese Foreign Minister Shigemitsu Mamoru. Shigemitsu described Japan's role as 'a bridge between East and West' at the General Assembly. Moreover, as if echoing British expectations, Shigemitsu expressed the hope that in the UN 'Japan would be able to exercise a useful and moderating influence in the Afro-Asian group'. It is with little wonder that Dixon cheerfully reported to Selwyn Lloyd, the Secretary of State for Foreign Affairs, that the 'Japanese Delegation may prove a valuable new friend of the United Kingdom in the United Nations'.[77]

In chairing the Afro-Asian Group meeting on the Suez Crisis in January 1957 and in subsequent General Assembly discussions on South Africa or the British colonies, Japan's behaviour in the UN was indeed a reliably moderating one for the UK.[78] An American political scientist, who analysed voting behaviour in the UN in 1960, described how the Afro-Asian Group had come to hold two centres of power, one in India and the other in Japan.[79] The British Liaison Officer to the Afro-Asian delegations in the UN also reported that 'the Japanese Delegation were a useful source of information about the more cagey members of the Afro-Asian Group, notably the Indonesians'.[80] Thus, in the UN, the UK regarded Japan as being relatively mild and a source of information on various aspects of Asian opinion. Such considerations doubtlessly lay behind the UK's support for Japan's election in 1958 as a non-permanent member of the UN Security Council.

Thus, British expectations for exerting influence indirectly through Japan grew, not only with regards to economic development, but also for political moderation, both in the Asian region and towards the Afro-Asian Group in the UN. In essence, the first and the fourth aspects of the British New Look for Asia, namely, to extend influence and co-ordination east of the Philippines, and to emphasize non-military aid to non-British and non-Commonwealth territories, were both linked to Japan. In addition, the aforementioned British political efforts to separate the strands of communism, anti-colonialism, and Moslem feeling within the Afro-Asian bloc were also partially pursued through the 'moderating influence' of Japan.

In tandem with the above policy approach, the fifth element of the New Look, that is, more vigorous publicity and diplomacy through personal exchanges with Asia, was also applied towards Japan after the Bandung Conference. Earlier in February 1955, when the Foreign Secretary, Anthony Eden, attended the inaugural meeting of SEATO in Bangkok, he disappointed Japan by declining an invitation to visit.[81] However, in September 1956, despite the aggravating situation of Suez Crisis, the British government sent Lord Selkirk, Chancellor of the Duchy of Lancaster, for a ten-day goodwill visit to Japan. This ministerial trip arose from repeated requests of the British Ambassador in Tokyo, who feared that the UK appeared to be cold-shouldering Japan at time when many other Commonwealth VIPs found time to visit. Selkirk carried a letter from Eden, now prime minister, to the Japanese prime minister, Hatoyama Ichirō, expressing regret at his inability to visit Japan the previous year and a hope to further friendly relations with Japan. In conversation with Shigemitsu, the Foreign Minister, Selkirk discussed UK support for Japan's membership of the UN and pending Anglo-Japanese issues such as Japanese war criminals, the UK's GATT waiver to Japan and the Commercial Treaty and Payments Agreement.[82] It is interesting to observe that, three years later, Lord Selkirk was to succeed Scott as Commissioner-General in South-East Asia.

In 1957, though the newly elected prime minister, Harold Macmillan, was unable to accept Japan's invitation, the UK government invited the Japanese Foreign Minister, Fujiyama Aiichirō, to visit in September. London hoped to positively influence Fujiyama and Kishi soon after their assumption of office.[83] British ministers and Fujiyama discussed the GATT waiver, China, British nuclear testing, and the Japanese proposal of a South-East Asia Development Fund. Though no substantial agreement was attained, both governments appreciated the closer discussions.[84]

British distrust of the 'valuable new friend'

In January 1958, this time at Japanese request, Fujiyama went to Singapore to meet Macmillan on his Commonwealth tour. Fujiyama proposed political consultation among the US, UK and Japan on international issues in Asia, such as the Indonesian or the Kashimiri problems. It is intriguing that the Kishi government was observed by the British Foreign Office staff as aspiring to a leading role in Asia and as regarding Britain as an effective political lever to influence the United States and South-East Asia, in order to raise Japan's own international status.[85] Two years later, the British ambassador to Japan even commented that 'they [the Japanese] would like to have us [the British] as useful friends, provided that it does not cost too much' and recommended that the UK government should adopt the same attitude towards Japan.[86]

However, Britain had long viewed Japan as a convenient economic and political instrument to help shoulder part of Britain's 'imperial obligations' and thus to retain London's influence in South-East Asia. The apparent mutual intention of using each other was a striking irony. For the UK government, naturally Japan could assist but must not be permitted to overshadow Britain's world role. Precisely as with the earlier example of the Colombo Plan, Britain consistently aimed to 'continue to play and to be seen to play, a major role' in South and South-East Asia.[87] A strong desire for a leading regional role was most likely the main reason behind the British rejection of Japan's plan for a South-East Asia Development Fund and the studied indifference to Fujiyama's proposal of tripartite consultation. In his draft letter of 1961 to the Commissioner-General, Macmillan aptly expressed the primary British objective in South-East Asia, namely to 'achieve a successful scaling-down of our objectives and commitments in the area with little damage to our prestige or general interests.'[88] With Malayan independence in 1957, self-government in Singapore as of 1959, and the British contemplation of similar moves in the Borneo territories in the background, this objective can be interpreted as one of dissolving formal empire, with all its costly obligations, while retaining an informal empire of influence in South-East Asia.

Despite the closer contacts and co-operation between Britain and Japan in Asia in the latter half of the 1950s, Britain still distrusted Japanese intentions. For example, in terms of cultural relations, although the British Council opened a Tokyo office in 1953, its annual reports were mainly negatively couched with terms such as 'failure' and 'inability' in the fore until 1957–1958.[89] Further, an Anglo-Japanese Cultural Convention was proposed intermittently from 1953 onwards, but did not materialize until December 1960.[90] In 1959, the British ambassador to Japan admitted that the two core obstacles inhibiting improved relations were trade competition and the memories of Japanese wartime atrocities.[91] Exemplifying this theme, in the same year, a member of the British Embassy commented, while drafting the Cultural Convention, that 'no loophole should exist through which the Japanese could stage semi-commercial exhibitions in the United Kingdom, e.g., of electronic equipment, under the guise of culture.'[92]

In addition, throughout the 1950s, British government officials continued to fear Japanese population pressure as a further possible stimulus for a Japanese export drive and expansion of markets and influence in South-East Asia, again to the detriment of British interests.[93] As mentioned above, it was also believed that Japan would try to exploit the Afro-Asian bloc in order to enhance Tokyo's standing in South and South-East Asia. In 1958, the British ambassador described Japan as a re-emerging global power, and the *Economist* of the same year stated that the 'Japanese fully expect to play once more a leading role in Asia and the world'.[94] In 1960, a Colonial Office official warned that one could not exclude 'the possibility of a revived Japanese interest' in North Borneo and Sarawak, which would sooner or later move out of British control under the international pressure for decolonization.[95] It was also reported to the Japanese Ministry of Foreign Affairs that 'so many [Britons] continue to believe that Japan is nursing an urge to rearm and again indulge in power politics whenever a suitable opportunity occurs'.[96]

All along, as Tanaka Takahiko has pointed out, the Kishi government began to explore further areas for Japanese engagement and considered regions as far as the Middle East and Africa. In his speech at the UN General Assembly in August 1958, Fujiyama demanded the withdrawal of Anglo-American forces from the Lebanon and Jordan, though this demand caused little friction with the UK due to Britain's own quick decision to pull out. During his visit to Britain in July 1959, Kishi expressed his hope that through co-operation with the UK in the UN, Japan could contribute to a peaceful solution of the nationalist-inspired political instability in the Middle East and Africa.[97] In preparation for Kishi's British visit, the Japanese government was reported to have offered assistance to the UK 'in containing Communism and in promoting healthy nationalism in the Middle East and . . . work[ing] out with us [the British] a common policy as regards the underdeveloped countries of Asia and Africa'.[98] The UK government politely welcomed these offers, but the British response was also guarded. In fact, on this latter offer from the Japanese government, one British high-level official in the Foreign Office commented that Japan tended to overestimate its influence in Asia. The British ambassador in Tokyo in turn interpreted it as Japanese hope that 'we [the British] can help them [the Japanese] in economic penetration and trade in those countries'.[99]

On the Japanese side, as seen above, while pledging to be a bridge between East and West and being responsive to local needs, Japanese proposals for development funds and consultation were always based on the utilization of Anglo-American resources and influence, rather than on the local South-East Asian opinion. Japan's neglect of local feeling and the bitter memories of Japanese occupation were typically demonstrated in December 1956, when the Japan–Malaya Singapore Association was established in Japan as an extra-governmental organization of Japanese Ministry of Foreign Affairs to promote friendship in preparation for Malayan independence. The first president, Aoki Kazuo, member of the House of Representatives, had been the wartime Minister for Greater East Asia and most of the leading inaugural members also held pre-war or wartime connections with Malaya.[100] In addition, the wording of the Japanese government's offer to the UK to contribute to promotion of 'healthy nationalism', as quoted above, was simply echoing the British imperial perspective of guiding 'adolescent' nationalism into constructive channels.

Conclusion

The British attitude towards Japan went through a structural change in the mid-1950s from one of guarding against a Japanese return to South-East Asia, to one of ushering in Japanese participation in regional economic stabilization and political moderation. The UK feared the growth of anti-British sentiment and the consequent loss of influence in the region. With the spread of anti-colonial nationalism and communist propaganda, Japan was more than willing to accede to British suasion as complementing Tokyo's own post-war objectives of resuming contacts with, and regaining acceptance back in to, South-East Asia. This trend was also related to the simultaneous shift in US–Japan relations from around 1954 as Japan sought to lessen reliance on the US, as South-East Asian scepticism towards American regional policies, as typified by SEATO, grew. As a result, Britain and Japan entered into co-operative relations vis-à-vis the region, with the fear of local antipathy in South-East Asia being common to both.

However, in practical terms, co-operation was more a marriage of convenience than anything earnest and genuine. On the one hand, despite Britain's intention to utilize Japanese economic and political influence to support informal empire in South-East Asia, London's pre-war distrust of Japan as an avaricious and unscrupulous trader was persistent even at the end of the 1950s. On the other hand, at the base of Japanese co-operation with Britain's South-East Asia policy lay Tokyo's own wish to expand Japanese influence and markets in the region and, wherever possible, with Anglo-American funding and support. In addition, though the UK introduced its New Look strategy in 1956 and the Japanese annual economic white paper published in the same year confidently stated 'it is no longer postwar',[101] their attitudes to South-East Asia show some continuity from their pre-war and wartime imperialism. Britain sought to maintain an informal empire in the region and Japan paid insufficient heed to local feeling when attempting to resume its pre-war or wartime connections with the region.

As a result, in the 1960s, both countries were to face difficult issues arising from local objections to these vestiges of imperialism. For Britain, it was the 1961–66 dispute over the closer association of Malaya, Singapore, and North Borneo, during which Indonesia accused London of continuing to pursue neo-colonialist policies by leading the formation of Malaysia. For Japan, it was a failure in mediating this dispute, together with the blood debt claim by Malaysia and Singapore demanding Japanese compensation for the murder of local Chinese residents by the Japanese army during the Second World War. In terms of bilateral Anglo-Japanese relations, the two countries had to wait until the 1960s for the development of more direct relations with increased political contacts and cultural exchanges.

Notes

1 The so-called 'Emergency' in Malaya was brought about in June 1948 by the uprising of Chinese communist guerillas against British Rule. The state of emergency was finally lifted in 1960.
2 Document 11 in A.N. Porter and A J. Stockwell, eds, *British Imperial Policy and Decolonization 1938–64: vol. 2, 1951–64*, London: Macmillan, 1989, pp.167, 171.
3 The US-led occupation policy towards Japan showed a gradual shift from late 1948 onwards from a punitive policy to leniency as the US found a growing necessity to keep Japan viable with less American input and retain it within the anti-communist bloc as the Cold War intensified. This about-face is often called the 'reverse course'.
4 SEATO was established in September 1954 as a collective security organization to withstand Soviet aggression in Asia. The initial members were the US, the UK, France, Australia, New Zealand, Thailand, the Philippines, and Pakistan. For insightful analyses of British policies towards SEATO and military commitments in South-East Asia, see Kibata Yoichi, *Teikoku no Tasogare*, Tokyo: Tokyo University Press, 1996; K. Hack, *Defence and Decolonisation in Southeast Asia*, Richmond: Curzon, 2001.

5 For pioneering analyses on British regional policies towards South-East Asia at the beginning of the 1950s, see N. Tarling, ' "Some Rather Nebulous Capacity": Lord Killearn's Appointment in South-East Asia', *Modern Asian Studies*, 20(3), 1986, pp.559–600; N. Tarling, *The Fall of Imperial Britain in South-East Asia*, Singapore: Oxford University Press, 1993; T. Remme, *Britain and Regional Cooperation in South-East Asia, 1945–49*, London: Routledge, 1995.

6 *British Documents on the End of Empire* (hereafter, BDEEP), B-3, Malaya, HMSO: London, 1995, Document 118.

7 The post of the Commissioner-General was created by amalgamating the posts of the Special Commissioner and the Governor-General for British Territories in South-East Asia (the latter had included Malaya, Singapore, and British North Borneo). MacDonald had been the Governor-General from April 1946.

8 National Archives, Kew (hereafter NA Kew), CO 1030/167/49, 'The Commissioner General [CG]'s Annual Conference in Singapore', undated (circa December 1955); see also NA Kew, FO 371/93024.

9 Also see Remme, *Britain and Regional Cooperation*, pp. 5–6.

10 C. Thorne, *Allies of a Kind*, London: Hamish Hamilton, 1978, pp. 157f, 538ff, 726.

11 For example, see BDEEP, B-3, Document 95. For a detailed analysis of the post-war British policy towards South-East Asia, with emphasis on regional co-operation and the role of the UK Commissioner-General and his annual conference, see Tomaru Junko, 'Tōnan Ajia no chiikishugi keisei to Igirisu (1941–1965)', *Kokusaihō gaikō zasshi*, 98(4), 1999, pp. 1–40.

12 Remme, *Britain and Regional Cooperation*, pp. 83–6; BDEEP, B-3, Document 196 (including quotation).

13 NA Kew, CO 936/350, Note by Parkes, Counsellor in Djakarta, enclosed in the letter from Morland (Djakarta) to Macmillan, 28 April 1955; PREM 11/2661, Scott, Commissioner General for the United Kingdom in South East Asia [CGSEA], to Macmillan, 6 May 1959.

14 NA Kew, DEFE 11/102, Minutes of a 10 Downing Street meeting of 3 February 1955, quoted in Hack, *Defence and Decolonisation*, p. 202.

15 Quotation from NA Kew, FO 371/11856, Note by Tahourdin, 29 December 1953. Also see BDEEP A-3-I, Document 138; DEFE 11/102, MacDonald to Eden, 8 February 1955, quoted in Hack, *Defence and Decolonisation*, pp. 201–2.

16 BDEEP, A-4-I, Document 4 and 5; A-4-II, Document 529.

17 BDEEP, A-3-I, Document 21. Hack, *Defence and Decolonisation*, p. 204. Kibata, *Teikoku no Tasogare*, pp. 247–9.

18 Hack, *Defence and Decolonisation*, pp. 202–3; NA Kew, CO 1030/1120, Draft letter from Macmillan to Lord Selkirk, CGSEA, August 1961.

19 For a detailed analysis of the change in UK attitude from opposition to a guarded encouragement of a Japanese economic role in Malaya and South-East Asia, see Tomaru Junko, *The Postwar Rapprochement of Malaya and Japan, 1945–61: the Roles of Britain and Japan in South-East Asia*, London: Macmillan, 2000.

20 NA Kew, FO 371/92642/FJ1127/14, MacDonald to Younger, Foreign Office [FO], 24 September 1951.

21 NA Kew, FO 371/99439/FJ11340/1, CGSEA to FO, 28 November 1951.

22 NA Kew, CO 1022/218, report from MacDonald to CO, 'Bukit Serene Conference – Japan', 28 November 1951.

23 NA Kew, FO 371/92642/FJ1127/17, Eden to MacDonald, 16 November 1951. Also see FO 371/92603/FJ1027/17, Dening to Strang, FO, 30 October 1951. Tomaru Junko, *The Postwar Rapprochement*, pp. 66–7, 71.

24 NA Kew, FO 371/92642/FJ1127/13, MacDonald to Younger, 24 September 1951; FO 371/115239/FJ1061/2, 'Draft brief for the Commonwealth Prime Ministers' Conference', February 1955.

25 Yoshida was premier from 22 May 1946 to 20 May 1947, and then again from 15 October 1948 to 7 December 1954.

26 Tomaru, *The Postwar Rapprochement*, Chapter 5, Section 4.
27 Ishii Osamu, *Reisen to Nichibei kankei*, The Japan Times: Tokyo, 1989, pp. 124–46.
28 Tanaka Takahiko, 'Anglo-Japanese Relations in the 1950s', in I. Nish and Y. Kibata, eds, *The History of Anglo-Japanese Relations, 1600–2000, vol.II*, London: Macmillan, 2000, pp. 203–34; 210.
29 NA Kew, FO 371/110410/FJ1023/1, Tokyo Embassy to Eden, 15 September 1954, and minute by Cortazzi.
30 For the rapid expansion of Malayan–Japanese trade from 1954, see Tomaru, *The Postwar Rapprochement*, pp. 50–1. Japan signed its first reparations agreement (with Burma) in November 1954.
31 For details on the British reaction to the Bandung Conference, see N. Tarling, ' "Ah-Ah": Britain and the Bandung Conference of 1955', *Journal of Southeast Asian Studies*, 23–1, 1992, pp. 74–111; Tomaru Junko, 'Bandon kaigi to Nichi'ei kankei', in Kitagawa Katsuhiko, ed, *Igirisu Teikoku to 20 Seiki vol. 4: Datsushokuminchika no jidai*, Kyoto: Minerva Shobō, forthcoming.
32 NA Kew, FO 371/116976/D2231/48, Lennox-Boyd to Eden, 11 January 1955; FO 371/116977/D2231/113, FO to UK High Commissioner, India, 18 February 1955; FO 371/116978/D2231/123, Draft telegram by FO to British overseas representatives, March 1955.
33 Tarling, 'Ah-Ah', pp. 108–110.
34 Tomaru, 'Tōnan Ajia', p. 16; 19–23.
35 The Afro-Asian Group began its joint activities in 1950 in the context of the Korean War as the 'Asia–Arab Group' and became the Afro-Asian Group with the subsequent participation of the Sub-Saharan countries of Liberia and Ethiopia from 1953. Okakura Koshirō, *Bandon kaigi to 50 nendai no Ajia*, Daitō bunka daigaku tōyō kenkyūjo: Tokyo, 1986, pp. 31–3; 317.
36 Matsumoto Saburō, 'Kokuren ni okeru Nihon no tōhyō taido ' in *Kokusai seiji*, no.1, 1963, p. 71; NA Kew, CO 936/316, 77, Commonwealth Relations Office [CRO] to UK High Commissioners, 10 March 1956; CO 936/354, 34, Note by Hanrott.
37 The Minister of State is the junior minister and is not a member of the cabinet.
38 NA Kew, FO 371/129342, Lord Reading, Minister of State, FO, to Scott, CGSEA, 3 January 1957. For a full analysis of the Suez Crisis, amongst many others, see K. Kyle, *Suez*, St. Martin's Press: New York, 1991; Wm. Louis and R. Owen, eds, *Suez 1956: The Crisis and its Consequences*, Oxford: Clarendon Press, 1989; and Sasaki Yuta, *Igirisu Teikoku to Suezu Sensō*, Nagoya: Nagoya University Press, 1997.
39 NA Kew, FO 371/129342/D1051/3, Bartlett, Straits Times Press, to Eden, 11 January 1957.
40 NA Kew, PREM 11/2661, Report of the CGSEA's Conference in December 1956 by Scott to Eden, 18 December 1956.
41 All quotations and the contents of conference proposals in this and the following paragraphs are from NA Kew, PREM 11/2661, Scott to Eden, 18 December 1956; see also FO 371/129343/D1052/1, 'Eden Hall conference, 1956' by CG's Office, 28 December 1956.
42 Ibid.
43 NA Kew, PREM 11/2661, Scott to Eden, 15 April 1956 and 1 June 1956.
44 A. Wainwright, *Inheritance of Empire*, 1938–55, Westport: Praeger, 1994, p. 170; C. Sanger, *Malcolm MacDonald*, Liverpool: Liverpool University Press, 1995, p. 367.
45 Sanger, *MacDonald*, pp. 79–80. After the Suez Crisis, MacDonald was told by former 10 Downing Street staff that his reports of India's bitter opposition to the British action was the third reason for the British withdrawal from Suez, after American criticism and the Russian threat of retaliation. Ibid., pp. 365–8.
46 OEEC was established in 1948, in order to co-ordinate the Marshall Plan, and was an antecedent of the OECD.

47 NA Kew, PREM 11/2661, Scott to Eden, 18 December 1956; see also FO 371/129343/
D1052/1, 'Eden Hall conference, 1956' by CG's Office, 28 December 1956.
48 *BDEEP, A-3-I*, document 66.
49 NA Kew, PREM 11/1804/D1631/28, FO to Ramsden, Prime Minister's Office, 1 October 1957.
50 NA Kew, FO 371/129343/D1052/5, Scott to UK representatives, 12 October 1957;
FO 371/129366, Marshall, FO, to Bentliff, CRO, 10 December 1957.
51 NA Kew, FO 371/116915/D1052/14, Minute by Haigh, FO, 21 September 1955;
BDEEP, A-4-1, Document 6.
52 '70th Anniversary 1934–2004', British Council homepage http://www2.britishcoun-
cil.org/history/history-70-anniversary/history-anniversary-landmarks.htm, accessed
on 13 April 2004.
53 F. Donaldson, *The British Council: the First Fifty Years*, London: Jonathan Cape,
1984, pp. 178–93. An independent committee of inquiry to review British overseas
information services was appointed by the UK government in the late 1952 under the
tenth Earl of Drogheda, the then Chairman of the Cinematograph Films Council. The
committee presented its report in July 1953, recommending more financial input and
Council reforms.
54 Sasaki, *Suezu Sensō*, p. 224.
55 *New Statesman*, 15 September 1956, quoted in Wm. Roger-Louis, ' The United Nations and the British Dimension of the Suez Crisis', paper presented at the conference
on The Role of the United Nations in International Politics, 20–21 December 2003,
Hokkaido University, Japan, pp. 23–43.
56 NA Kew, DO 35/10627, Report on the Afro-Asian Delegation [Afro-Asian Report]
at the 11th regular session of the United Nations General Assembly [GA], November
1956-March 1957.
57 NA Kew, DO 35/10627, Afro-Asian Reports at the 11th, 12th and 13th GA.
58 J. Darwin, *Britain and Decolonisation*, Macmillan: London, 1988, pp. 4, 70–3.
59 Hatoyama Ichirō succeeded Yoshida as Prime Minister from 10 December 1954 to
20 December 1956; he was in turn succeeded by Ishibashi Tanzan whose government
lasted for two months only.
60 NA Kew, FO 371/116975/D2231/7, minutes by Allen, 1 January 1955; see also FO
371/116076/D2231/68, Dening to FO, 26 January 1955 and FO to Tokyo Embassy,
28 January 1955. For details on the British attitude towards Japan's participation in,
and response to, the Bandung Conference, see Tomaru, 'Bandon'. For analyses of
the Japanese participation and American response, see Miyagi Taizō, *Bandon Kaigi
to Nihon no Ajia fukki*, Tokyo: Sōshisha, Tokyo, 2001; and K. Ampiah, 'Japan at the
Bandung Conference', *Japan Forum*, 7–1, 1995, pp. 15–24.
61 *BDEEP, A-3-I*, Document 21.
62 NA Kew, CO 1030167, 106, 'Japan', note for CGSEA's Conference, by Tokyo Embassy, 29 November 1956.
63 Kishi succeeded Ishibashi as premier on 25 February 1957 and remained in post until
15 July 1960.
64 NA Kew, FO 371/133598, FO minutes by Dalton, 25 July 1958, quoted in Tanaka,
'Anglo-Japanese Relations', p. 223.
65 NA Kew, FO 371/115239/FJ1061/2, 'Draft brief for the Commonwealth Prime Ministers' Conference', February 1955; FO 371/116915/D1052/5, 'Draft brief for Mr
Nabarro's debate with Mr. Kingsley Martin', April 1955; PREM 11/1910, 'Draft brief
for Prime Minister's Luncheon for Mr. Fujiyama', 27 September 1957. Also see *The
Times*, 13 December 1956.
66 On Kishi's South-East Asia policy, see Tomaru, *Postwar Rapprochement*, pp. 164–9;
181.
67 Text of speeches: Diplomatic Record Office, Tokyo (hereafter, DRO) A'-1051, Kishi
shushō Tōnan Ajia shokoku, Ōsutoraria, Nyū Jīrando hōmon kankei ikken (hereafter

Kishi Hōmon), vol. 3: Kakkoku shunō to no kaidan kiroku: Hirai to Fujiyama, 28 November 1957; Hinata to Fujiyama, 30 November 1957; pp. 79, 233f, 239f.

68 NA Kew, FO 371/133596/FJ1041/2, Tokyo to Lloyd, 10 June 1958.

69 DRO A'-1.5.1.5.-4 Kishi hōmon: shinbun ronchō, vol. 3, Yukawa to Fujiyama, 10 December 1957.

70 NA Kew, FO 371/166359/D1051/10, Selkirk to Macmillan, 24 January 1962; FO 371/175070/D1051/105, FO memorandum by South-East Asia Department, 29 October 1964. Tomaru, 'Tōnan Ajia', pp. 28–9.

71 Kokkai kaigiroku: dai 24 kai kokkai shūgiin gaimu iinkai, 61, Reply by Takasaki, 28 July 1956. Also see Tomaru, 'Bandon kaigi'.

72 Kawabe Ichirō, *Kokuren to Nihon*, Iwanami Shoten: Tokyo, 1994, pp. 45–6; *Asahi Shinbun*, evening edition, 7 June 1956.

73 DRO, A'-0376, 'Suezu mondai ni taisuru wagahō no taido ni kansuru ken', undated; Kokusai Kyōryoku Kyoku, 'Suezu mondai ni taisuru wagakuni no tachiba ni tsuite' 26 September 1956; Nishi Haruhiko, *Kaisō no Nihon gaikō*, Iwanami Shoten: Tokyo, 1965, pp. 166–75.

74 DRO A'-0376, Abstract of Foreign Minister Shigemitsu's press conference, 25 September 1956; DRO A'-0377, 'Record of conversation with Indonesian Consul in Tokyo', 7 November 1956; NA Kew, FO 371/121800/VR1091/940, Dixon to FO, 13 November 1956.

75 Kawabe, *Kokuren to Nihon*, p. 48.

76 NA Kew, DO 35/10627, 'Report on the Afro-Asian Delegation at the eleventh regular session of the UN GA [Afro-Asian Reports, 11th GA], November 1956–March 1957'.

77 NA Kew, DO 35/10627, Dixon to Lloyd, 11 January 1957.

78 DRO A'- 0377, Kase to Kishi, 25 January 1957; NA Kew, DO 35/10627, Afro-Asian Reports, 11th, 12th and 13th GA.

79 T. Hovet, Jr, *Block Politics in the United Nations*, Cambridge (Mass): Harvard University Press, 1960, p. 85.

80 NA Kew, DO 35/10627, Afro-Asian Reports, 13th GA.

81 *The Economist*, 26 February 1955.

82 NA Kew, FO 371/121047/FJ1054/1, Dening to Allen, 15 February 1956 and Minute by Allen, 18 February; FO 371/121047/FJ1054/2, Dening to Allen, 11 July; FO 371/121048/FJ1054/30, Draft letter from Eden to Hatoyama, September 1956; FO 371/121048/FJ1054/43, 'Record by the Earl of Selkirk of his meeting with Mr. Shigemitsu on Tuesday, September 25'.

83 NA Kew, PREM 11/1910, FO to Zulueta, 4 September 1957.

84 NA Kew, PREM 11/1910, 'Prime Minister Luncheon for Mr. Fujiyama on September 30', 27 September, *passim*; Tomaru, *The Postwar Rapprochement*, p. 179; Tanaka, 'Anglo-Japanese Relations', pp. 218–21.

85 NA Kew, FO371/133597, Lascelles to FO, 27 January 1958, quoted in Tanaka, 'Anglo-Japanese Relations', pp. 221–2.

86 NA Kew, FO 371/150561, Morland to FO, 12 January 1960, quoted in C. Braddick, 'Distant Friends: Britain and Japan since 1958', in Nish and Kibata, *The History of Anglo-Japanese Relations, vol. II*, pp. 263–312; p. 268.

87 Porter and Stockwell, *British Imperial Policy, vol. 2*, Document 4.

88 NA Kew, CO 1030/1120, Draft letter from Macmillan to Lord Selkirk, 14 October 1961.

89 As of 1958/59, British Council reports began to speak of 'steady progress'. NA Kew, BW 42/11, The British Council Japan Representative's Annual Reports, 1952/53–1962/63.

90 NA Kew, BW 42/12: Close, BC, Tokyo, to Controller of the BC, London, 28 January 1953; Phillips, BC Tokyo, to British Embassy Tokyo, 2 April 1959; White, BC London, to Leadbetter, Ministry of Education, 6 September 1961.

91 NA Kew, FO371/150561, Morland to FO, received 20 January 1960, quoted in C. Aldous, 'Eikoku suibō o kakusu kamen ka sono kokuin ka' in Tsuzuki Chushichi, Kusamitsu Toshio, and Gordon Daniels (eds) *NichiEi Kankeishi 1600–2000: 5 Shakai Bunka*, Tokyo: Tokyo University Press, p. 306.
92 NA Kew, BW 42/12, Mayall, Tokyo Embassy, to Speight, Cultural Relations Department, FO, 24 December 1959.
93 NA Kew, CO 1030/167, 'Japan' (Brief for Eden Hall Conference), by Tokyo Embassy, 29 November 1956; CAB 134/1644, 'Note by secretaries for Cabinet Committee on future developments in South East Asia', 20 June 1960.
94 *The Economist*, 8 March 1958, p. 32, quoted in Peter Lowe, 'Uneasy readjustment, 1945–58', in Nish and Kibata, *The History of Anglo-Japanese Relations, vol. II*, pp. 174–200; p. 194.
95 Aldous, 'Eikoku suibō', p. 306; NA Kew, CAB 134/1644, Martin, CO, to Allen, Singapore, Office of CGSEA, 18 May 1960, attached to Note by Secretaries, 23 June 1960.
96 DRO A'-0148, Memo from Tiltman, 5 May 1959, quoted in Braddick, 'Distant Friends', p. 267.
97 Tanaka, 'Anglo-Japanese Relations', pp. 222–5.
98 NA Kew, FO 371/141436/FJ1051/40, Landsdowne to Millar, enclosed in Trench to MacDermot, 16 June 1959, quoted in Braddick, *'Distant Friends'*, p. 266.
99 NA Kew, FO 371/141436/FJ1051/41, Trench to Heppel, 21 May 1959, quoted in Braddick, 'Distant Friends', p. 302 (note 23).
100 Tomaru, *The Postwar Rapprochement*, pp. 161–2. Out of the eight iron mines where operations began between 1951 and 1963 with Japanese participation, six had been operated by the Japanese either before or during the Second World War. Ibid., pp. 25, 27–32, 118.
101 Keizai Kikakuchō, ed., *Keizai Hakusho: Nihon keizai no seichō to kindaika: Shōwa 31-nendo*, Tokyo: Shiseidō, 1956, p. 42. This statement became a very popular catchphrase in Japan.

Part II

Japan's re-emergence in regional and international organizations

4 Japan at the Bandung Conference

An attempt to assert an independent foreign policy

Kweku Ampiah

According to H.W. Brands, 'Bandung as a metaphor lacks precision' because the membership was amorphous and defied a convenient definition. Nevertheless, the Conference, or, better still, what it stood for, challenged Yalta – the yardstick by which the spheres of influence of the superpowers were measured. As Brands reminds us,

> Yalta . . . required a focusing of attention and a narrowing of mind not least because it generated a siege mentality'. In essence, Bandung questioned the attitude of intransigence and overconfidence on the part of the superpowers by simply demanding 'a willingness to question premises and set ideology aside.[1]

This chapter is an account and analysis of events as they unfolded in relation to the Bandung Conference from the latter part of 1954 to May 1955, and provides us with an insight into how the US perceived Japan's motives in relation to the conference. Specifically, it informs us about the expectations that America had of Japan and supplies us with the signposts for evaluating Japan's own understanding of the conference, not to mention what it aimed to achieve from it. As a corollary, it sheds light on the nature of the US–Japan alliance as well as on Japan's relations with its neighbours.

The study is based essentially on US archival documents which inform us about the thought processes and decisions of top officials of the State Department, the US Embassy in Tokyo and the Japanese Ministry of Foreign Affairs (MoFA). What is manifestly evident in the study are Japan's initiatives in the mid-1950s (under the Hatoyama Ichirō administration) to reaffirm an independent foreign policy, away from encroachments from the State Department. The study is separated into five sections: US concerns about the Conference and a perceived shift toward neutralism in Japan; pre-conference consultations between the US and Japan; the composition of the Japanese delegation and America's concerns about it; the semblance of a working compromise between the US and Japan; and America's response to the Japanese performance at the conference.

The Bandung (officially the Asian–African) Conference of 18–24 April 1955 emanated from the Bogor Conference of 28–29 December 1954. The latter, which was also attended by the prime ministers of India, Indonesia, Burma, Ceylon, and Pakistan, was a by-product of the Colombo meeting of May of the same year. Before the meeting in Colombo there had been the shadowy and halting existence of the Asian Relations Organisation which emanated from the Asian Relations Conference of March 1947 – an event of great historical significance for a continent bursting out of its seams in its desire for international recognition and respect.

At the meeting in Colombo, the leaders of the five participating countries adopted a loosely worded agreement that pledged their five countries to neutrality in the conflict between the Communist bloc and the West.[2] Jawaharlal Nehru, the prime minister of India and the most influential of the leaders, had also intimated just before the Bogor Conference that the objective of the meeting in Bandung 'should be to create an atmosphere of co-operation and to put Asia and Africa more in the picture.'[3] This was necessary because, as he put it, 'the old balances no longer hold good'. More importantly, it was also agreed that the Bandung Conference should aim to contribute to the reconstruction of the economies of the participating countries. Consequently, the Colombo powers agreed to set up a committee for economic assistance and were determined to lay the foundations for the technological advancement of Asia, a proposal that the Japanese found rather attractive.[4] Japan's primary ambition at this stage was to rebuild its economy, which to all intents and purposes depended on the solvency of the economy of Japan's immediate neighbours. The raw materials to support the Japanese economy were to come from South-East Asia but the region was also viewed as a potential market for Japan's manufactured products.

As to the delegations at the conference, 13 (of the 29 countries invited) were led by their national heads of state and seven by foreign ministers. There were three princes, representing Saudi Arabia, Yemen, and Thailand. Cambodia sent a former king, and Japan a minister, as did the Gold Coast, although the conference organisers wanted the chief delegates to be the equivalent of a prime minister or a foreign minister.

There was certainly something manifestly intriguing about the Conference, as Brands points out. For example, it was designed to bond the participants together in their common struggle against marginalisation in international politics, and help them consolidate their aims and ambitions towards political sovereignty and economic development. Instead, it became infested with ideological and personality conflicts between the five organising members who apparently chose to prioritise national sovereignty over any chances for regional cohesion. The pro-West and anti-communist participants of the conference – Ceylon, the Gold Coast, Iran, Iraq, Pakistan, the Philippines, Japan, Jordan, Lebanon, Liberia, Libya, Saudi Arabia, South Vietnam, Sudan, Thailand, Turkey – openly disagreed with the non-aligned members – Afghanistan, Burma, Cambodia, Egypt, Ethiopia, India, Indonesia, Laos, North Vietnam, People's Republic of China, Nepal, Syria, and Yemen – who then candidly chastised the former for being subservient to the interests of America. Effectively, the participants were split up into two camps, reflecting the divisions of the Cold War.

The dichotomy of the above countries into 'aligned' and 'non-aligned' camps demands further elaboration since in reality they fell into three clearly discernible groups. On the one side was China and North Vietnam, the communist participants. On the other was a group of roughly ten countries whose sympathies were firmly with the capitalist West. These included Pakistan, Ceylon, Iran, Iraq, Japan, Lebanon, Pakistan, the Philippines, Thailand, and Turkey. The middle group (of which India, Burma, and Indonesia stood out) were the neutralists who customarily avoided involvement with one side or the other in the Cold War.

Japan, in many ways, stood out even among its cohort of ideological friends – the pro-West group of states – for it hovered, refusing to commit itself at the conference even on straightforward Cold War issues. At the same time, the Japanese delegation showed no inclination to support the cause of the newly emerging states. The issues of 'decolonization and self-determination' and even 'human rights' seemed beyond their conception, presumably because supporting those principles would have been seen as offensive to the Europeans, Britain and France in particular. As a result, Tokyo chose to respond mainly to non-contentious issues such as 'peace' and 'international co-operation'. Effectively, the Japanese delegation maintained a self-composed disposition on all the pertinent and troublesome issues that were dealt with at the Conference. Consequently, Japan pursued a policy of non-involvement on issues with potentially debilitating implications for its foreign policy. This, as argued here, was perhaps the beginning of Japan's reticent foreign policy, which might be seen as a formula to build Japan's prestige around issues that unite rather than divide.

US concerns about Bandung and 'a shift toward neutralism in Japan'[5]

The issue of Japanese participation in the conference was of immense strategic concern to the US, not least because Japan was its most important ally in East Asia. Moreover, within the State Department there were genuine concerns that Japan might be harbouring neutralist sentiments. This was made all the more pertinent because the Japanese public had been expressing serious concerns and doubts about the nature of the relationship between their country and the US. Nevertheless, the State Department, without much hesitation, mentioned Japan as one of the friendly states that would be participating in the Conference. This was because, according to the Department's working definition of neutralism, 'Japan [was] not neutral' and 'the probability that it [would] become neutral in the next few years appear[ed] small'. Yet doubts remained about Japan's sincerity as an ally, as shown in a State Department report on 'Nationalism in The Far East'.[6] Since the report is essential to our analysis it is worth examining some of its contents in detail. For example, it was noted that 'Japan . . . today relies heavily on the US for support, guidance and protection. In this situation there is general agreement in Japan that the nation must build its strength and, as it does so, strive for greater freedom of action.' Japan's over-dependence on the US was noted, and its frustrations about the situation were also mentioned. The report notes that, therefore, 'Japan's restiveness under US tutelage . . . and its fear of involvement in nuclear war are some of the important forces impelling' the country 'away from its twin conditions of weakness and dependence on the US'. It was further noted that 'these forces could eventually push Japan into a position of neutralism'. The 'significant, although far from dominant, groups working to this end' were identified as 'the many socialists, particularly left socialists . . . intellectuals, such as social science teachers and writers, leaders of the labour movement and internationalists'.[7]

A loss of confidence that the US would provide it with the opportunities for political and economic expression against the perceived communist threat might also have forced Japan to flirt with neutralist ideals, the State Department report noted. It also mentions the 'definite undercurrent of feeling' pushing Japan to 'steer clear of becoming entangled with either side' of the Cold War. All the same, Japan's determination to play a prominent role in international affairs cannot be underestimated. It was eager, for example, to serve as 'a peacemaker or bridge between the two sides', and its ambition 'to regain a leading position in Asia' remained as acute as ever.

Having noted the factors that might push Japan to the left, the report then, reassuringly, declares that the 'dominant forces and groups' in Japan were in favour of co-operation with the US and the free world because they believed such co-operation would continue to offer political and economic benefits well beyond communist abilities. The dominant forces were identified as 'the Conservative political elements, officialdom, the bigger businessmen and a generous cross-section of the population'. With regards to the course of action to be taken to prevent Japan from becoming neutral the report advised that the 'US should encourage Japan to attain greater national strength'. It also recommended that the United States 'should not interfere with Japan's efforts to establish limited political relations with the Soviet Union and trade with Communist China . . . particularly since Japan will probably appreciate its ties with the free nations more as it learns how little the communist nations have'. This was no doubt a reaction to Hatoyama's efforts to establish better relations with Japan's communist neighbours.[8] Finally, the report reaffirmed that 'the risk will be present for some time at least that Japan's recovery of strength could go in the direction of neutralism and ultra-independence rather than co-operation' with the West if the international and domestic circumstances should unexpectedly change the course Japan was following. It was in that context that the US viewed Japan's participation in the Bandung Conference.

Thus, on 5 January 1955, the US Embassy in Tokyo sent a telegram to Washington informing the State Department about the Japanese attitude to the impending conference.[9] It was noted that the Japanese had not been particularly forthcoming in outlining their views on how they would react if they were invited to the Conference. In addition, it established that 'the press has treated [the] conference with considerable caution'. Nevertheless, the telegram, signed by Ambassador John Allison, also intimated that a Japanese MoFA official, Tani Masayuki, had made some disparaging comments about the conference apparently because he felt the sponsors did not know its real purpose.

The following views as expressed in the telegram are particularly interesting and therefore deserve to be quoted extensively. First, the telegram notes that despite the lack of enthusiasm in Tokyo about the Conference 'in [the] end Japan [is] likely to decide on participation largely for reasons of enhancing its prestige in Asia'. It elaborates on why Japan cannot avoid the conference by affirming that the 'Japanese are deeply sensitive about isolation from mainstream Asian politics, and desirous of exploiting any opportunities to re-establish Japan's status as [a] major Asian power'. The other reason why Japan was more than likely to attend the Conference was because it 'offers such an opportunity as the first important post-war meeting Japan had been invited to attend.' Also crucial to the issue was the question of Japan's 'independence' and there were compelling domestic political factors at play here. As the telegram noted, 'particularly if [a] decision must be made prior to [the] March elections,[10] [the] government will be under strong political pressures to attend since rejection would be viewed as contrary to the "new" foreign policy of "independence" and [an] increas[ing] emphasis' on its affinity to Asia.[11]

All the same, Allison felt that since Japan was genuinely concerned about the American attitude towards attendance the Japanese were unlikely to act without close consultation with America. He further asserted that 'Japan would probably be hesitant about attending without at least the tacit consent of the US'. In the same breath, however, he warned that if the US should decide that it should decline the invitation 'great effort would be required to persuade Japan' to do so. In reality whether or not Japan went to the Conference, the telegram intimates, would depend on how the other anti-communist countries responded to their invitation. In other words, the 'decision of [the] other anti-communist Asian invitees to attend would . . . strengthen Japanese determination to accept [the] invitation'.

Similarly, the telegram warned that if Japan declined the invitation 'under pressure from the US' the decision might be interpreted as a result of US intervention. 'In that event, [the] US would be subject to strong public criticism for treating Japan as [a] puppet'. This, as the telegram affirmed, might force the government to assert the country's 'independence from the US on other issues in order to establish public prestige'. As is obvious from the above, the issue of the Japanese desire for independence from the US was of major concern to the US. It was also of immense concern to the PRC and India both of which wanted to liberate Tokyo from Washington's grip so that it could regain control of its own affairs and develop better relations with its neighbours.

As to the extent to which Japan would co-operate in the effort to combat the communists at the Conference, the ambassador's remarks were simply that it was impossible to forecast with any certainty 'until [the] domestic political situation clears up and [the] pattern of [the] conference [was] more clearly defined.' The telegram then notes that 'although it was relatively certain [that] Japan can, at least, be expected to side with [the] anti-Communist bloc where necessary, or not undertake actions which [would] alienate the US', it might be necessary for some influence to be applied in 'favour [of] innocuous compromises and against [the] adoption [of] controversial resolutions.' In other words, Japan should not be allowed into a situation where it might be forced to take a position against the interests of the US. Expecting Japan to assume a leadership role at the conference among the anti-Communists, on the other hand, was unlikely, Allison confirmed. He, however, also intimated that Japan has the 'capabilities and ambitions for [a] more prominent role in Asia'. Yet, he identified certain constraints on those ambitions. He alluded that 'Japan may be inhibited from this course by [a] reluctance to seem too "forward" at [its] post war "debut"' and by the concern that 'a strong stand [might be] misinterpreted as [an] indication [of] the resurgence [of] pre-war Japanese aggressiveness'. Besides, Japan's leaders may think that their country's 'prestige [may] be better built around issues which unite rather than divide' the Afro-Asian countries. They 'may also feel [that a] passive role among the anti-Communists [might] be necessary to satisfy domestic pressure for asserting some independence from [the] US'. He also suggested that it may be useful in the government's efforts to expand trade with the PRC, and settle problems with regards to fishing and reparations.[12]

That Japan's attitude at the conference would also be dictated by the performance of India and the PRC, was obvious. The soft tactics of the two countries might pre-empt the Japanese from taking a strong anti-Communist stand, Allison thought. The telegram then states that if the Japanese thought a more active role at the conference would not conflict with their ambitions for independence and prestige then 'it may be possible to awaken' their leadership potential. In sum, the Ambassador advised Washington not to try to 'dissuade Japan from attending the conference'. Instead, it should be encouraged to attend through consultations with the US government; and it should be inspired to play an active role in 'combating [the] Communists'. Allison also felt that if the Japanese were consulted at all stages of planning they might abandon their reluctance to play a more active role at the conference. Consequently, he asked to be allowed to engage the Japanese freely as partners about their preparations for the conference. 'It is particularly important that I be in [a] position [to] keep . . . Tani fully informed regarding pre-conference developments and [show] our desire [to] deal with [the] Japanese as partners in this', he pleaded.[13] As is clear enough, while the State Department viewed the conference with suspicion, Allison was exhorting Washington to let Japan attend.

The same day as the above telegram was despatched Ambassador Allison sent another message to Washington in which he expressed the concern of the Embassy of Pakistan in Tokyo that the Philippine government had declined the invitation to the Conference.[14] There were by then rumours that the Philippines and Thailand might not attend. Thus, officials at the Pakistan Embassy had made it known to Allison that their delegates might be isolated at the Conference if staunch anti-Communist countries such as the Philippines did not attend. In alerting Washington, Allison was also attempting to put pressure on the State Department to encourage participation by friends of the West. He was concerned that the 'premature' decision of the Philippines not to attend the Conference might be interpreted by some of the Asian countries as being a result of pressure from the US.

Indeed, officials of the Pakistan Embassy also hoped that Japan would be encouraged to attend the Conference since its participation 'would on balance be helpful to the anti-Communist countries'.[15] The indications from the above telegrams are that Ambassador Allison, like the heads of other missions in Asia, was using every opportunity available to him to get the friends of America to attend. Meanwhile, he was also trying to get Washington to respond positively.

However, the news that Foreign Minister Shigemitsu Mamoru favoured Japanese participation of the Afro-Asian conference made US Secretary of State John F. Dulles jittery. Shigemitsu had also apparently issued a statement alluding to the Japanese government's determination to reclaim and reassert the country's independence. Even worse was the fact that Shigemitsu had made the statement without consultation with the US, a serious offence in alliance politics, especially when the offence is committed by the junior partner. That Shigemitsu was aware of US scepticism about the Conference and would therefore consult the US before Japan made any concrete decisions about attending hardly, it seems, lessened Dulles' anxieties. Frustrated, Dulles wrote to the US Embassy in Tokyo to ascertain what exactly Shigemitsu had said.[16]

When the reply arrived Dulles responded that for the time being the Japanese government should not assume any public position on Japan's conference attendance. Since Japan had not received a formal invitation by then, the instruction caused no real problem. The response was, nevertheless, clearly indicative of Washington's anxieties about Japan's ambition to act freely in international politics. At the same time, it confirmed America's determination to continue orchestrating Japan's foreign policy. In response to Dulles, the US Ambassador in Tokyo wrote, among other things, to confirm that the Japanese were more than inclined to attend the Conference. Allison also persevered with his position that it would be best to have Japan attend.[17] He made reference to Tani's comments that 'in his opinion there was considerable merit in having as many non-Communist countries attend [the] conference as possible . . . otherwise Chou Enlai and Nehru will dominate [the] meeting' at the expense of the West. That was plain enough. Allison tried even harder this time. He affirmed that 'for [the] above reason, as well as for [a] strong desire of [the] government to be part of any Asian conference' Japan will accept the invitation 'unless a most persuasive reason can be adduced for not doing so'.[18]

To assuage the anxieties of the State Department, he confirmed that Tani had assured him that 'if Japan should accept [the] invitation it was his intention that [the] strongest possible delegation be sent and that it should be composed at least in part of officials who spoke English fluently so that they would be able to influence [decisions] taken at the conference'. Towards the end of the telegram, however, he reverted to his original strategy by stipulating that 'it would be difficult to persuade [the] Japanese government not to accept the invitation'. In a final act of persuasion he added that 'I think it would also be difficult to keep it a secret that we had attempted to dissuade [the] government from going'. He then signed off with the words, 'Our best interests would seem to be served by encouraging Japan to attend and giving [the] Japanese as much material as possible with which to counter Communist propaganda at [the] Conference'.[19] Allison seemed to have exhausted all his skills of persuasion by this time, but he would not give up.

Consultations between allies

Although the Japanese government was keen to respond positively to the invitation to the Conference and independently of the US, MoFA remained in steady consultation with the American Embassy about the Conference. When the formal invitation finally arrived on 25 January, the Ministry rightly informed the US Embassy.[20] It also provided the ambassador with a copy of the full text of the invitation as well as a copy of the Japanese government's brief (non-committal) statement that was issued in response to the invitation.[21] Arrangements were then made between MoFA and the Embassy for consultations on what attitude Japan should adopt. Following this, Allison requested immediate confirmation from Washington that it would not discourage Japanese and other Asian attendance to the Conference.[22] A 'response was needed *urgently*'[23] he wrote, 'so as not to give the press the impression that the Japanese government's delay in replying to the invitation was a result of American influence'. He warned that the 'Japanese government which now, with yesterday's dissolution of [the] Diet faces [a] bitter election campaign will be tempted to act independently without our final views'. Indeed Shigemitsu had been under immense pressure from the opposition parties to state how the government was going to respond to the invitation.[24] It is interesting to note that Washington had not responded to any of the telegrams that the embassy in Tokyo had sent it about the Conference since 5 January. Allison was obviously desperate for a response, preferably a positive one.

On 25 January, the day Allison sent his last telegram soliciting consent, State Department officials met in the Secretary of State's office about what to say to the friends of the US who were likely to attend the Conference. At the meeting, which involved Dulles, it was noted that Ambassador Allison had urgently requested instructions about how to conduct consultations with the MoFA. In response, the Secretary of State stipulated that 'our relationship with Japan would be served by consultation or *the appearance of consultation prior to our making a decision*'.[25] In other words, Japan would have to wait until the US made a decision about what it was expected to do in regard to the Conference. When the Department finally decided (in February) that its friends might go to the Conference it sent a message to Tokyo through its Embassy.[26] Among other things, Allison was to inform Japan of the possibility that the PRC may try to use the Conference to discuss the relationship between their two countries. It was also stipulated that Japan would need to put together a delegation that was highly competent and carefully instructed to handle whatever would be discussed at the Conference.

Allison wrote, on 3 March, to reassure Washington that his Embassy staff and MoFA officials had formed a 'Working Group' which would be meeting on a weekly basis to exchange views about the impending Conference.[27] The telegram he sent also contained a detailed description of what MoFA was doing in anticipation of the Conference. It also noted, however, that the Ministry was afflicted with indecision about what attitude Japan should adopt. The indecision was in part because 'one section [of the Ministry's working group] advocated close co-operation with' the West while the other section 'recommends' less commitment to any side. Apparently, MoFA was also divided over what stand Japan should take about the issue of trade with the PRC should it come up at the Conference.[28] Allison's telegram further intimated that the most disturbing issue for the Japanese, apart from the question of East-West relations, was its history as a colonial power. Because colonialism was designated as an agenda item, MoFA anticipated that further discussions about reparations might take place under the cover of the conference proceedings.[29] Evidently, Japan was being haunted by the legacies of its history as a colonial power.

The controversy within MoFA about tactics and what position to adopt at the Conference was won, it seems, not so much by those who wanted a non-controversial role in the conference but by no other person than the Foreign Minister, Shigemitsu. By all indications he was running the strategy for the Conference, and approved an overall policy of 'peaceful diplomacy'.[30] According to Allison, however, the Ministry's policy paper on the matter represented a compromise between the hawks and the doves within its own working group. Thus, while the general approach was to avoid coming across as an anti-Communist nation, on specific issues Japan seemed likely to adopt an anti-PRC stand. Among the key aspects of this policy was to place emphasis on the importance of the UN on all matters, including issues about economic development which were to be given much prominence.[31] The policy also recommended that Tokyo would 'avoid issues of direct interest to Japan which [were] controversial to countries in [the] area or [that] might lead to the criticism of Japan's pre-war and wartime actions'. A case in point was reparations, although the head of the Japanese delegation held talks, privately, with officials of some of the countries to which Japan owed reparations.[32]

As the date of the Conference inched closer, Dulles sent a message to the relevant embassies, including those in Ankara, Bangkok, Manila, and Tokyo, in which he insisted that it would be strategically useful for Japan to exchange views with Pakistan, Turkey, and Thailand about the Conference.[33] The Secretary of State thought that these countries were potentially capable of 'influencing Japan along constructive lines'. Such exchange of views, he wrote, 'could have important political effect in strengthening Japan's identification and co-operation with the free world participants at the conference'. Evidently, Dulles was worried that if Japan was not brought into check it might wander off and perhaps join the wrong crowd. Thus, the earlier Japan was approached by either Pakistan, Turkey, or Thailand and confirmed as an active member of the Western camp the better, Dulles suggested. Nevertheless, he was also careful to warn that the plan to get Japan firmly on the side of the West 'should not be attributed [to] the US's initiative'.[34] Instead, it should be explained as coming from the three countries that were merely taking advantage of the Conference to foster ties with Japan, he cautioned. Obviously, the master puppeteer was worried about offending the puppet, which was already agitating for an independent existence and platform.

He was also concerned about how the neutralists and communist countries would react to US initiatives to control Japanese foreign policy.

Curiously enough Dulles thought it would be 'inadvisable' for the Philippines to approach Japan although he wanted them to be included in all exchanges of views involving the pro-Western countries. This was necessary 'particularly since [the] Philippino delegation would be headed by General Romulo' who, as Dulles said, was 'likely to be one of [the] most effective spokesmen [of] the free world at Bandung'. The Secretary's message also contained suggestions for discussions involving Japan. As for priority issues to be considered, he noted that the pro-Western states should anticipate attacks on the South-East Asia Collective Defence Treaty and other Western bilateral regional defence arrangements and should therefore be ready to rebut any such attacks as well as justify these regional arrangements. Second, they should defend the advantages of remaining within existing international economic organizations such as GATT, the regional UN economic commissions, and specialised agencies of the UN and the Colombo Plan. This was meant to circumvent any attempts by the neutralists to establish breakaway regional economic organizations. As part of the State Department's tactical shift, Dulles also recommended that it would be desirable, when rebutting such proposals at the conference, '*not* to alienate the neutralist countries'.[35]

America's anxieties about the Japanese delegation

We noted above that as part of the plan to outwit the neutralists and communists at the Conference the State Department had instructed its friends to send a delegation composed of the best and the brightest. On 17 March, Allison reported to Washington that upon consultation with Mr Ozawa Takeo, head of the MoFA delegation to the 'Working Group', he had ascertained that Shigemitsu would lead the Japanese delegation to the Conference.[36] Ambassadors Kase Toshikazu and Ota Saburō (ambassador to Burma) were to serve as Shigemitsu's principal advisers. The telegram, however, revealed one problem still unresolved by the Japanese and this was the question of how Shigemitsu should handle any private interviews requested by Zhou Enlai at the Conference. By intimating that Shigemitsu was far from certain that he would meet with the Chinese premier privately, Ozawa (through Allison) gave Washington the assurance that nothing on that matter was decided yet. It is plausible, however, that Ozawa, by supplying that information, was in the first instance trying to see how the US would react to the news of a meeting between Zhou Enlai and Shigemitsu. At the same time, it also suggests a solicitation for instructions about how the chief Japanese delegate should handle private interviews (which seemed to have been already agreed to) with the Chinese premier. If these assumptions are substantially correct then one might be inclined to suggest that despite a determination to pursue an independent foreign policy the Hatoyama government lacked the confidence to operate freely, even at a regional conference.

By 31 March, the decision concerning who the chief Japanese delegate would be was still undecided. Shigemitsu's attendance had apparently been agreed by the Liberal Party, but on the condition that he was not absent from the Diet's discussion of the budget. However, since the Diet's consideration of the budget coincided with the Conference it was deemed highly unlikely that the foreign minister would go to Bandung.[37] The indications were, nevertheless, that the Asian Affairs Bureau of MoFA wanted Shigemitsu to head the delegation. Thus, Ozawa met with the Policy Committee of the Liberal Party and explained to them the importance of having the foreign minister attend the Conference.[38] He also persuaded the press to underline the importance of Shigemitsu's attendance in response to the government's proposal to send Takasaki Tatsunosuke as the chief delegate. In any case, by this time MoFA was desperate for a firm decision about the chief delegate, in part because they were embarrassed about the vacillation and indecision.

News about problems relating to the composition of the Japanese delegation arrived at the Secretary of State's office on 29 March.[39] The US Embassy pointed out that it was 'almost impossible that Shigemitsu' would attend the Conference. At the same time, Tani had been excluded as leader of the delegation because he could not be given the ministerial rank required of the leader of the delegation. Thus, as noted by the Embassy, the indecision about who would head the Japanese delegation was creating tensions within the Ministry. Ozawa, for example, was deeply frustrated. He was particularly worried that the inability to decide a leader quickly would be seen as an indication that Japan would not be sending a strong delegation to the Conference.

Some resolution to the leadership question had to be found, and soon enough MoFA arrived at a decision about who the chief representative of the Japanese delegation would be. On 1 April, the secretary of state was informed that Takasaki Tatsunosuke (Minister of International Trade and Industry and Director General of the Economic Deliberation Agency) had been selected as head of the Japanese delegation, with Tani as Chief Deputy given Takasaki's lack of experience in international diplomacy and poor command of English.[40] Although there was no mention of other members of the delegation it was noted that it might include representatives of the major parties. These, including members of the Socialist parties, would serve as advisors to the delegation. The inclusion of Socialist politicians in the delegation, as one can imagine, was bound to cause some consternation within the State Department. When eventually the full list of the Japanese delegation arrived at the American Embassy in Tokyo the latter made brief evaluative comments about the more important members of the delegation and sent the list to Washington.[41] The comments were really an assessment of how the delegates would fare confronted by the neutralists and communist sympathisers, of which Japan itself, at least from the American perspective, had plenty.

The Embassy was not pleased with the composition of the Japanese delegation. Takasaki, it was noted, was 'primarily a businessman and not [an] experienced diplomat' and therefore had 'little knowledge of [the] major problems likely to arise at the conference'. Consequently, it was felt that he 'was likely to act as [a] figurehead'. A note attached to the list of delegates further recorded that Takasaki could 'not . . . deal on equal terms with such men as Nehru or even Romulo or Prince Wan'. In other words, faced with Zhou Enlai's diplomatic antics Takasaki would not stand a chance, the implication being that Takasaki could not be depended on to defend the interests of the US. Consequently, the Japanese representatives were found to be 'not as strong a delegation' as 'Japan could have sent'. Nevertheless, the delegation was perceived as 'generally competent'. The staff might have been able, but the fact that it did 'not include any of the top men in the MoFA Asian Bureau' was perceived as a serious weakness. Yet, the telegram contained a message that the State Department would have found reassuring. This was that any view of the representatives from the political parties 'will reflect their personal biases and should not be interpreted as official views of the Japanese government.'[42] The implication was that the views expressed by the representatives of the Socialist parties should not be taken to heart.

The comments about the other principal members of the delegation are equally instructive. Tani was referred to as an 'experienced diplomat' and perceived as the one who 'will probably make [the] decisions for the delegation'. He was also referred to as a 'close friend of Shigemitsu', and seen as likely to 'be co-operative in dealings he may have with US representatives'. Kase Toshikazu, Japanese ambassador to the UN, on the other hand, had apparently been recently given the post of ambassador in preparation for attending the Conference. The biographical notes on him noted that he was a Harvard graduate with fluent English, and the principal confidant of Shigemitsu, although ambitious and vain. Accordingly, he 'might not be above twisting facts or manipulating situations to suit his own interests'. Ota Saburō was the ambassador to Burma and a career diplomat. He apparently left MoFA in 1947 to serve as Mayor of Yokosuka. As a result he was said to be active in domestic political circles. Another principal member of the delegation, Wajima Eiji, was formerly head of the Asian Affairs Bureau of the Ministry. He had, however, been posted to Indonesia as Ambassador at the time of the Conference, and was seemingly well known and liked by the staff of the American Embassy in Jakarta. Asakai Koichirō was the last of the prominent delegates commented on. He was said to be an able diplomat who was, at the time, the head of the Economic Bureau of MoFA. Like Wajima he had good English and was 'generally co-operative'.[43]

Meanwhile, consultations between the American Embassy in Tokyo and the Ministry continued as planned. On 14 April the two groups met for the seventh time to discuss the Conference.[44] At that meeting Ozawa alluded to some of Takasaki's concerns about the delegation he would be leading. Takasaki was apparently worried that the Diet members might prove 'troublesome at [the conference] since they might take [a] position [different] from that of the delegation'. He was therefore 'anxious to exercise control over [the] Diet men during the conference'. The problem was that, as a figurehead, Takasaki was not sure 'how he could do so'. That could not have been too surprising to officials of the State Department. What might have been of some concern to them was perhaps the fact that they had been given the assurance by Allison that the views of the political representatives would have no bearing on the Japanese government's position, and that the views of the politicians would merely represent their personal biases. What had somehow become obvious by now (through Takasaki's expressed concerns) was that, regardless of whether their views would carry any weight or not, some of the socialists – especially Sone Eki (on the right of the Social Democratic Party, SDP) and Sata Tadataka (on the left of the SDP) – could be a nuisance. Suffice to say, it had become apparent that perhaps these representatives (who were officially designated as 'political advisers') were not going to 'serve primarily as observers who will watch the proceedings of the conference and report back to their individual parties the final results' after all.[45] Indeed during the Conference, five of the Diet members had a two-hour meeting with Zhou Enlai during which the Chinese premier is said to have asked them to transmit his views directly to Hatoyama and Shigemitsu. It seems Zhou 'found Takasaki too taciturn'.[46]

The semblance of a compromise

With or without a strong delegation, Japan had its own agenda for attending the Conference. The Japanese reactions to US expectations of how Japan should conduct itself are therefore interesting. Allison had been taking note of aspects of Japan's supposedly enigmatic behaviour. He confirmed, for example, that Ozawa did 'not mention any Japanese plans for bilateral discussion[s]' with the countries that Dulles mentioned in an earlier telegram, and further alluded to another problem.[47] He observed that Japan was reluctant to have its delegation join Turkey in making a proposal to discuss the Formosan situation at the Conference. Apparently Japan was also against joining with Pakistan to make laudatory statements about SEATO, as recommended by Dulles. Ozawa had informed Allison that it would be tactically wrong and therefore inadvisable for Japan to make comments about SEATO because 'Japan was not geographically part of Southeast Asia and therefore not covered' by SEATO. He also informed Allison that on the question of the two Chinas, Shigemitsu 'was anxious to push hard' on settling the conflict peacefully. In other words, Tokyo would not be the 'carrier' of America's belligerent policies.[48]

All the same, Allison formed the impression that the Ministry 'now seems to be coming to [the] view that [the conference] will be on balance [a] useful meeting – particularly if Japan can avoid committing herself on controversial questions', as they planned to.[49] Ozawa was of the opinion that the Conference would be useful to Japan in its attempts to establish top-level contacts with the other countries in the area. It would also help Tokyo to ascertain, as Ozawa thought, 'what the countries in the region . . . [thought] about Japan'. Invariably, the question of expanding economic relations with the region also needed prodding and the Conference would provide Tokyo with the opportunity to do so. On security issues as well, Ozawa felt the Conference would provide Tokyo with an insight into regional views, particularly the Formosa crisis.

The seventeenth meeting between the Embassy and the Ministry, however, revealed what seemed like important changes in the Japanese attitude to the Conference as far as the US was concerned. These were, incidentally, favourable to the US because they revealed that Japan would seek, first, to avoid the formation of an Afro-Asian bloc (as matters important to the region were also of world-wide concern and not limited to any particular geographical area) and, second, to replace Nehru and Zhou Enlai's Five Principles with a 'Peace Declaration' which would reflect the framework of the United Nations Charter.

The idea behind the latter point was to make the objectives of the Conference identical with those of the UN.[50] Linking the Afro-Asian conference to the UN was part of Japan's attempt to make the event less intimidating to the European countries and the US.[51] In addition, Ozawa also intimated that Japan desired to always side with the aligned group of states at the Conference. The Japanese delegates might therefore have separate consultations with Pakistan, and were prepared to discuss procedures and positions with delegates from Thailand, Turkey and the Philippines, as Dulles expected.

At a meeting with Tani, Allison was given further assurances of Japan's intention to co-operate with the US, and pursue a peaceful resolution of the problems in East Asia.[52] Ozawa also informed him that the Ministry had 'studied carefully records of the behaviour and tactics of [the Peking] delegation at the Geneva Conference' where they were, apparently, at their best. That had been necessitated by, it seems, a determination on the part of Japan to try and counter Chinese influence at the Conference. Consequently, Allison started to express satisfaction with Japan's preparations for the Conference. These positive signals to America notwithstanding, the overall Japanese strategy, as intimated by Ozawa, remained unchanged. It was simply that Japan should 'refrain from taking a positive stand on delicate issues'.[53] However, neither would Japan take a negative stand on any delicate issues. This was based on Shigemitsu's recommendation for 'a soft, non-controversial tone . . . even in response to Communist propaganda'.[54]

America's response to the Japanese performance at the conference

Tani returned from the Conference believing that Japan 'did not do badly'. In his capacity as the chief informant to the US Embassy, upon returning to Tokyo he duly informed Allison of what was supposedly his greatest achievement. Zhou's request for a second meeting with Takasaki was cancelled by Takasaki, apparently on Tani's advice. The expectation was that the Americans would be immensely grateful for this. Evidently Tani, or perhaps MoFA, was attempting a form of damage limitation exercise in regard to Japan's reputation with the US. At the very least, it was an attempt to appease the US and wish away any American misgivings about Tokyo's performance at the Conference, but the State Department was not fooled by this rather mediocre attempt at appeasement. As it noted, the Japanese 'most profusely explained away the "coincidence" of Takasaki and [Z] hou being seated beside each other for a photograph'.[55] Evidently, the Department was not impressed.

To the delight of the State Department, the Conference was dominated neither by the neutralists nor by China. Nevertheless, it pronounced the Japanese performance as 'rather insignificant'. Thus, when it came to rewarding the defenders of American interests at the Conference the Department excluded Japan. A memorandum from the Far Eastern Department to the under-secretary of state stated, rather matter-of-factly, that:

> The Secretary of State intends to call in the Ambassadors of certain countries, primarily those which were particularly friendly toward the United States at the Asian-African Conference, to express satisfaction and elicit any comments they may want to make regarding the outcome of the conference. [The] FE (Far Eastern) Department has not recommended that Ambassador Iguchi [Sadao] be included among those to be called in since *we do not consider that Japan's role at the conference was positive enough to warrant a special expression.*[56]

With regards to the Philippines, on the other hand, it was suggested that the secretary of state should see General Romulo personally and 'compliment him on his vigorous advocacy of free world principles and effective exposition of the subversive tactics of world communism'. It was also to be noted that Romulo 'helped to channel the activities of anti-Communist representatives into constructive channels'.[57] As planned, the Secretary of State met with Romulo and showered him with compliments.[58]

It was also agreed that the ambassadors in Manila and Bangkok would send 'laudatory statements from the Secretary' to the host governments. Alternatively, the ambassadors, using their own discretion, should 'convey orally to Prince Wan [of Thailand] and Romulo an expression of appreciation'. The ambassadors of Pakistan and Ceylon to Washington were amongst those invited by the Secretary of State for 'compliments'. With respect to Japan, diplomatic etiquette still demanded that despite the rather inconsequential 'Japanese contribution at the conference . . . an informal word of appreciation' for MoFA's co-operation with the American Embassy in Tokyo would be in order.[59] Thus, the State Department wrote that 'The United States appreciates the opportunities afforded by the Japanese Government for a very useful exchange of ideas prior to the Bandung conference.' The Department was also 'gratified to note certain similarities between ideas expressed by the Japanese to our Embassy at Tokyo prior to the conference and the final communiqué issued at the close of the conference, and [assumed] that Japanese influence was responsible to some degree for the rather moderate tone of the final communiqué.'[60] These comments were designed to keep Japan content within the alliance for, after all, Tokyo was Washington's most important ally in East Asia.

Conclusion

The Bandung Conference was a damnable itch in the side of the US until it ended. As is evident from the above analysis, it evinced and exaggerated American anxieties about the Cold War in Asia, in part because it confronted Washington with the trauma of possibly losing its allies and friends in the region. For example, the widely-held perception that pan-Asianism (countervailing racial and anti-colonial ideals) was working hand in glove with neutralism was strongly felt within the State Department. This sharpened the Secretary of State's neurosis about the Conference. Thus, as Dulles confessed, he felt depressed about the evolving turn of events in the region.

That Washington initially did not want its friends to attend the Conference is obvious enough. Its initial reaction was outright negativity, but it subsequently came to accept it in a form of 'benevolent indifference'.[61] When it became apparent that it could not prevent some of its friends from attending, and having considered the potential dangers of not being represented at all at the Conference, it took the other extreme approach, that is, a U-turn. The revised position was that its friends may attend the Conference but should do so with the best possible delegation and only after consultation with Washington. That, invariably, necessitated the State Department's frantic search for a strong and capable leader for the pro-American countries that would attend the Conference. The objective was to find someone who could stand up to Zhou Enlai and Nehru. At the same time the State Department was determined not to cast its friendly governments 'in the role of agents rather than equal partners of the United States' – a delicate and tricky act to attempt to follow. Basically, Washington was jittery about being perceived world wide as having 'sought before and during the conference to exercise influence on the conference proceedings through its friends'. Moreover, it was concerned that this 'would diminish the prestige of the friendly governments concerned and would be exploited by the communists and used by supporters of Neutralist policies to promote their philosophy'.[62]

Despite its earlier protestations, the overall US assessment of the Conference was a positive one. According to one observer, 'the official line endeavour[ed] to give a balanced consensus between the extremes of those who think Bandung was an unqualified success for the United States and those who class it as an unqualified success for Chou en lai'.[63] Ultimately, however, the State Department saw the moderate tone of the Bandung Communiqué as a victory for the West and attributed this to the outspoken espousal of the cause of the West by its friends (especially Turkey, Lebanon, Iraq, Pakistan, Thailand, Ceylon, and the Philippines) at the Conference. As a result the Department became almost reverential about the outcome of the Conference and complimented some of its friends, in particular General Romulo, for their good work.

The overall view within the Department, however, was that Japan's contribution in that regard was almost negligible.[64] In fact, as shown above, Japan was a source of concern for the State Department not least because it was perceived to be harbouring 'neutralist sentiments'.[65] It was also noted that the desire on the part of Tokyo to regain a leadership role in Asia was enough to make Japan adopt a rather reticent posture at the Conference. Indeed MoFA had made it clear to Allison that Japan would not be drawn on issues relating to Formosa or, for that matter, SEATO. Tokyo was therefore determined to avoid being the carrier of America's belligerent policies at the Conference. The State Department also noted Hatoyama's burning desire for independence to limit US encroachment on Japanese foreign policy. That Takasaki represented Japan as its chief delegate at the Conference, despite America's list of grievances against him, could itself be seen as a testament of an attempt on the part of Japan to assert an independent foreign policy, one that, as Shigemitsu put it, was 'Japan-centred'.[66] The relevance of this stance becomes even more obvious when juxtaposed to the fact that in the case of the Philippines, the State Department managed to replace Carlos Garcia, who was the Philippine government's first choice as chief delegate, with Romulo because the State Department felt that Garcia 'might be played upon by the Neutralists if not the Communists'.[67] In any event, the State Department did not deem Tokyo's role at the Conference positive enough for any medals. Nevertheless, an informal word of appreciation for Tokyo's 'co-operative attitude prior' to the Conference was duly expressed, even though as a mere footnote.

Notes

1 H.W. Brands, *The Spectre of Neutralism: The United States and the Emergence of the Third World, 1947–1960*, New York: Columbia University Press, 1989, pp. 2–4.
2 National Archives, Kew (hereafter NA Kew), FO 371/116977, 'Southeast Asia, 4448', 6 January 1955.
3 G. H. Jansen, *Nonalignment and the Afro-Asian States*, New York: Frederick A. Praeger, 1966, p.172.
4 Diplomatic Record Office, Tokyo (hereafter DRO), 'Ajia-Afurika kaigi e no Nihon no sanka mondai', B'6.1.0.24–1, B'0049, 0017–0018: Telegram from Kimura Toshio (Minister of Legation) to Shigemitsu, 29 May 1954.
5 R.W. Rinden, 'Nationalism in the Far East', Eisenhower Library, File Folder no.9, Bandung, Box 2, Planning Coordination Group Series, White House Office NSC Staff: Papers, 1945–61.
6 Ibid. For further accounts of Japan's flirtation with neutralism in the early post-war era see Yamaguchi Fusao, *Chūritsu: kono minzoku no kadai*, Tokyo: Gendaijin sōsho, 1959; Maebashi Kakuzō, Yamate Haruyuki (eds), *Chūritsu wa genjitsu dekiru ka*, Tokyo: Sanichi shobō, 1961; J. A. A. Stockwin, *The Japanese Socialist Party and Neutralism: A Study of a Political Party and its Foreign Policy*, London: Melbourne University Press, 1968.
7 Rinden, 'Nationalism in the Far East'.
8 US National Archives, Washington: Department of State central files (hereafter NA Washington) 670.901/1–455 Memorandum from Young to Robertson, Sebald and Baldwin, 'US Asian Policy and Communist China', 4 January 1955.
9 NA Washington, 670.901/1–555, Telegram 1596 from Tokyo to Secretary of State, 5 January 1955.
10 The elections were actually held in February.
11 NA Washington, 670.901/1–555, Telegram 1596 from Tokyo to Secretary of State, 5 January 1955; *Gaimuiin kaigiroku*, 2, Kanpō, 31 March 1955, p. 8; *Gaimuiin kaigiroku*, 2, Kanpō, 11 March 1955, p. 5.
12 Ibid.
13 Ibid.
14 NA Washington, 670.901/1–555, Telegram 1597 from Tokyo to Secretary of State, 5 January 1955.
15 Ibid.
16 NA Washington, 670.901/1–855, Telegram 1375 from the Department of State to the American Embassy, Tokyo, 8 January 1955; NA Washington, 670.901/1–1855, Telegram 1641 from Tokyo to Secretary of State, 18 January 1955; *Gaimuiin kaigiroku*, 2, Kanpō, 11 March 1955.

17 NA Washington, 670.901/1–1255, Telegram 1663 from Tokyo to Secretary of State, 12 January 1955.
18 Ibid.
19 Ibid.
20 NA Washington, 670.901/1–2555, Telegram 1778 from Tokyo to Secretary of State, 25 January 1955.
21 NA Washington, 670.901/1–2555, Telegram 1781 from Tokyo to Secretary of State, 25 January 1955.
22 NA Washington, 670.901/1–2555, Telegram 1778 from Tokyo to Secretary of State, 25 January 1955.
23 Author's emphasis.
24 NA Washington, 670.901/1–2555, Telegram 1782 from Tokyo to Secretary of State, 25 January 1955.
25 NA Washington, 670.901/1–2555 CS/E Memorandum of Conversation, 'Afro-Asian Conference', the Secretary's Office, 25 January 1955. Author's emphasis.
26 NA Washington, 670.901/2–1555 From the State Department to the US Embassy, Tokyo, 15 February 1955.
27 NA Washington, 670.901/3–355, Telegram 2139 from Tokyo to Secretary of State, 3 March 1955.
28 Department of State, 'Developments relating to the Bandung Conference', *Intelligence Report*, 6830.4, 1 April 1955, p. 8; Miyagi Taizō, *Bandon Kaigi to Nihon no Ajia fukki: Amerika to Ajia no hazama de*, Tokyo: Sōshisha, 2001, pp. 78, 85.
29 Department of State 'Developments relating to the Bandung Conference', *Intelligence Report*, 6830.4, 1 April 1955, p. 8.
30 NA Washington, 670.901/3–1155, Telegram 2218 from Tokyo to Secretary of State, 11 March 1955.
31 Ibid.
32 Masashi Nishihara, *The Japanese and Sukarno's Indonesia: Tokyo-Jakarta Relations, 1951–1966*, Honolulu: University Press of Hawaii, 1976, pp. 42, 56.
33 NA Washington, 670.901/3–2355, Telegram 1409 from Department of State to US Embassies, 23 March 1955.
34 Ibid.
35 Emphasis in the original.
36 NA Washington, 670.901/3–1755, Telegram 2288 from Tokyo to Secretary of State, 17 March 1955.
37 *Gaimuiin kaigiroku*, 2, Kanpō, 11 April 1955.
38 NA Washington, 670.901/4–155, Telegram 1596 from Tokyo to Secretary of State, 1 April 1955.
39 NA Washington, 670.901/3–2955, Telegram 1636 from Djakarta to Secretary of State, 29 March 1955.
40 NA Washington, 670.901/4–155, Telegram 2486 from Tokyo to Secretary of State, 1 April 1955 (10:54 am).
41 NA Washington, 670.901/4–855, Telegram 2486 from Tokyo to Secretary of State, 8 April 1955.
42 Ibid.
43 Ibid.
44 NA Washington, 670.901/4–1455 CS/E Telegram 2622 from Tokyo to Secretary of State, 14 April 1955.
45 Ibid.
46 NA Washington, 670.901/4–2755, Telegram 2761 from Tokyo to Secretary of State, 27 April 1955.
47 NA Washington, 670.901/4–155, Telegram 2486 from Tokyo to Secretary of State, 1 April 1955 (10:54 am).
48 Ibid.

49 NA Washington, 670.901/4–855, Telegram 2575 from Tokyo to Secretary of State, 8 April 1955.
50 NA Washington, 670.901/4 1455, Telegram 2627 from Tokyo to Secretary of State, 14 April 1955.
51 NA Washington, 670.901/3–1155, Telegram 2218 from Tokyo to Secretary of State, 11 March 1955.
52 NA Washington, 670.901/4–1455, Telegram 2626 from Tokyo to Secretary of State, 14 April 1955.
53 NA Washington, 670.901/4–855, Telegram 2572 from Tokyo to Secretary of State, 8 April 1955.
54 NA Washington, 670.901/3–1155, Telegram 2218 from Tokyo to Secretary of State, 11 March 1955; *Gaimuiin kaigiroku*, 2, Kanpō, 31 March 1955, p. 8.
55 NA Washington, 670.901/4–3055, Memorandum from Young (PSA) to Robertson (FE), 30 April 1955.
56 NA Washington, 670.901/5–255, From Sebald (FE) to the Under Secretary, 'Comment to Ambassador Iguchi re Asian–African Conference', 2 May 1955, author's emphasis; NA Washington, 670.901/4–2755, From Young to Sebald, 'Proposed action to express appreciation of support [for] free world principles by friends of the United States at Bandung', 27 April 1955.
57 NA Washington, 670.90/4–2855, From W. J. Sebald to the Secretary of State, 'Talks with representatives of governments which participated in the Asian-African Conference', 28 April 1955.
58 NA Washington, 670.901/5–2455, 'Memorandum of conversation between the Secretary of State and General Romulo', 24 May 1955.
59 NA Washington, 670.901/5–255, From Sebald (FE) to the Under Secretary, 'Comment to Ambassador Iguchi re Asian–African Conference', 2 May 1955.
60 Ibid.
61 NA Washington, 670.901/4–1255, Circular 598 from Dulles to American Embassies, 12 April 1955.
62 NA Washington, 670.901/4–2755, From Young to Sebald, 'Proposed action to express appreciation of support [for] free world principles by friends of the United States at Bandung', 27 April 1955.
63 NA Washington, 670.901/4–3055 Memorandum from Young (PSA) to Robertson (FE), 'Asian–African Conference developments', 30 April 1955; NA Kew FO 371/116984, 67969, Memorandum (by G. R. Laking) for the Secretary of State of External Affairs, Wellington, 5 May 1955.
64 NA Washington, 670.901/5–255, From Sebald (FE) to the Under Secretary, 'Comment to Ambassador Iguchi re Asian–African Conference', 2 May 1955.
65 R.W. Rinden, 'Nationalism in the Far East'.
66 *Gaimuiin kaigiroku*, 2, Kanpō, 31 March 1955, p. 8; *Sangiin kaigiroku*, 11, Kanpō, 28 April 1955, p.114.
67 NA Washington, 670.901/2–1755, From W. J. Sebald to the Secretary of State, 17 February 1955.

5 Japan's entry into ECAFE

Oba Mie

Introduction

This chapter investigates the process by which Japan gained entry to the Economic Commission of Asia and the Far East (ECAFE), a significant step towards Japan's post-war re-engagement with its Asian neighbours. Existing studies have examined Japan's role in post-war Asian regional conferences and organizations such as the Bandung Conference and the Colombo Plan, but Japan's involvement in ECAFE has yet to be the object of detailed scholarly attention.[1] While some studies have considered Japan's participation in ECAFE in the context of the organization's history, few have examined it in the context of Japanese policy towards Asia during the early post-war period.[2]

Participation in ECAFE, the first regional organization in Asia and one of the sub-organizations of the United Nations (UN), would enable Japan both to engage the emergent sovereign states of Asia and to return to international society. Defeat in the Second World War cost Japan its colonies in Asia and the Pacific, and deprived it of its rights as a sovereign state. In other words, Japan was no longer a direct participant in regional affairs and international society. The US conducted Japan's external relations and dominated the occupation through the Supreme Commander of Allied Powers (SCAP).[3] Even under occupation, however, significant themes such as returning to international society, and building new relationships with Asia, emerged in certain Japanese elite circles. After the 1951 San Francisco Peace Treaty, the question of how best to secure a new position for Japan in post-war Asian and international society became all the more urgent.

After the Second World War, many Asian countries gradually regained their independence from the European and North American colonial powers. This process fundamentally changed the way in which Japan would need to approach its future relations with the region. This newly emerging Asia provided much of the context for the establishment of ECAFE. Ultimately, Japan's entry into ECAFE depended on whether Asian countries would accept Japan's re-emergence.

For many Japanese officials, building ties with Asia meant that Japan would adopt a special role in Asia rather than simply entering Asian regional society.

Several studies have shown that, even during the Allied occupation, Japanese officials began to plan an Asia policy that was not completely in accord with that of the United States.[4] Despite defeat, loss of empire and drastically reduced diplomatic capacities, many in the Japanese government nonetheless believed that Japan should and could contribute to regional development, industrialization and the raising of living standards. This vision formed the basic tenet of Japanese policies towards Asia and was a key stimulus in Japan's efforts to enter ECAFE.

Equally, Japan was also keen to enter international organizations such as the UN and its sub-agencies, namely the United Nations Education, Science and Culture Organization (UNESCO), the International Labour Organization (ILO), the International Monetary Fund (IMF), and the International Court of Justice (ICJ). Since entry to such organizations would symbolise Japan's return to international society, Japanese anxiety to gain membership to these bodies at such an early stage should not be underestimated and its attempts to enter ECAFE should be examined in this context.[5]

The process of Japan's admission to ECAFE can be divided into three stages. First, Japanese officials and technicians informally attended as advisors to SCAP representatives; second, in 1952, Japan became affiliated with ECAFE as an associate member; finally, Japan obtained full membership in 1954. This chapter begins with a brief description of ECAFE and analyses the above three stages in turn.

ECAFE: The emergence of Asian regionalism

The historical background to ECAFE helps to explain why Japan's entry is of importance for contemporary scholarly investigation. ECAFE was established as a regional commission of the United Nations Economic and Social Council (hereafter, ECOSOC or Council) in 1947. Its main purposes were to serve as an arena wherein member nations could meet on a regular basis to exchange opinions on regional economic and social issues, and to assist in the economic reconstruction and development of Asia. Decisions at each ECAFE session had to be endorsed by ECOSOC. More specific features and purposes of ECAFE were stipulated in the terms of reference in November 1951, which was adopted at the fourth session. These were to:

(a) Initiate and participate in measures for facilitating concerted action for the economic reconstruction and development of Asia and the Far East, for raising the level of economic activity in Asia and the Far East and for maintaining and strengthening the economic relations of these areas both among themselves and with other countries of the world;

(b) Make or sponsor such investigations and studies of economic and technological problems and development within the territories of Asia and the Far East as the Commission deems appropriate;

(c) Undertake or sponsor the collection, evaluation and dissemination of such economic, technological and statistical information as the Commission deems appropriate;

(d) Perform such advisory services, within the available resources of its secretariat, as the countries of the region may desire, provided that such services do not overlap with those rendered by the specialized agencies or the United Nations Technical Assistance Administration;

(e) Assist the Economic and Social Council, at its request, in discharging its functions within the region in connection with any economic problems, including problems in the field of technical assistance.[6]

The restoration of political sovereignty in Asia was one of the major impulses to regional co-operation for economic development.[7] The Republic of China (RoC), India, and the Philippines sought to establish programmes of economic co-operation schemes, and saw success with the formation of ECAFE at the March 1947 ECOSOC session. Western delegates remained more or less sceptical about the idea of establishing an economic commission for Asia.[8] With its first session held in Shanghai in June 1947, ECAFE became the first post-war regional organization in Asia supported, as it was, by a burgeoning Asian political consciousness.

To understand the process of Japan's accession to ECAFE, its unique membership system requires some explanation. Membership was not limited to Asian nations. The founding members included four Asian countries (Republic of China, India, the Philippines, and Thailand), as well as six non-Asian countries (Australia, France, the Netherlands, the Soviet Union, the United Kingdom, and the United States). The member nations of ECAFE fell into three categories: (1) full regional members; (2) associate regional members (constituting a zone known as the 'ECAFE region'); and (3) full non-regional members. The last category comprised those nations that possessed or had possessed colonies in Asia (US, UK, France, and the Netherlands) and those with strong interests in Asia (Australia and the Soviet Union). Under this status, New Zealand joined in 1948. Associate membership was given to those territories which fell within Asia, but were non-self-governing or non-member states of the United Nations. Associate member nations could participate in all ECAFE activities, but did not hold voting rights, nor could they have their representatives appointed as chairman or vice-chairman at ECAFE sessions.[9]

Within ECAFE, regional (full and associate) members attempted to prevent non-regional members from dominating decision making, as they held that Asian views and concerns should carry the greater weight. This sentiment culminated in the Lahore Agreement, adopted at ECAFE's seventh session in 1951, which declared that regional members would take their own decisions on regional economic problems, and that non-regional members would refrain from voting against economic proposals which predominantly concerned the region and enjoyed the majority support of regional members. The Lahore Agreement, in essence a gentlemen's agreement, affirmed that the primary purpose of the Commission was to serve the interests of its regional members.

In addition to a burgeoning political consciousness in Asia, the Cold War further deeply coloured debates in ECAFE and ECOSOC. The 1949 establishment of the People's Republic of China (PRC) and the June 1950 outbreak of war on the Korean peninsula heightened rivalries between East and West, and between pro-Western and non-aligned countries. Such Cold War tensions inevitably affected discussions within the Commission on matters such as how to define Asia as region, and how to promote intra-regional co-operation.

Occupied Japan and ECAFE: informal and indirect participation

The Japanese were already participating in ECAFE activities, with American support, prior to the 1952 restoration of Japan's independence. The fifth session of ECOSOC in July 1947 enabled ECAFE to promote consultation between SCAP and ECAFE 'for the purpose of mutual information and advice on matters concerning the economy of Japan' in relation to Asia.[10] Consequently, SCAP began sending its representatives to ECAFE sessions and committees, who then forwarded their observations to the Japanese government.

Asian members of ECAFE could not ignore Japan's economic potential to assist in their reconstruction and development. In late 1947, the ECAFE Secretariat submitted to the second ECAFE session a preliminary report entitled *Survey of Reconstruction Problem and Needs*. The Report pointed out that Japanese economic weakness in the immediate post-war period would provide other Asian countries with an opportunity to industrialize in the short term but that in the long run, a stagnant Japan would negatively impact upon economic stability and development in the ECAFE region.[11] Subsequent reports focused on encouraging trade between Japan and Asia, and promoting Japanese technical co-operation with the region.

In July 1948, an interim report identified areas in which ECAFE could assist Japanese economic growth and regional co-operation by, for example:

(a) Arranging finance to facilitate import/export trade with Japan;
(b) Determining and executing as early as possible any reparations removal, as an integral part of the industrial development plans in the ECAFE region;
(c) Utilizing Japanese technical personnel wherever practicable in the development of projects in the region.[12]

At its third session, ECAFE adopted a resolution affirming the value of the Japanese economy to the reconstruction and development of the ECAFE region.[13] This principle was reaffirmed at the fourth session in December 1948.

In addition to trade, Japanese technical assistance was also expected. With positive encouragement from SCAP, the ECAFE executive secretary, Dr P. S. Lokanathan, wrote to the Far Eastern Commission in March 1949 pointing out the urgent need for Japanese technical assistance, as certain ECAFE countries were anxious to secure Japanese technicians for both private and government projects.[14] Emphasising this need, he also went to Tokyo to negotiate for technical support with SCAP in late May 1949. Simultaneously, the Indian Liaison Mission in Tokyo pressed SCAP to allow the despatch of Japanese experts to service Indian technical requirements.[15] In August 1949, SCAP sent a memorandum to the Japanese government and the heads of foreign missions in Japan, permitting the deployment of Japanese technicians in the ECAFE region.[16] In this manner, even though under occupation, Japan began informal participation in ECAFE activities.

The attendance of Japanese officials at the first sub-committee on Iron and Steel, held in August 1949, as technical advisors to SCAP, was a milestone for Japan's involvement in ECAFE.[17] Thereafter, Japanese officials and businessmen increasingly attended ECAFE committees in this manner. Such participation culminated in Japanese attendance at a full session of ECAFE in Lahore in January 1951, though still retaining the designation of technical advisor to SCAP. Two factors enabled Japan's informal and indirect participation in ECAFE. First, the United States wanted to strengthen the economic and political ties between Japan and Asia, especially South-East Asia. Washington aimed at revitalizing the Japanese economy in order to promote economic growth in South-East Asia, hoping thereby to prevent the expansion of communist influence in the region.[18] The framework of the Commission would lend itself to the achievement of such objectives.[19] Second, South-East Asia itself recognized the potential of Japan to promote economic development in the region, even though the memory of Japanese wartime atrocities remained strong.

Nonetheless, Japanese indirect participation in the Commission was neither unanimously accepted nor totally welcomed by all member nations. For example, the Philippine delegation to the fifth session submitted a draft resolution insisting that ECAFE adopt some means to prevent a revitalized Japanese economy from threatening world peace.[20] Furthermore, when Dr Sherwood M. Fine, the US representative, insisted at the May 1950 Committee of Industry and Trade at Bangkok that Japan's trade with Asia be promoted according to the Most Favoured Nation (MFN)[21] principle, delegations from the United Kingdom, France, and British Malaya expressed their fears pertaining to potential Japanese competition in their newly reclaimed markets. Despite this, the Committee resolved that trade with Japan be promoted lest Japanese economic stagnation have a negative influence.[22] Moreover, at a January 1952 meeting of the Industry and Trade Committee held in Lahore, British and Soviet delegates prevented Japanese participants from making a statement. Okita Saburō, one of Japan's observers, bitterly referred to this event later as follows:

> Japan was not yet independent and our position was as advisor to SCAP. However, Japan's status in the world was much lower than it had been. For example, our attempt to speak at the meeting was resisted. Furthermore, the host country presented gifts to all of the representatives at session, but it did not present anything to those of us from Japan. These events indicated that Japan's standing in the international society was so pitiful at that time. We felt so small attending meetings for that month.[23]

Despite such misgivings, Japan welcomed US and Asian plans for its participation in ECAFE. Japanese government agencies such as the Ministry of Foreign Affairs (MoFA) and the Economic Stabilization Board keenly translated and circulated numerous papers and reports supporting the significance of Japanese involvement in ECAFE. Japanese officials regarded Japan's participation in ECAFE as both a tool for building ties with the newly independent countries of Asia and as one means of carrying out Japan's regional policies.

Gaining associate membership

The Japanese government attempted to realize direct participation in ECAFE as soon as possible after the 1951 Peace Treaty, a move encouraged by SCAP; the ECAFE Secretariat, especially Dr Lokanathan; and some Asian nations, particularly Pakistan. It is notable that Japan's admission to associate membership (in 1952) was approved before the Peace Treaty came into force. While only UN members in the ECAFE region were eligible to be full members, Japan, still technically under occupation, was permitted associate membership only. Even for this to happen, first Paragraph Two of the Terms of Reference, which defined the Asian region, had to be amended to include Japan, and, second, ECAFE had to formally adopt a resolution to admit Japan. Furthermore, such steps had to be recognized at both ECAFE and ECOSOC sessions. Japan's associate membership was approved at the eighth session of ECAFE in January 1952,[24] and Japan was formally admitted at the fourteenth session of ECOSOC in June of the same year. This section will examine in detail the process by which Japan gained its associate membership.

The Japanese government was anxious to enter ECAFE as an associate member, regarding the organization as an instrument to both strengthen political and economic ties with South-East Asia and to contribute to international co-operation.[25] More specifically, MoFA spelled out key advantages. Namely, Japan would be granted direct input into the economic recovery and development schemes of member states and would be provided with opportunities to directly participate in the processes of their planning and management; Japan would obtain information and data pertinent to the economic situation in the ECAFE region; and, through the promotion of technical assistance, Japan might expand its exports of capital goods to South-East Asia in the future.[26]

Japan and SCAP began to jointly prepare for Japan's associate membership application prior to the conclusion of the Peace Treaty in the context of strengthening ties between Japan and South-East Asia. Concrete planning took place over June and July 1951.[27] One tangible outcome of such planning was the US–Japan joint mission to South-East Asia in July 1951.[28]

After the conclusion of the Peace Treaty, Japan's intention to gain ECAFE associate membership was obvious and the ECAFE Secretariat responded positively. In early September 1951, MoFA representatives in Bangkok reported that some South-East Asian officials, such as D. G. Pascur of the Secretariat's Industrial Division, welcomed a rapid Japanese affiliation due to the vital role of Japan's industrial power in restoring and developing Asian economies.[29] In addition, other members of the Secretariat were also said to be in favour of establishing the ECAFE Secretariat in Tokyo. Support for Japan clearly existed, but was by no means unanimous, as debate over the amendments to Paragraph Two of the Terms of Reference clearly showed. In November, MoFA representatives in Bangkok reached an agreement with Dr Lokanathan whereby Paragraph Two would be amended at the thirteenth session of ECOSOC in December 1951. Consequently, the Japanese government asked some ECOSOC member governments, specifically the Philippines, India and Pakistan, to support the amendment.[30] Pakistan accepted the request and promised to sponsor the proposal,[31] and India agreed to support any proposal for the inclusion of Japan as an associate member.[32] The Philippines, however, merely acknowledged the request.[33] Despite this tempered support, the thirteenth session of ECOSOC failed to agree to an amendment of the Terms of Reference and decided to postpone discussion until May 1952. The Philippines objected to Pakistan's proposal on the grounds that the Filipino delegate had not received any instruction on the matter. In addition, India and the US wanted to postpone discussion.[34]

The Japanese government and Lokanathan planned to obtain Japan's associate membership even if the thirteenth session of ECOSOC did not amend the Terms of Reference. Pakistan also submitted a proposal to the Secretariat in early December 1951 to include Japan as associate member, which also approved an amendment to Paragraph Two of the Terms of Reference and requested ECOSOC to approve the amendments to these Terms.[35] Pakistan emphasized the importance of Japan's affiliation with ECAFE as follows:

> The member governments of the ECAFE have paid continued attention to the possibilities of maximizing trade with Japan, as the importance of Japan's industrial potential in relation to the economic development of the Asian countries is patent as is also Japan's need of raw materials for the rehabilitation of its own economy. The change in the international status of Japan arising from the recent Peace Treaty with this country make it necessary to reconsider the question of future consultation between the ECAFE and Japan. It is indispensable that the mutual co-operation, which has been established between Japan and the countries of the region by consultations referred to above, should be continued and intensified.[36]

The Japanese government submitted its application for associate membership of ECAFE on 23 January 1952,[37] slightly prior to the opening of the eighth session of ECAFE, and attached SCAP's letter of endorsement.

At the eighth session, the Pakistani proposal was discussed. At the outset, the Burmese chairman, U Kyaw Thein, minister of Commerce, Industry and Mines, welcomed the participation of Japanese observers.[38] However, the Representative of the Philippines, C. Balmaceda, secretary of the Department of Commerce and Industry, reiterated his objections to Japan's admission to associate membership in this session. He insisted that amendment of Paragraph Two to include Japan in

East Asia was acceptable, but that Japan could not become an associate member because it was not responsible for its own international relations until the Peace Treaty came into force.[39] Other delegates, however, disagreed and advocated accepting Japan as an associate member as soon as possible. The Ceylonese representative, G. G. Ponnembalam, minister of Industries, Industrial Research and Fisheries, replied that the Philippines' observations were technically correct, but warned ECAFE against permitting mere technicalities to prevent the active co-operation of Japan.[40]

The Pakistani delegation parried the Philippines' objection by replying that the draft resolution aimed not to propose Japan for associate membership but rather to make Japan eligible for associate membership as soon as possible.[41] The Thai representative, M.C. Sakol Varavarn, adviser on ECAFE matters to the government, supported Pakistan, referring to the necessity and importance of Japan's entry as an associate member as soon as possible.[42] Dr Lokanathan said that SCAP recognized that the Japanese government had full authority to assume any obligations the Terms of Reference might impose. The US representative, Merrill C. Gay, minister and economic adviser to the Assistant Secretary of State for Far Eastern Affairs, also insisted that Japan had been given responsibility in international affairs with regards to commercial matters even though the Peace Treaty had not come into force, and that Japan had already secured entry to several international organizations, such as FAO, ILO, WHO and UNESCO.[43] The RoC's Foreign Office representative, V. S. Pan, said that despite the fact that the RoC had been the main victim of Japan's pre-war colonial policy in Asia and had yet to sign a peace treaty with Japan, the RoC would not vote against Japan's admission.[44] The representatives of both Vietnam and Burma also expressed their approval for Japan's admission, recognizing Japan's potential contribution to economic development in the ECAFE region.[45] After some debate, the Pakistani proposal was adopted by majority vote.[46]

At the fourteenth session of ECOSOC held in New York in June 1952, not only Pakistan, but also the UK, Sweden, the RoC, Egypt, the US, and even the Soviet Union, expressed support for Japan's associate membership, though the Filipino delegate maintained his objections.[47] Eventually, the recommendation from the eighth session of ECAFE to amend Paragraph Two of the Terms of Reference was adopted unanimously while the vote for Japan's associate membership was passed with only the Philippines abstaining.[48]

Towards full membership

In June 1953, the Japanese government put forward its reasons for seeking full membership as a means of 'co-operating more closely with the United Nations and contributing more effectively to the prosperity of Asia'.[49] Associate membership was regarded by MoFA as sufficient to participate in ECAFE's various operations, but the desire for full membership stemmed from the need to obtain a higher position and status in the Asian region. For example, Japan would be able to invite ECAFE to base its secretariat in Tokyo, bringing with it the credit of a UN office in Asia located in the Japanese capital.[50] Full membership would also bolster Japan's application to enter the UN.[51] Again, Cold War tensions were reflected in the Soviet Union and the United States potentially using their respective vetoes to block the entry of rivals belonging to the opposing bloc. Regional issues, such as the volatile situation in Indochina and the virtual dissection of the Korean peninsula, made discussing the criteria for full membership more complex. The prospects for Japan's application for membership to the United Nations were bleak under such conditions. Since, in principle, a full member of ECAFE should also be a member of the UN, Japan's request for full ECAFE membership would be all the more difficult to realize.

The promotion of associate members to full membership was first discussed at the ninth session of ECAFE held in Bandung in February 1953.[52] Japan's application was not the sole topic of discussion. Apart from Japan, the full range of associate members constituted Ceylon, Nepal, Cambodia, Laos, Vietnam, and South Korea. The Cambodian representative, H. E. Sonn Voeunsai (director-general of Royal Railways of Cambodia), submitted a draft resolution, to which A. Khaleeli, the Pakistani representative (Industrial Development Commissioner and Secretary to the government of East Pakistan), proposed the insertion of a clause stating that 'any associate member which is responsible for its own international relations, may on application to the Commission, be admitted as a member of the Commission' under the Terms of Reference.[53] The aim of both resolutions was to allow associate members to participate in ECAFE as full members. Cambodia, Pakistan, and others regarded the promotion of associate members to full members as an effective means to encourage Asian pre-eminence in this regional organization.[54]

However, some members did not accept the draft resolution. The Thai representative, Sakol Varavarn, said that ECAFE should not make any recommendations to ECOSOC, but should merely welcome measures taken by ECOSOC to promote greater and more active participation of the associate members in the works of the Commission. To that end, he referred to a prior ECAFE meeting where the question of PRC representation was side-stepped on the grounds that higher authorities in the UN were discussing it.[55] An Indonesian representative, A. P. Makatita, objected that the effect of the Cambodian draft resolution would be to drastically alter the Terms of Reference on membership without sufficient debate.[56]

S.S. Nemtchina, the Soviet representative, criticized the colonial powers for only wanting to grant full rights to their puppets such as Bao Dai or Synghman Rhee.[57] Nemtchina's remarks indicated the Soviet Union's suspicions that the Western powers were attempting to get pro-Western but non-UN member countries into the UN by providing them with full membership of ECAFE. The US representative, Merrill C. Gay, flatly denied such charges.[58]

Khaleeli submitted a revised resolution which recommended to ECOSOC that full membership of ECAFE be granted to those associate members who were responsible for their own international relations and who apply to ECAFE for such membership.[59] Although, Indonesia and the Soviet Union reiterated their objections, it was nonetheless adopted with ten approving, one objecting and two abstaining.[60]

At the fifteenth session of ECOSOC, the United States and the United Kingdom proposed a joint draft resolution to grant Cambodia, Ceylon, Japan, South Korea, Laos, Nepal, and South Vietnam full membership by adding these countries to the list of the full members of ECAFE.[61] However, this draft resolution met with stern resistance. The Soviet representative reiterated the same objections as at the ninth ECAFE session, that is, that the resolution aimed to include the French puppet, Bao Dai, in order to dominate ECAFE. Poland followed the USSR's line. On the other hand, France and the United States adamantly supported the admission of associate members as full members to ECAFE, which meant that the non-UN members in ECAFE obtained voting rights. In contrast, however, at the fourteenth session of ECOSOC they had opposed the suggestion that non-UN member nations in Eastern Europe should obtain the right to vote in the Economic Commission for Europe (ECE).[62]

Such objections served to symbolize the intensifying confrontation between the two camps. On the other hand, some member nations, including India, Sweden, Yugoslavia, and Argentina, expressed their doubts as to the legitimacy of the joint US/UK draft resolution in the context of the founding principles of the UN and its organizations. They held serious reservations as to whether ECOSOC possessed the authority to establish membership criteria for UN agencies. Sweden and Yugoslavia asserted that the question of full ECAFE membership was inextricably intertwined with UN affiliations. For ECOSOC, resolving the membership issue proved to be an intractable problem given the impact of Cold War tensions on UN debates. They argued that ECOSOC credibility would suffer if it awarded voting rights to associate members by granting them full membership without giving the same rights to non-UN members in Europe at the ECE.[63]

These debates on full membership of ECAFE were one aspect of the general question of whether non-UN members could enter into either the Asian or the European regional commissions as full members. On 24 April, it became clear that the US, the UK, France, and Australia approved the resolution; while the USSR, Poland, and Sweden objected and India abstained. Yugoslavia approved the admission of only Japan and Ceylon, while the Philippines recognized that of Ceylon, South Korea, and Nepal, but abstained in the case of Japan.[64] India proposed to shelve all discussion of non-UN member affiliation with the regional commissions. The session eventually adopted the Indian proposal, and decided that further discussion would be postponed until the next ECOSOC session.

Prior to the fifteenth session of ECOSOC, the Japanese government was sanguine about its prospects for full membership after the adoption of the resolution at the ninth session of ECAFE at Bandung. The government believed that the fifteenth session would readily admit associate members, including Japan, to full membership since the members of ECOSOC included the seven ECAFE members in favour of the motion.[65] Washington was as optimistic as Japan. Likewise, ECAFE's executive secretary, Dr Lokanathan, was also positive.[66] Consequently, the Japanese government was visibly shocked by the adverse decision and hoped that the sixteenth session would instead admit Japan as a full member. Unfortunately, the sixteenth session, held in December 1953, did not address the question of full membership of non-UN members in the regional economic commissions, and decided to postpone the discussion once more.

Failure awoke the Japanese government to the importance of full membership. It planned to reiterate its support for the motion for ECOSOC to admit associate members as full members in the tenth session of ECAFE to be held in Kandy, Ceylon in February 1954. In addition, Japan invited ECAFE to hold its next session in Tokyo. Moreover, Japan attempted to change the criterion that the chairman was to be elected from the representatives of full members only, to one that enabled representatives from associate members to become chairmen. Were this change to be effected, a Japanese representative could act as chairman even if Japan were not admitted as a full member.

The Japanese representative, Ōta Ichirō, presented two draft resolutions at the tenth ECAFE session. One stated that 'ECAFE urges ECOSOC to reach a decision enabling the Commission to admit to its membership those associate members who are responsible for their own international relations'.[67] The second proposed an amendment to procedures to allow representatives to be chosen as chairmen from the combined pool of full and associate members. The Soviet representative objected to the first draft resolution, but not the second. The Japanese proposal to host the next session was unanimously accepted.[68] Indonesia and India also pointed out that their delegations had voted against a similar resolution in Bandung in April 1953. Ultimately, however, by a show of hands both draft resolutions were adopted.[69]

As groundwork for the seventeenth session of ECOSOC, Japan requested that non-Soviet-aligned member countries support the promotion to full membership of ECAFE associate members to avoid a repeat of events at the fifteenth and the sixteenth sessions. At the seventeenth session, France, Pakistan, and the US proposed yet another draft resolution based on earlier drafts. India countered, suggesting that the affiliation of Laos, Cambodia, and South Vietnam be postponed. The USSR reiterated that it could not accept the draft resolution submitted by the three countries, but remarkably approved the affiliation of Japan, Nepal, and Ceylon on the condition that the PRC was admitted to ECAFE. The French, Pakistani, and American draft resolution was adopted with 14 approving, two objecting (the Soviet Union and Czechoslovakia) and two (India and Yugoslavia) abstaining. As a result, seven countries, including Japan, became full members of ECAFE.[70]

Discussion of an amendment to procedures was redundant since Japan, now a full member, would be able to host the next session of ECAFE with Japanese acting as both chairman and vice-chairman. The eleventh session of ECAFE was held in Tokyo from late March to early April 1955. Hosting this session marked Japan's evolving position in Asia.[71] Takasaki Tatsunosuke, Director General of the Economic Deliberation Agency (later the Economic Planning Agency) headed the Japanese delegation at this ECAFE session. He was unanimously elected as chairman of this session.[72] Prime Minister Hatoyama Ichirō gave an opening address, expressing Japan's enthusiasm on gaining full membership, to contribute even more fully to ECAFE aims and activities.[73]

Conclusion

The establishment of ECAFE symbolized the clear success of a newly independent Asia in creating its own regional body and demonstrated a burgeoning regionalism. This chapter examined the process of Japan's admission to ECAFE, which was divided into three stages: Japan's informal and indirect participation during the occupation; its accession as associate membership; and, finally, entry as a full member. For Japan, entry into such regional organizations provided a vehicle for greater involvement in the region. Many Japanese firmly believed that Japan could contribute to the improvement of Asia's economic prospects. Moreover, joining ECAFE also represented Japan's gradual return to the international society.

However, Japan confronted various obstacles at each stage, not least the antipathy of some Asian countries, especially the Philippines, towards Japan due to Japan's wartime behaviour. Further, the United Kingdom, Australia, and some Asian countries were concerned about the promotion of trade between Japan and ECAFE region given the stiff competition they had faced from Japan in pre-war Asian markets such as textiles. Moreover, the confrontation between the two Cold War camps sometimes prevented Japan from easily participating in ECAFE. This especially hampered Japan's attempts to gain full membership.

On the other hand, other powers and agencies encouraged Japan's affiliation with ECAFE at each stage. The US, pursuing a containment policy, supported Japan's involvement in ECAFE in order to revitalize Japan and enable its return to Asia in a manner consistent with newly emerging regionalist norms. Given Cold War rivalries, strong support from the US and other Western counties was indispensable. Japan's involvement in ECAFE accorded with US policy to reorientate Japan's economic links and raw material supplies away from the now communist North-East Asia to that of South-East Asia. In this context it is important to observe that many ECAFE member states were South-East Asian, some of whom regarded Japan as important to the economic development of the region.

The ECAFE Secretariat always supported Japan's affiliation with ECAFE and its co-operation with ECAFE objectives, based upon the view that Japanese participation and engagement was indispensable for the revitalization and development of the ECAFE region. Dr. Lokanathan, who was influential in Secretariat decision making, was especially eager to promote Japan's participation in ECAFE activities.

During the latter half of the 1950s, Asian ECAFE members became increasingly interested in promoting regional co-operation through, for example, the Intra-Regional Trade Talks (1959), the Mekong River Development Plan (1957), the Asia Highway Plan (1958) and so forth. Proposals to strengthen Asian regionalism gathered momentum in the early 1960s and included discussions on establishing an Organization for Asian Economic Co-operation. Although this body was never established, the discussions themselves led to the founding of the Asia Development Bank in 1966. These developments showed that ECAFE provided Asia with a significant forum in which to promote regionalism from the 1950s to the mid-1960s. Japan was deeply engaged in the development of regional co-operation within and beyond ECAFE. It was Japan, for example, that proposed the Intra-Regional Trade Talks in 1957, and Okita Saburō was an advocate of the Organization for Asian Economic Co-operation. Thus, the study of Japan's role in ECAFE reveals that the promotion of Asian regionalism was a core element of Japan's evolving foreign policy in the 1950s.

Notes

1 For details of Japan's participation in the Bandung Conference, see Miyagi Taizō, *Bandon Kaigi to Nihon no Ajia fukki: Amerika to Nihon no hazama de*, Tokyo: Sōshisha, 2001. On Japan's entry into the Colombo Plan, see Hatano Sumio, 'Tōnan Ajia kaihatsu o meguru Nichi-Bei-Ei kankei: Nihon no Koronbo puran kanyū o chūshin ni' in Kindai Nihon kenkyūkai ed., *Nenpō kindai Nihon kenkyū 16: Sengo gaikō no keisei*, Tokyo: Yamakawa, 1994, pp. 215–242.
2 Olson refers to ECAFE in the context of Japanese policy towards Asia in L. Olson, *Japan in Postwar Asia*, Westport, CT: Praeger, 1970. Yokoi describes Japan's participation in ECAFE in the context of British policy towards Japan in Yokoi Noriko, *Japan's Postwar Economic Recovery and Anglo-Japanese Relations, 1948–1962*, London: RoutledgeCurzon, 2003, pp. 104–5. For details on the activities and politics of ECAFE, see D. Wightman, *Toward Economic Cooperation in Asia: The United Nations Economic Commission for Asia and the Far East*, New Haven and London: Yale University Press, 1963; United Nations, *ECAFE: Twenty Years of Progress* (E/CN.11/766 Rev.1), 1967; and L. P. Singh, *The Politics of Economic Cooperation in Asia: A Study of Asian International Organizations*, Columbia, MO: University of Missouri Press, 1966.
3 SCAP refers both to the supreme commander, General Douglas MacArthur, and to the administrative organs which he headed.
4 Nakamura Takafusa, 'Nichi-bei "keizai kyōryoku" kankei no keisei' in Kindai Nihon kenkyūkai (ed.) *Nenpō kindai Nihon kenkyū 4: Taiheiyō Sensō: Kaisen kara kōwa made*, Tokyo: Yamakawa, 1983, pp. 279–302. Watanabe Akio, 'Southeast Asia in US-Japanese Relations' in A. Iriye and W. I. Cohen (eds) *The United States and Japan in the Post-War World* Lexington, Kentucky: University Press of Kentucky, 1989, pp. 80–95. Suehiro Akira, 'Keizai sai-shinshutsu e no michi' in Nakamura Masanori (ed.), *Sengo kaikaku to sono isan: Sengo Nihon senryō to sengo kaikaku*, Tokyo: Iwanami Shoten, 1995, pp. 211–252. Inoue Toshikazu, 'Sengo Nihon to Ajia gaikō no keisei', *Nenpō Seijigaku, 1998: Nihon gaikō ni okeru Ajiashugi*, Tokyo: Iwanami, 1998, pp. 129–147.
5 Japan joined UNESCO in July 1951, ILO in November 1951, IMF in August 1952 and IJC in April 1954.
6 ECAFE, E/CN.11/29 Rev.3, 15 November 1951.
7 Wightman, *Economic Cooperation* p. 8.
8 For details on the establishment of ECAFE, see Wightman, *Economic Cooperation*, pp. 13–18 and Singh, *The Politics of Economic Cooperation*, pp. 15–25.
9 According to the Rules of Procedure, ECAFE shall 'elect from among its representatives a Chairman and a Vice-Chairman who shall hold office until their successors are elected in the next session'. ECAFE, *Rules of Procedure*, E/CN.11/2 Rev.9, 24 February 1953.
10 ECAFE, *Terms of Reference*, November 1951, Paragraph 10. This was deleted when Japan was admitted as an associate member later.
11 ECAFE, *Survey of Reconstruction Problem and Needs*, E/CN, 11/39, 23 October 1947. This report was translated into Japanese by Economic Stabilization Board in March 1948.

12 ECAFE, *Interim Report and Recommendations on Industrial Development by the Working Party*, E/CN.11/82, 6 May 1948, p. 102.

13 ECAFE, *Resolution*, E/CN.11/113. 11 June 1948.

14 The Far Eastern Commission was established in February 1946 in order to determine the occupation policies of Allied powers towards Japan. The Commission was composed of ten Allied powers: the United States, the United Kingdom, RoC, Soviet Union, Australia, Canada, France, India, Holland, New Zealand, and the Philippines. In November 1949, Burma and Pakistan also joined. The Far Eastern Commission was technically the supreme decision-making agency over GHQ and SCAP. However, this Commission usually merely confirmed GHQ and SCAP decisions, and had but slight influence on occupation policies.

15 The Indian Liaison Mission was the overseas agency of the government of India during the occupation era, given that Japan, as an occupied nation, could not technically receive embassies.

16 For details on the despatch of Japanese experts to the ECAFE region for technical assistance, see ECAFE, United Nations Programme of Technical Assistance for Economic Development, Report by the Executive Secretary, E/CN. 11/200, 6 September 1949.

17 Ogiwara Tōru, *Nihon gaikōshi (30): Kōwago no gaikō (II) Keizai (I)*, Tokyo: Kajima Kenkyūjo Shuppankai, 1972, p. 266.

18 The United States began to soften its attitude toward Japan in 1948, a process referred to as the reverse course. In addition, after the communist victory in China in 1949, South-East Asia came to be regarded by SCAP and the US government as a vital area to counter communist infiltration. M. Schaller, *The American Occupation of Japan: The Origins of the Cold War in Asia*, Oxford: Oxford University Press, 1985, pp. 122–63.

19 Some officials in SCAP and the Department of State began to plan Japan's regional integration with Asia in 1948 in the hope that this would encourage economic development and diminish the communist threat. See Schaller, *The American Occupation*, pp. 141–63.

20 *Kokusai Shūhō*, 1 November 1949, 43, p. 2.

21 MFN is the provision in a commercial treaty which extends trading benefits equal to those accorded any third state.

22 *Kokusai Shūhō*, 6 June 1950, 73, p. 4.

23 Okita Saburō, 'Dai 17 kai Ekafe sōkai no inshōki', *Ekafe Tsūshin*, 296, 1 April 1962, p. 29.

24 ECAFE Eighth Session, Official Records, 29 January – 8 February 1952, E/CN.11/344, 21 April 1952, p. 35.

25 Diplomatic Record Office, Tokyo (hereafter, DRO), B'-0045, 'ECAFE e no kamei shinsei no ken ni kanshi kakugi kettei no ken', 12 January 1952.

26 DRO, B'-0045, 'ECAFE ni kansuru setsumeisho', 10 January 1952.

27 DRO, B'-0045, Kokusai kyōryoku ikka 'Ekafe sanka to Nichi-Bei gōdō misshon ni kansuru ken', 26 June 1951.

28 Nakamura, 'Nichibei keizai kyōryoku kankei no keisei', pp. 295–6.

29 DRO, B'-0045, 'ECAFE kankei kaigi no ken', Telegram from Suzuki (Bangkok) to Foreign Minister Shigeru Yoshida, 57, 6 September 1951; and 'Nihon no ECAFE sanka ni kansuru ken', from Suzuki to Masutani Hidetsugu, 7 September 1951. The office of the ECAFE Secretariat was located in Bangkok, so that in effect MoFA representatives in the Office of the Japanese Government Overseas Agency in Bangkok acted as liaison to the ECAFE secretariat.

30 DRO, B'-0045, Telegram from Foreign Minister to Secretaries in Karachi and New Dehli, 'Nihon no ekafe kamei ni kansuru ken', 10 December 1951.

31 DRO, B'-0045, Letter from Dhaudhri (Ministry of Foreign Affairs of Commonwealth Relations, Karachi, Pakistan) to Hiroshi Uchida, 22 December 1951.

32 DRO, B'-0045, Letter from Indian Liaison Mission in Tokyo to the Ministry of Foreign Affairs, 27 December 1951.

33 DRO, B'-0045, Letter from Philippines Mission in Japan to Ministry of Foreign Affairs, 27 December 1951.

34 Prior to the decision at the thirteenth ECOSOC session, Japan and the ECAFE Secretariat secured, in agreement with SCAP, Japanese attendance at future sessions as independent observers rather than as functionaries of SCAP. Thus, in November 1951, Lokanathan invited SCAP to nominate representatives to attend the eighth session of ECAFE and other meetings such as the sub-committee on Electric Power, the sub-committee on Iron and Steel and the fourth session of the committee on Industry and Trade to be held in January and February in Rangoon. Since SCAP had no intention of attending these sessions, the invitation was, in effect, one to the Japanese government. DRO, B'-0045, Letter from Lokanathan to Chief, Diplomatic Section, SCAP, 3 November 1951; Letter from H.W. Rand, Deputy Chief, Diplomatic Section, SCAP to Lokanathan, 7 December 1951.

35 ECAFE, Draft resolution proposed by Pakistan delegation, Eighth Session, 29 January 1952, Rangoon, Burma, E/CN.11/328, Add. 2., 29 January 1952; ECAFE, From J. Farukhi, Under Secretary to the Government of Pakistan to the Executive Secretary, ECAFE, *Amendment to ECAFE's Terms of Reference for Closer Association of Japan with the Commission*, 5 December 1951, E/CN.11/328, p. 3.

36 From J. Farukhi, Under Secretary to the Government of Pakistan to The Executive Secretary, ECAFE, 'Amendment to ECAFE's terms of reference for closer association of Japan with the Commission,' 5 December, 1951, in E/CN.11/328, p. 3.

37 ECAFE, E/CN.11/328 Add.1, p. 2.

38 ECAFE Eighth Session, Provisional Summary Record of the Ninety-First Meeting, E/CN.11/SR.91, 29 January 1952, p. 5, and ECAFE E/CN.11/344, p. 28.

39 ECAFE Eighth Session, Provisional Summary Record of the Ninety-First Meeting, E/CN.11/SR.91, 29 January 1952, p. 5.

40 Ibid., pp. 6–7.

41 Ibid., p. 7.

42 Ibid., p. 8.

43 Ibid., p. 9.

44 Ibid., pp. 9–10.

45 Ibid., p. 11.

46 Ibid., p. 13.

47 DRO, B'-0045, 'Ekafe kanyū no ken', Telegram from New York to Tokyo, 13 June 1952.

48 DRO, B'-0045, 'Nihon no Ekafe kanyū ni kansuru ken', Telegram from New York to Tokyo, 108, 10 June 1952.

49 DRO, B'-0045, Letter to Sir Winston S. Churchill, Acting Secretary of State for Foreign Affairs, 26 June 1953.

50 DRO, B'-0045, 'Ajia oyobi kyokutō keizai iinkai kamei no ken', Telegram from Tokyo to Geneva, 20 June 1953.

51 DRO, B'-0045, 'Ajia oyobi kyokutō keizai iinkai kamei no ken', Telegram from Foreign Minister Okazaki to Consul in Geneva, 23 June 1953.

52 ECAFE Ninth Session, Official Records, 6–14 February 1953, E/CN/363, 15 April 1953, p. 9.

53 Ibid., pp. 151–3.

54 Wightman, *Economic Cooperation*, p. 52.

55 ECAFE Ninth Session, Official Records, 6–14 February 1953, E/CN/363, p. 154.

56 Ibid., p. 155.

57 Ibid., pp. 156–7.

58 Ibid., p. 164.

59 Ibid., p. 165.

60 Ibid., pp. 166–7.
61 ECOSOC, E/L.504. 23 April 1953. The draft resolution was slightly revised in response to a proposal by Australia with regards to a procedural issue, ECOSOC, E/L.505, 24 April 1953.
62 The ECE and ECAFE were established simultaneously at the 1947 ECOSOC session.
63 'Ekafe jun kamei koku no seishiki sanka ni kansuru ken', Telegram from New York to Tokyo, 30 April 1953.
64 DRO, B'-0045, 'Waga kuni to no ekafe kamei ni kansuru Bei-Futsu kyōdo teian no shingi jōkyō ni kansuru hōkoku no ken', Telegram from New York to Tokyo, 52, 24 April 1953.
65 DRO, B'-0045, 'Ekosoku ni okeru ekafe jun-kōseikoku no seishiki sanka ni kansuru ken', Telegram from Tokyo to New York, 27 March 1953, 25.
66 DRO, B'-0045, 'Ekafe kamei mondai ni kansuru ken (Rokanasan naiwa)', 19 April 1953.
67 ECAFE/SR.137, 18 February 1954, p. 8.
68 Ibid., p. 3.
69 Ibid., p. 11.
70 'Nihon to nana kakoku no ekafe seishiki kamei', *Kokusai Shūhō*, 272, 27 April 1954, p. 1.
71 Olson makes a similar point, but places greater emphasis on the economic aspect, see Olson, *Japan in Postwar Asia*, p. 23.
72 ECAFE, Eleventh Session, Official Records, E/CN.11/408, p. 42.
73 DRO, B'2–3–7,1–3–6 'Opening Address by His Excellency Mr. Ichiro Hatoyama, Prime Minister of Japan,' and 'ECAFE dai 11 kai sōkai kaikaishiki ni okeru sōri aisatsu', 28 March 1955.

6 Japan's struggle for UN membership in 1955

Kurusu Kaoru

Introduction

In late 1956, after a five-year struggle, Japan was finally admitted to the United Nations (UN). This chapter focuses on the issues surrounding Japan's bid for membership during the tenth General Assembly (GA) in 1955, examining the reasons for Japan's failure to be admitted at that time. Historians have hitherto described the process of Japan's entry to the UN from the perspective of the Japanese government.[1] This chapter, however, illustrates the way in which the changing international situation in the first half of the 1950s contributed to the difficult process of Japanese admission to the UN. In particular, it pays close attention to the positions of the US, USSR and Republic of China (RoC) regarding the Canadian proposal that would have seen Japan and Outer Mongolia, amongst others, gain admission to the UN on the basis on universal membership.

Cold War politics, differing perceptions of the changing role of the UN in international affairs, in addition to the issue of Chinese representation in the UN, ultimately combined to prevent Japan's admission in 1955. In considering the strategic positions of the US and USSR, this chapter demonstrates how Japan's membership to the UN was a secondary factor in their considerations. Thus, for example, for the Dwight Eisenhower administration, the issue of Japan's UN membership was a low priority in 1955 owing to America's obsession with the realpolitik of the Cold War, particularly its strategic concern over the People's Republic of China (PRC). In addition, the US government could not keep pace with the rapid shift towards the 'universality' of the UN, conspicuous among other small and middle-size countries. By contrast, the Soviet Union, with its new 'peace offensive' strategy took advantage of this opportunity, and fought hard for admission of Outer Mongolia and four other Soviet satellites. It also used the issue of Japanese admission to the UN as leverage in the faltering negotiations with Tokyo on USSR–Japan normalization.

The chapter begins with some background to Japan's bid for membership, followed by an explanation of the Canadian proposal for a multi-member 'package deal' and the initial response from UN members. The chapter then describes in detail the various manoeuvres of the American, RoC and Soviet governments in their attempts to resolve their differences, and concludes by offering some explanations for their actions.

Developments prior to the tenth session of the General Assembly

Since 1950, there had been deadlock on the issue of UN membership, to which, with the exception of Indonesia, no new member had been admitted. In general, the Western powers believed that the East European states, proposed by the Soviet Union as candidates for membership, lacked the qualifications as stated in Article Four of the Charter (whereby members must establish sufficient internationally-recognized status and be regarded as peace loving). The Western nations withheld their support in the Security Council (SC), which consequently failed to recommend the East European states to the General Assembly.[2] In retaliation, the Soviet Union repeatedly vetoed the applications of Western candidates. Thus they had continuously denied Japan's admission to the UN since its initial application in 1952.

In the meantime, the US Department of State (DS) proposed several schemes for 'associate membership' for Western applicants, including Japan, but these did not come to fruition. By early 1955, however, new windows of opportunity opened for the Hatoyama government regarding Japanese membership: (i) the possibility of linkage to the issue of Beijing's representation; (ii) the Bandung initiative; (iii) the inauguration of bilateral diplomatic talks between the Soviet Union and Japan; and (iv) the Canadian initiative for a package deal based on the principle of universal membership.

Possibility of linkage to Beijing's representation

The problem of Chinese representation gradually emerged in the UN in the early 1950s. The British government was one of its major proponents, calling for the idea of linking People's Republic of China (PRC) representation to Japan's admission. By the spring of 1954, London held that the policy of supporting RoC representation in the UN would soon become untenable, given British diplomatic recognition of the PRC in 1950. It preferred to see Beijing represented in the UN as a more practicable means of dealing with East Asian issues.[3] Nonetheless, on 10 September 1955, the British Foreign Office (FO) informed the US by telegram that the British government, 'after considerable hesitation and reluctance', had agreed to the moratorium on Chinese representation (whereby the British government would support US policy on the exclusion of representatives of the PRC). The telegram added, however, that this 'had been a hard decision', and there was 'strong political feeling in both parties that the time has come to admit the Chinese Communists'.[4]

The US administration was strongly opposed to the idea of admitting Beijing into the UN in exchange for Japanese admission.[5] Having persuaded the UK to hold to the 'moratorium arrangement',[6] Washington also proposed several 'associate membership' schemes for Japan, which would have enabled de facto Japanese membership, without impinging upon the issue of Chinese representation. In short, this latter issue might have served as an effective tool to admit Japan into the UN, had the Americans not stymied the possibility of a linkage between Chinese and Japanese entry to the UN.

The Bandung initiative

The Bandung Conference for the Promotion of World Peace and Co-operation was held in April 1955. In addition to its significance in demonstrating the solidarity of Asian and African countries, it urged that UN membership be granted to seven countries: Cambodia, Ceylon, Japan, Jordan, Laos, Libya, and Nepal (the 'Bandung Seven'). It was agreed that Turkey, as a non-permanent member of the Security Council, should initiate action as soon as possible.[7] The Ceylon government had hoped that the Bandung Conference would change the nature of international relations so dramatically that the Soviets would be unable to oppose entry of the Bandung Seven.[8] Indeed, the acting Soviet ambassador in Karachi indicated that the Soviet Union would possibly support Japanese entry to the UN.[9]

The attitude of the British government gradually changed in the wake of Bandung, adopting the view that the UN should be more 'universal' and enjoy greater representation from Asia.[10] Confronted by de-colonization in Asia and Africa, the British government came to accept that it would never be reversed.[11] Britain's ties with Commonwealth countries also forced it to realistically assess the new movement in international politics, especially in the UN.

Japan also placed its hopes on the Bandung framework, since it lacked any effective means of its own to realize admission to the UN. Not only were the Bandung countries (the Bandung group) prepared to respect Japan's aspirations, but their influence over the major powers seemed increasingly useful for Japan's UN diplomacy. At the UN Conference in San Francisco in 1955, the Japanese Ministry of Foreign Affairs (MoFA) attempted to persuade other delegates that in order to make UN membership universal, they should endeavour to break the deadlock and accept all candidates.[12] This was supported by the delegations of 29 countries, mainly from the Bandung group. MoFA anticipated that the Bandung group's influence would pressurize the Soviets to support issues raised by the Asian and African countries.[13] However, in 1955, it became apparent that the Western countries did not wish the UN admission issue to be resolved solely by the Bandung group, which led to the Canadian initiative of a universal package in an attempt to break the deadlock.

Bilateral diplomatic talks with the Soviet Union

Another window of opportunity for Japan's admission to the UN was created by the Hatoyama cabinet's new diplomatic initiative towards the Soviet Union. Upon its inauguration on 10 December 1954, the Hatoyama government announced that it would commence talks on diplomatic normalization with the Soviet Union. Bilateral negotiations began in London in June 1955, and there was some expectation on the Japanese side that the negotiations would quickly pave the way for Japan's admission to the UN by removing Soviet opposition. However, when the negotiations reached a stalemate in the summer of 1955, the Soviets announced that they would agree to Japan's admission only upon the establishment of diplomatic relations. As the newly-formed Liberal Democratic Party strengthened

Japan's territorial claim to the Northern Territories,[14] the likelihood of the Soviets accepting Japan's individual admission to the UN decreased. By the time the Canadian package deal was proposed in October 1955, bilateral negotiations had stalled on the territorial issue. As long as there was no progress in bilateral negotiations, Japan had no other option but to consider the Canadian proposal.

The Canadian initiative for universal membership

The Canadian draft proposal for a universal package to admit 17 countries was placed on the informal agenda of the GA in mid-August 1955. Latin America, the Bandung group, and even Australia supported the proposal. The British Commonwealth Relations Office (CRO), however, was concerned about a possible split within the Commonwealth due to Ceylon's place within the Bandung group.[15] Nonetheless, at the end of August, the British government concluded that the Canadian proposal should be supported, in order to avoid any antagonism that might emerge between the Bandung countries and the Europeans.[16] In October 1955, the Canadian proposal was circulated informally among the pro-Western delegates in the GA with a view to gaining their endorsement of the admission of the group of 18 (now including Franco's Spain, which had submitted its application in September). Spain was expected to gain wide support from the Latin American countries in addition to the US domestic constituencies with Spanish or Latin American origins. Later the draft proposal sought to gain co-sponsorship of the Netherlands, Norway, Brazil, Australia, Peru, New Zealand, and Iraq. The GA, 'having noted the growing general sentiment in favor of the universality of the UN membership', requested the Security Council (SC) to consider the pending application of the 18 states.[17]

Reactions to the Canadian proposal

On 20 October 1955, Britain's prime minister, Anthony Eden, formally reached a decision to support the Canadian proposal, considering it preferable to a 'deadlock'.[18] Britain still wished to avoid the admission of Outer Mongolia and Albania, but nonetheless made it known that, in the worst case, Outer Mongolia's admission would be accepted. In fact, the establishment of diplomatic relations between India and Outer Mongolia in December 1955 made it easier for the British to accept Outer Mongolia's entry. The FO never ruled out the possibility that US might also agree to Outer Mongolia's admission. The main reason, however, for the British decision to approve the package deal derived from the pressures brought to bear by Commonwealth countries such as Canada, Australia and Ceylon.

Domestically in the US, the State Department was divided on the membership issue. The apparent success of the Bandung Conference had caused the US to reassess its position on UN membership. The Secretary of State, John F. Dulles, suggested at first that the US should take advantage of the Bandung statement calling for the admission of the Bandung Seven. By June 1955, however, there was a split of views within the State Department. The Bureau of Far Eastern Affairs and North Eastern Asia sought prompt SC action for admission of the Bandung Seven, possibly with Turkish sponsorship.[19] The Far Eastern Bureau's main concern was to deny Beijing UN representation. For this purpose, the Bureau wished to avoid a Canadian package deal, for fear that the entry of Soviet satellites to the UN would become a pretext for the PRC's admission.[20] The International Organizations Affairs Office (IOA) and the Bureau of European Affairs, however, supported the idea of a package deal.[21] The IOA also recognized, in late August, that the admission of the Bandung Seven alone would strengthen the anti-colonial and neutralist forces in the UN. To defend against such a risk, Britain, France, and other European members would be forced to press for the admission of West European candidates (Italy and Portugal), even at the cost of admitting the Soviet satellites.[22] The IOA concluded that it was desirable to bring the maximum number of states into the UN. Hence, in their view, the US response should be either the admission of all applications except Outer Mongolia, or all pending applicants including Outer Mongolia. In the latter case, however, the IOA faced a dilemma. The official US position was that Outer Mongolia was a puppet of the Soviet Union and not a sovereign state. In addition, Outer Mongolian entry into the UN would undoubtedly raise the issue of Chinese representation. Thus, the decision on Outer Mongolia had to be taken on the basis of whether its exclusion would constitute the sole obstacle to an agreement on the admission of all other applicants.[23]

With regard to the other permanent members of the Security Council, France, engrossed in its struggle with Algeria, was not in a position to be concerned about UN membership. However, it was generally thought that the French reaction would not be positive because of the implication for is own colonies. Taipei's position was still unclear, but, for the time being, the RoC felt the need to co-operate with the position of the Western capitalist bloc.

Following the circulation of the Canadian draft proposal, the situation in the GA moved quickly in favour of a universalist settlement, a development which had not been fully anticipated by the US State Department. A meeting of representatives from the UK, the US and France took place on 24 October 1955. The British secretary of state for foreign affairs, Anthony Nutting, referred to a rising tide in favour of a solution, in part due to the Soviets who had been 'fishing around and dropping hints' about their willingness to support a group of 18, including Japan and possibly Spain. The British official described this as a behind-the-scenes prior agreement between the West and the Soviet Union to 'promote, support or acquiesce in admission of membership of group of 18'.[24]

Overture to US policy failure

Confronted with this pressing situation, the US representative to the UN, Henry Cabot Lodge, stated in a message to the State Department that 'my motive is more to prevent damage to the US than to solve the membership question'.[25] Lodge told Dulles that the US appeared to be 'losing popularity with Italy and other nations over the membership', and he asked for Dulles' approval to adopt the position of admitting all applicants except Outer Mongolia. This meant that the US was taking a defensive rather than offensive line in controlling the situation, and it had to make every effort to limit the damage in the face of pressure from Canada and other smaller states.

The Soviets were increasingly inclined to accept admission of all candidates, even Japan. On 3 November 1955, the first secretary of the Soviet Embassy, Leonid Zamyatin, approached the senior political advisor to the US Mission at the UN, John McSweeney. Zamyatin insisted on some sort of solid assurance regarding the admission of their candidates, albeit in a private or informal way.[26] The next day, the Soviet Foreign Minister, Vyacheslav Molotov, did not dissent when the British delegation suggested that an obvious solution would be to admit all candidates.[27] McSweeney indicated to the US Mission that Washington should give an answer soon.[28] The US Mission increasingly took the view that the US should take the initiative, and, explaining this position, Lodge commented that 'the situation is developing here in such a way that we will be confronted with a proposal of this sort in any event and will have to accede to it or incur considerable unpopularity throughout the world.' The increasing pressure from the governments of Italy, Ceylon, Spain, and Japan also needed to be considered.[29]

On 4 November, Lodge concluded that the US should draw up a draft press statement, and he asked for Dulles' authorization. Based on a report that the Soviets would withhold their veto, Lodge argued that the US should vote for the admission of thirteen free countries and raise no objection to the entry of Albania, Bulgaria, Hungary, and Romania, but Outer Mongolia would not be admitted.[30] The admission of thirteen free nations greatly outweighed that of the four Eastern European states.[31]

Dulles was worried that the failure to admit the Bandung Seven as well as Italy, Spain, Portugal, Austria, and Ireland could invite very serious consequences, particularly with regard to the Italians and the Latin Americans.[32] In terms of international and domestic pressure on the US, Latin America was expected to be far more influential than Japan.[33] On 5 November, an urgent personal message was delivered from Dulles to the British foreign secretary, Harold Macmillan. Dulles wrote, 'I am disposed favorably to consider package membership arrangement in UN. I do not see, however, how we can bring ourselves to swallow Outer Mongolia.'[34] On 7 November, Dulles asked Macmillan to inform the Canadians and the British delegation of this point. Macmillan instructed his delegation to go slow on Outer Mongolia.[35]

President Eisenhower had a relatively favourable view towards the package deal in general and could not see any 'great defeat for the Americans' by its acceptance.[36] For him the countries involved were small nations, and the US could win the admission of Italy and Japan, thereby raising their morale in the context of the Cold War. Although the US administration reached the conclusion that it would accept the package deal in general, Dulles was still firmly opposed to the admission of Outer Mongolia.[37]

In the GA, the smaller countries, led by Latin America and Canada, moved towards a solution of the membership issue. On 9 November, the Peruvian representative to the UN, Victor Belaunde, met Lodge and handed him a letter addressed to Dulles. Belaunde attempted to persuade Lodge to accept Outer Mongolia, stating that failure to solve the membership problem would produce a profound crisis in the UN. He warned that any veto in the Security Council would go against established views, and that the blame would be placed on any permanent member who applied their veto power. Lodge reiterated that the US could not accept Outer Mongolia.[38]

The US, Taipei, and the Outer Mongolia question

Japan was only one of many candidates seeking entry to the UN, and its admission had never been the highest priority for the major powers. For the FO, Ceylon and Italy were the most important. For the US, the UN itself did not hold much importance, much less the issue of membership. Moreover, in the absence of diplomatic relations, the Soviets were opposed to Japanese admission, if considered individually. Thus from a Japanese point of view, the only hope was the package deal, although this would deny Tokyo any room for manoeuvre. The question of Japan's future membership was, therefore, in the same boat as many other countries. However, in this case Japan was only a third-class passenger, and most likely to fall overboard. This section will explore how the package deal was scuppered by the RoC's use of the veto, and how Japan failed in its attempt to enter the UN in 1955.

On 8 November, the RoC representative to the UN, Tingfu Tsiang, informed Lodge that his instructions were to veto Outer Mongolia, although his government could accept the four East European satellites.[39] At this point, the US was still sympathetic toward the RoC's position but ultimately underestimated Taipei's strength of opposition.

On 10 November, the Canadian foreign ministry warned MoFA about the possibility of Taipei vetoing Outer Mongolia's admission.[40] The Japanese were concerned that this could jeopardize the package deal as a whole. The Japanese ambassador to Taipei, Yoshizawa Kenzō, obtained from the RoC foreign minister, George Yeh, confirmation of the possibility of veto.[41] The Japanese ambassador to the UN, Kase Toshikazu, believed that Japan could rely on the US to persuade the RoC not to use the veto.[42] The Japanese ambassador to the US, Iguchi Sadao, conveyed his wish to the Assistant Secretary for Far Eastern Affairs, Walter Robertson, that Japanese admission should be effected through the good offices of the US.[43] Iguchi also added that once Japan entered the UN, the Soviets would lose a bargaining chip in the USSR–Japanese bilateral negotiations in London. Robertson assured Iguchi that the US would make every effort to ensure Japanese membership.[44]

On 10 November, the Canadian draft based on the principle of universal membership was formally proposed in the GA. Paul Martin, the Canadian representative to the UN, expressed his belief that the Soviets were prepared to 'go a long way'. In other words, they would not use their veto.[45] On the following day, Martin told

Tsiang about the proposal, explaining that it would be backed by 25 nations. By this time, Tsiang was convinced that a deal had been made in Moscow in October between Molotov and the Canadian minister of external affairs, Lester Pearson, and that Canada must have obtained British support too. Tsiang told Martin that his instructions to veto Outer Mongolia were not open to negotiation.[46]

Confronted with the Canadian proposal and the possibility of Taipei's veto, the US State Department debated several options. Dulles considered supporting the package deal, but excluding Outer Mongolia, so that Taipei would not have to use the veto. Lodge was positive, and hoped he could issue the previous draft press statement of November 4.[47] The advantage of this option was the possibility of maintaining Taipei's seat in the SC, but the disadvantage was that the US would have to persuade the Soviets and others to accept a package without Outer Mongolia. The second option was based on the more pessimistic scenario that Taipei's expected veto would trigger a Soviet veto of Spain or Japan. In such a case, the US should certainly win sufficient support from friendly countries in the GA to block the admission of the four Soviet satellites.[48] Of course, the third option would be to accept all Soviet candidates, including Outer Mongolia, but this was out of question.

In the meantime, the FO was prepared to openly express its support for the Canadian proposal. When a meeting of representatives from the US, UK and France took place in Geneva in early November,[49] Macmillan expressed his concern that if Outer Mongolia were not admitted, the Soviets might be tempted to veto Spain. If the Canadians tabled the proposal, London, under increasing attack from the Ceylonese press, would have to support it in order to admit Ceylon. If it were a question of all or nothing, the British government would accept membership of all 18 countries, including Outer Mongolia.

On 13 November, Molotov and Dulles discussed the problem of membership in Geneva. Dulles informed Molotov that the US would not exercise the right to veto in the SC.[50] Referring to the package deal, Molotov mentioned that the USSR had certain reservations regarding Japan and Spain but that, nevertheless, a solution would be possible. Dulles stressed that, if Molotov dropped the reservations about Japan and Spain, he might find a way to accept the satellites, but he was not prepared to accept Outer Mongolia. Molotov indicated that American difficulties regarding Outer Mongolia were the same as the Soviets' regarding Spain.[51] By now it was clear to Dulles that the Soviets were prepared to accept a package including Japan and Spain, but that it would be impossible for them to consider any package deal without Outer Mongolia.[52] The FO noted that the US did 'not seem to realize that Mr. Molotov is unlikely to accept Spain, unless Outer Mongolia is included'.[53]

Dulles informed Lodge that unless the State Department was prepared to accept the onus for rejecting any package proposal, they should quickly produce a US counter-proposal for the admission of 17 countries, and try to rally support, particularly from the Latin Americans, to nullify the Canadian proposal. Later the same day, Lodge stated at a press conference that the US would not veto but only abstain on the issue of Soviet satellites and added that Outer Mongolia could not possibly be accepted.[54] The Soviet ambassador to London, Y.A. Malik, strongly criticized the US for excluding Outer Mongolia, and said there would be no room for compromise.[55] Dulles was increasingly concerned about the poor publicity the US was attracting due to its continued opposition to Outer Mongolian admission.[56]

On 16 November, the Canadian proposal was tabled with 25 co-sponsors in an Ad Hoc Political Committee.[57] When the British representative to the UN, Sir Pierson Dixon, was informed that Martin intended to submit the resolution, Dixon objected, since he felt it was still premature in light of the unsettled Outer Mongolian issue, but Martin was determined to proceed. Lodge warned Martin of the catastrophic results if the membership solution collapsed as the result of a RoC veto.[58] In particular, he was concerned about Anglo-American discord that would arise from the reopening of the issue of Chinese representation should Taipei veto.[59]

In the meantime, the Soviets had told the British that the US was the only country preventing agreement, and that London should act as a mediator.[60] Later Kuznetsov announced at a press conference that the USSR would firmly support the 18-country package, but would resort to a veto unless the US co-operated as well.[61] General opinion within the UN supported the Canadian proposal, and members began to realize that the US was hampering the overall agreement.

Faced with the high probability that the Canadian proposal would be supported widely in the GA, Lodge and Dixon began to worry about the consequences of Taipei's actions. At one point, Lodge even stated that one more satellite nation (that is, Outer Mongolia) was not too much for the UN to swallow. He believed that the State Department should do everything to prevent a complete breakdown, which would probably occur if Taipei were to veto.[62] This did not mean, however, that Lodge had come to accept Outer Mongolian membership. He told the FO that due to the tremendous difficulty of weakening the RoC's resolve, he wanted Britain to work as mediator to persuade the Soviets to drop Outer Mongolia from the package. Having already publicly accepted the package, however, the FO was reluctant to respond to Lodge's appeal.[63]

Meanwhile, when the RoC ambassador to the US, Wellington Koo, asked whether the US was prepared to support the RoC in vetoing Outer Mongolia, the Assistant Secretary for Far Eastern Affairs, Walter Robertson, replied they were doing all thay could to ensure Outer Mongolia would be excluded. Robertson went as far as to say that the US found it difficult to believe that Outer Mongolia would have sufficient support to even make the veto necessary and observed that, as a last resort, the US might have to ask the RoC government to abstain rather than veto Outer Mongolia's admission.[64] Ambassador Koo gained the impression that the American attitude regarding the possibility of Taipei's veto was not firmly fixed, because the Americans still hoped to discover another way of excluding Outer Mongolia from the UN.[65]

To prevent Taipei from using its veto, the US tried first to gain support for its own package. Lodge was very slow to recognize that new developments in the UN had already made it next to impossible to exclude Outer Mongolia. According to Kuznetsov, Moscow still had problems with Spanish and Japanese entry to the UN, and was adamant that they could not consider any solution except the admission of all 18 countries. He hinted that if Outer Mongolia were dropped, the USSR would require Spain to be dropped.[66] Kuznetsov announced at a press conference that the Soviet Union would approve the candidates on condition that all be admitted.[67] The Soviet position was reiterated via Malik to the Chairman of the Latin American caucus, Jose Vincente Trujillo (Ecuadorian representative to the UN), that unless Outer Mongolia was admitted, the USSR would veto Spain.[68] This prompted Belaunde to urge the US government to accept the 18-country proposal.

US–Taiwan negotiations

Having failed to get Outer Mongolia dropped from the package, the State Department was obliged to convince Taipei not to use its veto. Ironically, in so doing, the US government itself had to accept the 18-country package. Lodge, still optimistic, keenly observed that the RoC was already fully aware of the dangers of the situation, and that Taipei may not wish to take the threat of veto to the extreme, since this would in turn jeopardize its own status in the UN. Thus, the US urgently needed to persuade Chiang Kai-shek to respect the common interests of both countries.[69]

After a number of conversations between Lodge and Tsiang, however, Lodge understood that Taiwan would definitely veto Outer Mongolia. Lodge explained to Tsiang that the veto would gravely endanger Taipei's overall position, not to mention its seat in the UN. Tsiang simply replied that it could not be helped. This prompted Lodge to write to the State Department suggesting that President Eisenhower approach Chiang Kai-shek personally.[70] Finally on 21 November, the State Department formally asked Taipei to refrain from the veto.[71] In a 22 November letter to Chiang Kai-shek, Eisenhower stressed that since 'the thirteen free nations ardently desire admission', it was 'worthwhile to pay the price of five satellites to get the thirteen non-satellites.' He emphasized that 'we cannot simply interpose a veto to block arbitrarily the will of the great majority,' and 'to use it now would strengthen the Communist cause and do grave damage to our influence in the UN.' He also added that 'It would not be necessary to vote for membership you disapproved of but only to abstain', reminding Chiang that 'the issue is so important to us both.'[72]

On 23 November, the US Embassy in Taipei reported that President Chiang was being influenced largely by domestic considerations, particularly by the reaction in the legislative Yuan.[73] Yeh also admitted that the Chiang government was emotionally involved in the matter. Chiang went as far as to remark that trends in the past year or so made the entry of the Chinese communist regime into the UN inevitable, and that the RoC might as well get out of the UN and stop making so much trouble for the US government. Yeh had the distinct impression that US interest in, and willingness to support, Taipei was definitely waning. President Chiang left Taipei on a scheduled visit to Sun Moon Lake, but he consequently prolonged his holiday there until 14 December in order to avoid direct involvement in the matter of Outer Mongolia.[74] In the meantime, on 26 November, a reply from Chiang Kai-shek was delivered to Eisenhower. The State Department finally came to understand that Taipei's objection to Outer Mongolia sprang not only from the UN representation issue, but also, and perhaps more importantly, from domestic pressures and Taipei's concern about national prestige.

In late November, it became widely known that the RoC insistence on the veto was delaying a solution, which made the Chiang administration increasingly unpopular both domestically and internationally. Lodge was still seeking to prevent Outer Mongolia's entry without the use of a veto, and asked other nations if they would abstain from voting on Outer Mongolia. However, most indicated that this would be impossible, which Lodge soon came to recognize as a fairly universal GA sentiment.[75] In fact by this time, the State Department was resigned to the fact that if Outer Mongolia's entry was prevented by organized abstentions, the US would be blamed.[76] In light of Chiang's response of 26 November, Lodge suggested that a State Department official should visit Taipei in order to demonstrate to other countries that the US was attempting to dissuade Taipei from using the veto.[77]

On 28 November, Eisenhower sent a second letter to Chiang Kai-shek, warning him that it would be an abuse of the RoC's veto power were they to use it against the will of the majority of SC members.[78] Taipei, however, issued a formal press statement the following day announcing that it would veto Outer Mongolia. On hearing this, the US Information Agency issued a press release criticizing Taipei's attitude. This caused Yeh to remark later that this 'departure of established policy under which differences between the two countries had been dealt with discreetly' was rather frustrating; subsequently, Taipei further stiffened its position.[79]

The FO recognized that there was nothing either the British or US government could do to stop the Taiwanese, and nor was there any way to shift the blame to the Soviets.[80] The Soviets could not lose: either the proposed package deal would be accepted, or the RoC would use its veto thereby damaging its reputation. Every manoeuvre the State Department tried was in vain. Lodge proposed the admission of the 17 nations while referring Outer Mongolia's application to the Council's Committee on Admission of New Members. Peru's Belaunde, however, said he would not do this, and at the first meeting of the Good Offices Committee decided that there should be no discrimination against any of the applications. Secretary of State Nutting also told Lodge 'we absolutely cannot do it.' Nutting instead asked for American reaction to a possible introduction of a British proposal in the SC. They explained that the rationale for such a proposal was that it would be less difficult for Taipei to support a proposal raised by the British government than the one offered by the Soviets.[81] Nevertheless, Lodge said candidly that his personal reaction to the British proposal was negative.[82]

The State Department's change in policy and Taipei's isolation

On 1 December, an Ad Hoc Political Committee meeting in the GA was held and discussion began on the Canadian proposal. A Soviet committee member announced that the USSR would support the Canadian proposal. On the same day, Lodge wrote that there was no way for the US to avoid accepting the 18-nation package:

> An 18 applicant solution seems like the least objectionable outcome in view of the fact that events since my last wire have moved so fast that we cannot either shelve the membership question or have it fail without serious consequences which would include a great share of the blame for US and a determined effort by numerous delegations to expel the Chinese should they use their veto. The possibility of 17 package proposal which would have been so effective is now, I fear, outdistanced by events. This means that we should, whatever the Chinese do, vote for an 18 state resolution in the SC.[83]

A few days later, Malik told Kase that the Soviets had decided to vote for the admission of Japan and Spain.[84] It was a remarkable breakthrough, and it appeared that the USSR was serious this time. For example, it had asked Greece, which was against the inclusion of Albania, to vote in favour of all 18 applicants.[85] On 7 December, the Ad Hoc Political Committee approved the Canadian draft resolution by 52 to 2 (Cuba and the RoC objected) with five abstentions (the US, Belgium, France, Greece, and Israel).[86]

Meanwhile, Dulles issued urgent instructions to the US Embassy in Taipei to persuade Chiang and Yeh to follow US advice and emphasised the importance of the two presidential letters.[87] Pressure from the US and other countries (including Japan) in early December appeared to have an effect, and Taipei began to show some flexibility. Chiang, for example, mentioned the possibility that an alternative to a veto could be worked out. Yeh wished to avoid using the veto but, at the same time, regretted that the US was sending mixed signals and that he had not been informed earlier about its change of position.[88]

Nonetheless, Chiang asked Eisenhower again if there was any possibility of a 17-country package excluding Outer Mongolia.[89] Robertson warned Ambassador Koo in Washington that Eisenhower was concerned that neither Chiang nor Yeh realized the full implications of what they were doing. He told Koo that the US was not happy about letting in five satellites, but it simply would not ignore the opinions of a large majority in the UN by using a veto. He requested that Taipei understand this situation and show greater patience.[90]

Why did Chiang Kai-shek's administration so adamantly reject Outer Mongolia's membership in the UN? The standard explanation is that Taipei was concerned about who would represent China in the UN. Some governments, including the British, were already of the opinion that Beijing should represent China. Taipei regarded Outer Mongolia's admission as a Soviet manoeuvre to isolate Taipei, which would eventually lead to its replacement by Beijing in the UN. A second explanation derives from Chiang Kai-shek's desire to reclaim what he viewed as lost territory. The RoC government had claimed territorial sovereignty over Outer Mongolia since February 1945, when the KMT accepted a US–Soviet deal to make the Soviets wage war against Japan in exchange for Outer Mongolia's independence based upon the Sino-Soviet Treaty of Friendship and Alliance. After the Sino-Soviet Treaty became null and void, the RoC reclaimed sovereignty over Outer Mongolia. Outer Mongolia's admission in the UN meant the Taiwanese would have to relinquish their claims and recognize Outer Mongolia's independence. A third explanation stems from Taiwan's concerns about national prestige and RoC domestic politics. Chiang's understanding was that the Soviets had used Outer Mongolia as a base for incursions into China to aid communist rebellion, resulting finally in the communist occupation of mainland China. In Chiang's mind, Outer Mongolia symbolically represented the core of the RoC's national interests. He believed that he would lose political legitimacy, not to mention the support of his domestic constituencies, if Outer Mongolia were to be recognized internationally. In fact, Chiang's 26 November letter to Eisenhower verified that his persistence regarding this issue was linked to a combination of the second and third explanations, that is, the territorial claim and national prestige.[91]

Washington misinterpreted the RoC position by assuming that the reason for its stubbornness was due to concern over the Chinese representation issue.[92] The miscalculation of Taipei's motives sprang from the State Department's own Cold War-contextualized obsession with the Chinese representation issue.[93] In retrospect, it can be said that consideration of this risk finally compelled the Americans to accept Outer Mongolia's admission on 16 November. The US stressed that, if Taipei did not change its mind, and vetoed Outer Mongolia because it feared losing representation in UN, it would lead to an even quicker loss of their seat because of the damage it would do to their reputation. Taipei, however, had come to the conclusion that, sooner or later, it would lose its seat anyway. Taipei therefore decided to accentuate its status as a sovereign state by appealing to its national constituencies.

Disarray in US domestic politics

The State Department could not build a consensus among domestic political actors, especially Congressional members, and there was a danger that they might send the wrong signal to Chiang. While the US Ambassador to Taipei, Karl Rankin, was discouraged by the Chinese from going to Sun Moon Lake to present the president's second letter in person, Chiang was having a meeting with six US congressmen who were urging Chiang to pursue his initial position. The study commission of the House Foreign Affairs Far East Sub-committee[94] drafted the following statement:

> The members of the study commission are greatly alarmed and desire to report the gravity with which our friends in the Far East view the 'package

deal' despite their strong desire to see Spain and other free world allies as members. The Far East Subcommittee unanimously wishes to urge that our country not compromise a moral principle and US historical righteousness.[95]

After receiving this statement, Dulles demanded that Ambassador Rankin do all he could to persuade the Sub-committee members to lobby Chiang.[96] At the same time, Dulles tried to clarify the US position by contacting the Sub-committee members present in Tokyo. He sent a telegram to the US ambassador to Tokyo, John Allison, asking him to deliver a message to the chairman of the study commission, Clement Zablocki, conveying the State Department's position and appealing for help in convincing Chiang.[97] The study commission was, however, far from willing to change Chiang's mind. On the contrary, during their stay in Taiwan, they pledged their full support and assured Chiang that his moral position was completely sound. Congressman Walter Judd even suggested that it was solely the attitude of the Soviet Union that was keeping Japan out of the UN, and that Taipei was completely justified.[98]

The study commission's statement was put together during its trip around South Asia, but the conversations with Chiang and other officials encouraged them to formally issue their draft statement.[99] After some eight weeks of travel, the study commission arrived in Taiwan, shocked and alarmed at the expansion of the communist sphere of influence, and were correspondingly sensitive to any evidence of what might appear to them as new communist successes. Ambassador Rankin conveyed to Dulles that the study commission felt that the UN membership issue was a secondary consideration compared to the dire importance of supporting Taiwan as an essential ally in the fight against Communist expansion. Chiang, of course, concurred with this view.[100]

Ambassador Rankin was finally allowed to meet Chiang for the first time at Sun Moon Lake on 8 December.[101] Chiang maintained that the RoC regarded the situation more seriously than the US, which seemed to be preoccupied solely with the issue of Chinese representation in the UN. For the RoC it was a far more serious question, its place in the UN stemming from its symbol as a bastion of anti-communism. Chiang had been convinced that the US government and others had made a deal behind his back. He described the package deal as a British project, with the clear implication that the British government was again trying to lead the US towards recognition of Beijing.[102]

On 12 December, the study commission sent a response to Dulles. It rebuffed Dulles, saying that 'we feel compelled to urge that the US reconsider its position.'[103] During their visit to Tokyo, the study commission met with Prime Minister Hatoyama. Byrd raised the issue of the package deal and hoped that Japanese government would understand that the true villain in this matter was the Soviet Union and not the RoC. Judd went so far as to say that there were many Americans in the Congress who disapproved of the present US administration's stance on the issue. After this meeting, the Foreign Minister, Shigemitsu Mamoru, called Allison to renew his request for US intervention with regards to Taipei.[104]

The vote on admission and aftermath

On 10 December, a Security Council meeting was held during which Brazil and New Zealand presented a joint draft resolution. It provided for a SC recommendation to the GA to admit the 18 specified countries to the UN on the condition that a vote would be taken on each of the countries named in the resolution, on each paragraph of the resolution, and then on the resolution as a whole.

On 13 December, the Security Council held a vote on the Brazil- and New Zealand-sponsored proposal outlining the procedures for admitting the 18 candidates. It was decided by eight votes to one (the RoC objected), with two abstentions (Belgium and the US) to give the draft resolution priority over all proposals. A vote was then taken in the SC in accordance with the stipulations of the resolution. As expected, Taipei's representative vetoed Outer Mongolia. The USSR, in retaliation, vetoed all 13 Western countries. Western states abstained on the resolution as a whole. Thus no country was recommended for admission into the UN. However, quite unexpectedly, on the morning of 14 December, the Soviet Deputy Foreign Minister, Kuznetsov, asked for an urgent meeting of the SC. He wished to withdraw the Soviet delegation's vetoes of the day before and proposed the admission of 16 countries, leaving the question of Japanese and Outer Mongolian membership until the next session of the GA, when, the Soviets hoped, the two countries would be accepted.[105]

Lodge was in favour of going ahead with the proposal the same day, since 'this would give the Japanese less time to make a fuss'.[106] The Foreign Office considered their amicable relations with Japan and raised the idea that 'Japan's name should be proposed (and subsequently vetoed by the Russians)'. During the recess it was agreed that the US should propose the addition of Japan. The Soviets raised no objection to this procedure.[107] The US amended the proposal by adding Japan to the package, and the USSR vetoed the Japanese application (against 10 votes in favour). The USSR then submitted a second draft resolution including Outer Mongolia and Japan, which was not accepted because of 10 abstentions. In the voting on the final package of the 16 countries, although the RoC, US and Belgium abstained from voting for or against certain individual states, there were no opposing votes cast, and the whole package was approved by eight votes in favour. In this way, the SC was able to recommend admission of the 16 countries to the GA.

Lodge wanted a SC resolution recommending that the GA admit Japan at the eleventh session. Kuznetsov issued a statement in which he expressed his desire to see Japan admitted to the UN at the eleventh session. Turkey insisted the plenary of the GA should not meet to admit the 16 countries until the US resolution was dealt with. However, the Turkish proposal gained no support from other nations because it was seen as damaging to the deal which had already been agreed upon. On 14 December, the GA formally admitted the 16 countries to the UN.[108]

For the time being, the SC members decided to defer consideration of the US proposal on Japanese admission until the following meeting. The British delegation then proposed a draft resolution, expressing the belief that Japan was fully qualified for membership and the hope that Japan would soon be admitted to the

UN.[109] Discussion of Lodge's draft resolution and several others continued in the SC until 21 December, when the SC finally accepted the draft resolution submitted by the British delegation. After unsuccessfully pushing for the adoption of a draft resolution that would link Outer Mongolia to Japan on the issue of membership, the Soviet representative recorded an abstention on the British resolution.

Japanese Ambassador Kase, however, feared Japan might again be linked to Outer Mongolia and summarily vetoed in the eleventh GA session as well.[110] On 16 December, a Japanese minister called the State Department with a last-minute appeal for US arbitration with Taipei in an effort to have them forgo their veto against Outer Mongolia, thus making possible an arrangement with the Soviets for Japan's admission to the UN during the tenth GA. The State Department explained it would be impossible to change Taipei's attitude.[111]

New developments: bilateral diplomatic normalization talks and Japan's admission in 1956

There was a general feeling in Japan that it had 'missed the bus'. Not only had Japan lost the only opportunity of a package deal which should have enabled Japanese admission before the conclusion of a peace treaty with the Soviet Union, but, to make matters worse, there was now also a possibility that the Soviet Union might link the admission of Outer Mongolia and Japan, resulting in another RoC veto. To avoid such a situation, Japan's admission would have to become acceptable to the Soviets on its own merit. It was believed in MoFA that once diplomatic relations were established with the Soviet Union, it would be difficult for them to oppose Japanese entry or even continue to link it with Outer Mongolia.

MoFA's policy, therefore, was to launch a more active and enthusiastic campaign for Japanese admission to prevent the Japanese application from being linked to the Outer Mongolian application and to the Chinese representation issues, and to gather maximum support from member countries to prevent the Soviets from casting a veto.[112] To create this support, MoFA perceived the importance of approaching the Afro-Asian group. It also targeted the Commonwealth members in anticipation of gaining their support.[113]

Japanese socialists in the Diet attacked the Hatoyama cabinet for its stubborn stance adopted during the negotiations with the Soviet Union and for being too dependent on the US. They sponsored a no-confidence resolution against Shigemitsu, though this failed to gain enough support. Against such criticism, Shigemitsu emphasized that Japanese policy towards the US should not be changed and that the government should not make major concessions in the negotiations with the Soviets, sticking to its demand for the return of the Northern territories.[114] He warned the Cabinet that a Soviet veto on the UN issue would become leverage in the negotiations too. In fact, as long as the bilateral talks faced a deadlock, MoFA would remain anxious about the possible Soviet rejection of Japanese admission.

In the summer of 1956, Hatoyama's adoption of the so-called 'Adenauer formula' (suspending territorial issues while achieving diplomatic normalization) provided hope that the deadlock could be broken. After Shigemitsu's fruitless mission to Moscow, Hatoyama sent a letter to the Soviet prime minister, Nikolai Bulganin, in which Japan set out five conditions, including Soviet support for Japan's admission in the UN, that would need to be satisfied before resuming the talks on diplomatic normalization in Moscow.[115] Two days later Bulganin accepted Hatoyama's conditions.

During the Moscow talks, the Soviet delegation endorsed Japanese admission to the UN without any pre-conditions.[116] Still sceptical, Hatoyama proposed that Japan and the Soviet Union should exchange letters to assure the latter's unconditional support for Japanese admission. On 19 October 1956, after letters of agreement were exchanged,[117] the Joint Declaration on diplomatic normalization was signed by Bulganin and Hatoyama. However, it was not clear whether Soviet endorsement would become effective before the treaty had been ratified. Despite MoFA's grave concern over the Soviet posture, other governments were rather optimistic about Japanese admission to the UN. Among them, the British government predicted at the end of May that Japanese admission would be certainly achieved in the eleventh session of the GA.[118]

In early November, MoFA finally believed it had won Soviet support for their application. By December, the Japanese government had obtained categorical assurance from Bulganin that Russia would now support Japan unconditionally.[119] On 12 December, when the Joint Declaration came into force, the Security Council adopted a Peruvian draft resolution that recommended Japan's admission to the General Assembly. On 18 December, the General Assembly admitted Japan unanimously.

Conclusion

Japan's failure to be admitted during the tenth General Assembly session mirrored its weak status in the international community during this period. The second package deal proposed by the Soviets on 14 December might well be described as an organized conspiracy to exclude Japan and Outer Mongolia in exchange for the admission of the other 16 countries. The Foreign Office concurred with the *Asahi Shinbun's* 'healthy self-reflection' that Japan's allies, especially the US, were not prepared to support it to the extent of vetoing the whole package of 16 countries put forward by the Soviets on the last day. The fact that the GA was prepared to pass the Soviet proposal with an enormous majority can be attributed in part to Japan's inadequate measures to convince the smaller nations of its case, particularly the nations of South-East Asia.[120]

Why did the Soviets omit Japan from the final 14 December package? It was, most likely, in order to balance out the exclusion of the Soviet candidate, Outer Mongolia. The Soviets had frequently indicated that Spain would be dropped if Outer Mongolia were omitted, but consideration for Latin America, paired with the US domestic objections to a revised package without Spain, probably caused the Soviets to change their tactics and leave Japan out instead. The Soviets needed Latin American votes in order to achieve success in their 'peace offensive'. Moreover, the Soviets would have considered the attractive possibility of using

Japanese admission as a means to influence the Russo-Japanese bilateral negotiations to their advantage.

Japan's entry into the UN coincided with a gradual change in the UN's nature, from being a wartime alliance of great powers to more of a universal organization. Naturally, this change influenced the process by which Japan was accepted into the UN. At first, MoFA tried to secure Japan's admission through the support of Western countries, especially the US. However, as early as 1953, new forces in the form of the smaller states in Latin America, Asia, and the British Commonwealth emerged in the GA and the Cold War deadlock abated to some extent. The Soviet Union took advantage of this trend and succeeded in astutely handling the membership issue in the tenth General Assembly. The US State Department, in stark contrast, could not prevent the collapse of the 18-country package because of its preoccupation with making a stand against the emergence of communist China. Generally speaking, however, the new movement in the GA eventually worked in Japan's favour, and UN members agreed that Japan should be admitted during the following year's session.

In the bilateral diplomatic talks of 1956, the Soviets often used the issue of Japanese admission to the UN as diplomatic leverage, and Japan was influenced by the changing nuance of Soviet wording. However, if the Soviet Union had blocked the Japanese application in 1956, it would have run counter to the Soviets' own efforts in terms of the 'peace offensive.' The conclusion of a diplomatic relationship with the Soviet Union was an important factor in Japan's entry to the UN, but it would be more appropriately considered as a final step to complete the process.

Notes

1 Studies on Japan's entry into the UN include: Inoue Hisaichi, 'Kokuren to sengo Nihon gaikō' in *Nenpo kindai Nihon kenkyū*, 16, Tokyo: Yamakawa, 1994, 189–214; Ikeda Naotaka, 'Kokuren daijū sōkai ni okeru Nihon kamei mondai', *Kokugakuin daigaku daigakuin bungaku kenkyūkai kiyō*, no.32., 2000, 419–437; Ikeda Naotaka, 'Kokusai rengo "jun kamei mondai" to gaimushō', *Kokushigaku*, no.170, 2000, 69–1000; Lian Pan, 'The Formation of Japan's UN Policy in the early Postwar Era 1946–57', *Kokusai seiji keizai kenkyū*, September 1999, 17–41.

2 Admission to the UN required a Security Council recommendation with a majority of seven votes in favour (the SC then consisted of 11 members, including five permanent members). Approval of the SC recommendation by the General Assembly would then require a two-thirds majority.

3 National Archives, Kew (hereafter NA Kew), UN 22516/21, FO 371/117470, UK Delegation to UN, Memo 'The Admission of New Members to the UN', 13 May 1955.

4 Telegram from Mission at UN to DS, 260, 10 September 1955, *Foreign Relations of the United States* (hereafter *FRUS*) *1955–1957*, vol. XI (United Nations and General International Matters), Washington, D.C., 1988, p. 302.

5 NA Kew, UP 123/6, FO 371/112341, P. M. Crosthwaite, UK Delegation to UN, Admission of New Members, 24 April 1954.

6 Memo of a Conversation between Counsellor of British Embassy and Special Assistant for UN Affairs in Bureau of European Affairs, DS, 25 February 1955, *FRUS 1955–1957*, p. 263.

7   Memo from Assistant Secretary of State for IOA (Key) to Deputy Under Secretary for Political Affairs (Murphy), 26 May 1955, *FRUS 1955–1957*, pp. 274–5.

8   Diplomatic Record Office, Tokyo (hereafter DRO), B'-0040, 0136, Yuhki (Colombo) to Shigemitsu, 158, 14 June 1955.

9   DRO B'-0040, 0138, Yamagata to Shigemitsu, 163, 24 June 1955.

10   NA Kew, UN 22516/21, FO 371/117470, UK Delegation to UN, 13 May 1955.

11   C. Cross, *The Fall of the British Empire*, London: Paladin, 1970, pp. 290–3.

12   DRO B'-0040, 140–141, Katsuno (San Francisco) to Shigemitsu, 40, 25 June 1955.

13   DRO B'-0040, Matsudaira to Shigemitsu, 207, 27 July 1955, pp. 200–1.

14   The Northern Territories refers to the four islands off the northeast coast of Hokkaido which the Russians occupied at the end of World War II, and which successive Japanese governments have attempted to reclaim.

15   NA Kew, UN 22516/46, FO 371/117472, Commonwealth Office to FO, 19 August 1955.

16   NA Kew, FO 371/111708, Office of High Commissioner for Canada, Memo Admission of New Members to UN, 29 August 1955.

17   Mission at UN to DS, 161, 26 October 1955, *FRUS 1955–1957*, pp. 316–17.

18   NA Kew, FO 371/117475, Foreign Office to UK Delegation to UN, 1480, 22 October 1955.

19   Memo from Director of Office of UN Political and Security Affairs (Popper) to Key, 2 June 1955, *FRUS 1955–1957*, pp. 277–9.

20   Memo from Deputy Assistant Secretary of State for Far Eastern Affairs (Sebald) to Secretary of State, 8 June 1955, *FRUS 1955–1957*, pp. 282–3.

21   Memo from Key to Dulles, 7 June 1955, *FRUS 1955–1957*, pp. 280–1.

22   Memo from Deputy Assistant Secretary State for IOA (Wainhouse) to Dulles, 24 August 1955, *FRUS 1955–1957*, pp. 292–3.

23   Memo from Popper to Key, 2 June 1955.

24   Mission at UN to DS, 160, 24 October 1955, *FRUS 1955–1957*, pp. 314–15.

25   Mission at UN to DS, 161, 26 October 1955.

26   Memo from Senior Political Adviser to Mission at UN (McSweeney) to IOA Staff of Mission at UN (Joseph Sisco), 3 November 1955, *FRUS 1955–1957*, pp. 319–20.

27   NA Kew, UN 22516/151, FO 371/117476 UK Delegation to Meeting of Foreign Ministers to FO, 4 November 1955.

28   Memo from McSweeney to Sisco, 3 November, 1955, op. cit.

29   Mission at UN to DS, 217, 4 November 1955, *FRUS 1955–1957*, pp. 321–3.

30   Delegation at Foreign Ministers meetings in Geneva to DS, 188, 5 November 1955, *FRUS 1955–1957*, pp. 328–9. The position of France in the SC had not been clarified, but the DS believed France would not contradict the will of the great majority.

31   Mission at UN to DS, 4 November 1955, op. cit.

32   Dulles to DS, 50, 7 November 1955, *FRUS 1955–1957*, p. 333.

33   IOA office staff's analysis on the Congressional reaction concluded that the inclusion of Austria, Finland and Portugal would have general Congressional approval. Japan would be received with less enthusiasm but the overall reaction would be favourable. Memo 30 September from Morton to Wilcox, Attachment to Memo from Sisco to Lodge, 6 October 1955, *FRUS 1955–1957*, p. 311.

34   Embassy in Austria to the Embassy in UK, 125, 5 November 1955, *FRUS 1955–1957*, p. 326.

35   Embassy in Austria to the Embassy in UK, 125, 5 November 1955, op. cit., footnote 2.

36   Acting Secretary of State to Dulles, 58, 5 November 1955, *FRUS 1955–1957*, p. 327.

37   Dulles to the Mission at UN, 37, 8 November 1955, *FRUS 1955–1957*, p. 337.

38   Mission at UN to DS, 251, 9 November 1955, *FRUS 1955–1957*, pp. 341–2.

39 Delegation 237 from USUN, DS, Central Files, 310.2/11–855, 8 November 1955, *FRUS 1955–1957*, vol. XI, p. 338 (footnote).
40 Matsudaira to Shigemitsu, 277, 10 November 1955 cited in Ikeda, 'Kokuren daijū sōkai ni okeru Nihon kamei mondai,' p. 427.
41 Embassy in RoC to DS, 355, 23 December 1955, *FRUS 1955–1957*, pp. 463–7.
42 Kase to Shigemitsu, 368, 22 November 1955, cited in Ikeda, 'Kokuren daijū sōkai ni okeru Nihon kamei mondai,' p. 428.
43 Memo of Conversation between Iguchi and the Assistant Secretary of State Far Eastern Affairs, 19 November 1955, *FRUS 1955–1957*, pp. 384–5.
44 Sakamoto Kazuya 'Nisso kokkō kaifuku kōshō to Amerika', *Kokusai seiji*, 105, January 1994, pp. 144–62.
45 Mission at UN to DS, 266, 10 November 1955, *FRUS 1955–1957*, pp. 343–5.
46 Despatch from Embassy in RoC to DS, 229, 23 December 1955, *FRUS 1955–1957*, pp. 463–7.
47 Mission at UN to Delegation at Foreign Ministers Meeting at Geneva, 15, 12 November 1955, *FRUS 1955–1957*, pp. 349–50.
48 DS to Dulles at Geneva, 81, 11 November 1955, *FRUS 1955–1957*, pp. 345–7.
49 Memoir of Conversation, Secretary's Office, Geneva, 12 November 1955, *FRUS 1955–1957*, pp. 347–9.
50 Based on the increasing unpopularity of the veto, Dulles announced in October that the US would not veto the membership issue.
51 Memo of Conversation, Secretary's Suite, Geneva, 13 November 1955, *FRUS 1955–1957*, pp. 351–5.
52 Dulles to DS, 74, 13 November 1955, *FRUS 1955–1957*, pp. 355–6.
53 NA Kew, UN 22516/191, FO 371/117477 I.T.M. Pink, FO, New Members of UN, 12 November 1955.
54 Mission UN to DS, 279, 13 November 1955, *FRUS 1955–1957*, pp. 356–8.
55 Kase to Shigemitsu, 345, 14 November 1955, cited in Ikeda, 'Kokuren daijū sōkai ni okeru Nihon kamei mondai,' p. 423.
56 Consul General Tatsuki to Shigemitsu, 614, 16 November, cited in Ikeda, 'Kokuren daijū sōkai ni okeru Nihon kamei mondai,' p. 424.
57 The draft was revised to substitute the phrase 'widest possible membership' for the word 'universality'.
58 Mission at UN to DS, 302, 16 November 1955, *FRUS 1955–1957*, pp. 369–70.
59 Embassy in UK to DS, 2256, 1 December 1955, *FRUS 1955–1957*, pp. 413–14.
60 NA Kew, UN 22516/179, FO 371/117477, UK Delegation to UN to FO, 1182, 15 November 1955.
61 From Kase to Shigemitsu, 355, 17 November 1955, cited in Ikeda, 'Kokuren daijū sōkai ni okeru Nihon kamei mondai,' p. 425.
62 NA Kew, UN 22516/180, FO 371/117477, FO UN New Members, 16 November 1955.
63 NA Kew, UN 22516/180, FO 371/117477, FO UN New Members, 17 November 1955.
64 Memo of a conversation between Koo and Robertson, 17 November 1955, *FRUS 1955–1957*, pp. 373–4.
65 Despatch from Embassy in RoC to DS, 23 December 1955.
66 NA Kew, UN 22516/194, FO 371/117477, UK delegation to UN to FO, 1207, 18 November 1955.
67 Despatch from Embassy in RoC to DS, 23 December 1955.
68 Mission at UN to DS, 316, 19 November 1955, *FRUS 1955–1957*, pp. 383–4.
69 Mission at UN to DS, 309, 18 November 1955, *FRUS 1955–1957*, pp. 374–9.
70 Mission at UN Lodge to DS, 314, 19 November 1955, *FRUS 1955–1957*, pp. 379–80.

71 Embassy in RoC to DS, 229, 23 December 1955, op. cit.
72 DS to Embassy in RoC, 304, 22 November 1955, *FRUS 1955–1957*, p. 388.
73 Embassy in RoC to DS, 490, 23 November 1955, *FRUS 1955–1957*, pp. 394–5.
74 Ibid.
75 Telegram from Mission at UN to DS, 26 November 1955, *FRUS 1955–1957*, pp. 388–91.
76 Mission at UN to DS, 368, 28 November 1955, *FRUS 1955–1957*, pp. 404–06.
77 US Delegation at UN, Eyes Only for Dulles, 363, 27 November 1955 *FRUS 1955–1957*, footnote, p. 404.
78 DS to Embassy in RoC, 369, 28 November 1955, *FRUS 1955–1957*, pp. 406–7.
79 Embassy in RoC to DS, 229, 23 December 1955, op. cit.
80 NA, Kew UN 22516/220, FO 371/117478, FO to UK delegation to UN, 1851, 30 November 1955.
81 Mission at UN to DS, 390, 30 November 1955, *FRUS 1955–1957*, pp. 410–12.
82 Dulles gradually became tired of Lodge who was out of step with UN politics. NA, Kew UN 22516/220, FO 371/117478, FO to UK Delegation to UN, 1852, 30 November 1955.
83 Mission at UN to DS, 400, 1 December 1955, *FRUS 1955–1957*, pp. 415–16.
84 Ikeda, 'Kokuren daijū sōkai ni okeru Nihon kamei mondai,' p. 430.
85 NA Kew, UN 22516/257, FO 371/117479 British Embassy, Ankara to UN Political Department, FO, 6 December 1955.
86 Belgium abstained because it was against Spain. France abstained out of concern over colonial issues. Greece was against Albania. Israel was against Jordan.
87 DS to Embassy in RoC, 329, 2 December 1955, *FRUS 1955–1957*, pp. 419–20; DS to Embassy in RoC, 333, 3 December 1955, *FRUS 1955–1957*, p. 422; DS to Embassy in RoC, 335, 5 December 1955, *FRUS 1955–1957*, pp. 425–26; DS to Embassy in RoC, 341, 6 December 1955, *FRUS 1955–1957*, p. 436.
88 Embassy in RoC to DS, 511, 1 December 1955, *FRUS 1955–1957*, pp. 412–13.
89 Embassy in RoC to DS, 317, 3 December 1955, *FRUS 1955–1957*, pp. 423–24.
90 Memo of a Conversation between Koo and Robertson, 6 December 1955, *FRUS 1955–1957*, pp. 427–31.
91 DS to Mission UN, 374, 26 November 1955, *FRUS 1955–1957*, pp. 401–04.
92 This belief was also shared by the British government: NA Kew, UN 22416/202, FO 371/117478, UK Delegation to UN to FO, 182, 23 November 1955. In fact, the UK and US had already discussed a deal by which Taipei would not oppose admission of Outer Mongolia in exchange for a guarantee that Taipei would not be excluded from the UN before 1957: UN 22516/248, FO 371/11478, UK Delegation to UN to FO, 1328, 8 December 1955.
93 Sano Masafumi 'Hatoyama naikaku no Chūgoku seisaku to Amerika' in *Nijū seiki kenkyū* 3, December 2002, pp. 45–74.
94 This was a bipartisan group of Representatives including Chairman Clement Zablocki, Ross Adair, Robert Byrd, Marguerite Church, John Jarman, Walter Judd and Richard Wigglesworth.
95 Telegram from Embassy in RoC to DS, 6 December 1955, *FRUS 1955–1957*, pp. 434–35.
96 DS to Embassy in RoC, 349, 8 December 1955, *FRUS 1955–1957*, pp. 439–40.
97 DS to Embassy in Japan, 1200, 8 December 1955, *FRUS 1955–1957*, pp. 440–1.
98 Embassy in Japan to DS, 1315, 9 December 1955, *FRUS 1955–1957*, pp. 441–2.
99 Embassy RoC to DS, 528, 6 December 1955, *FRUS 1955–1957*, pp. 434–5.
100 Embassy in RoC to DS, 541, 10 December 1955, *FRUS 1955–1957*, pp. 442–3.
101 Embassy RoC to the DS, 533, 8 December 1955, *FRUS 1955–1957*, pp. 436–9.
102 Despatch from the Embassy in RoC to DS, 355, 23 December 1955.
103 Embassy in Japan to DS, 214, 12 December 1955, *FRUS 1955–1957*, pp. 444–5.
104 Embassy in Japan to DS, 218, 13 December 1955, *FRUS 1955–1957*, pp. 449–50.

105 At first the Indian delegate, Krishna Menon, told the British delegation that the new Russian proposal would exclude Spain and Outer Mongolia. NA Kew, UN 2257/1, FO 371/123736, UK Delegation to FO, 'Summary of Events Leading up to the Admission of 16 to the UN', 7 January 1956. Dixon commented that 'the final decision by the Russians to back down except in regard to Japan came as a surprise to me' and that 'the Americans agreed to the Soviet proposal to admit sixteen was extraordinary'.

106 NA Kew, UN 22516/279, FO 371/11747, Delegation to UN to FO, 1381, 14 December 1955.

107 The US document explains this with slightly different nuance: Lodge promptly submitted an amendment to add Japan to the Soviet draft resolution.' Editorial Note, *FRUS 1955–1957*, vol. XI, p. 451.

108 UN Document A/RES/365, 16 December 1955.

109 NA Kew, UN 22516/282, FO 371/117479, UK Delegation to UN to FO, 1390, 15 December 1955.

110 Delegation to UN to FO, 1381, 14 December 1955.

111 DS to Embassy in RoC, 368, 16 December 1955, *FRUS*, p. 455.

112 DRO B'-0043 0003, 'Kokuren kamei jitsugen no tame no hōsaku ni kansuru ken,' Kokusai Kyōryoku Kyoku, 16 April 1956.

113 DRO B'-0043 0018, Kurino, 'Kokuren kamei mondai ni kansuru jimukan kaigi no ketsuron', Kokkyō Ikka, 9 May 1956; Memo from Wilcox to Dulles, 26 October 1956, *FRUS*, p. 475.

114 Telegram from the Embassy in Japan to DS, 1385, 17 December 1955, *FRUS*, pp. 457–9.

115 Tanaka Takahiko, *Nisso kokkō kaifuku kōshō no shiteki tenka*, Tokyo: Hitotsubashi University Faculty of Law, 1993, pp. 273–4.

116 Ibid., p. 301.

117 The letter of agreement stated that the 'USSR will support Japan's request for admission to membership in the UN'.

118 NA Kew, UN 2257/53, FO/371/12738, From UK Delegation to UN to FO, 146, 29 May 1956.

119 NA Kew, UN2257/90, FO371/123739, From UK Delegation to UN to FO, 1585, 7 December 1956.

120 NA Kew, UN 22516/339, FO 371/117480, British Embassy in Tokyo to Secretary of State for Foreign Affairs, 222, 21 December 1955.

Part III

Japanese and US domestic constraints on foreign policy

7   The Lucky Dragon Incident of 1954

A failure of crisis management?[1]

John Swenson-Wright

International crises rarely, if ever, happen in isolation. Certainly there are few instances in which a country's policy makers, at the moment of an unforeseen catastrophe or diplomatic disaster, are able to respond instantaneously and with complete attention, undistracted by competing issues of comparable importance. The Lucky Dragon Incident of 1954, in which the 23 crew members of a Japanese fishing vessel were exposed to radioactive fall-out following the testing of a US hydrogen bomb in the Pacific, was a major disruption to relations between Washington and Tokyo. In the words of one observer, it imposed 'the most serious strain on Japanese-American relations since 1945'.[2] The US government, and its apparent failure to give adequate consideration to Japanese grievance, angered public opinion in Japan, and subsequent scholarly analysis has often been sharply critical of American actions.[3]

Such criticisms may have been overstated. The emotional intensity of the Japanese reaction to the Incident is readily understandable, in light of the psychological and physical scars left by the bombing of Hiroshima and Nagasaki. However, to view it at face value would be to neglect the various efforts within the Eisenhower administration, both in Washington and Tokyo, to handle the crisis constructively. Moreover, studies of the Incident may have been drawn on too narrow a canvas, missing, or at least giving insufficient attention to, the wider context. Historians have, perhaps, assumed too readily that policy makers could or should have viewed events with the same degree of dispassionate clarity that access to the archives and the benefit of hindsight provides.

In the context of 1954, four sets of factors need to be appreciated when judging the decisions of the Eisenhower Administration in relation to Japan, namely: the broader policy considerations associated with nuclear weapons testing; the reliability of existing scientific knowledge relating to nuclear technology as a whole; concern for adequate security co-operation between allies; and the overall conflict between international communism and the Western alliance.

Stressing these factors is not a basis for exonerating or excusing US actions. Mistakes occurred and, in certain respects, the crisis could have been handled more effectively and sensitively, and with less disruption to alliance relations. Nevertheless, explicitly taking these factors into account, while extending the analysis both before and beyond 1954 to highlight the antecedents to the crisis and subsequent developments, provides a more complete picture of events. It also reveals the importance of psychological and propaganda techniques in America's Japan policy at this time, as well as the recognition by US officials that Japanese domestic political instability (itself, in part, the product of American actions stemming from the 1945–52 occupation), seriously constrained the United States in developing a strong alliance with Japan. Japanese internal bureaucratic tensions as well as the lack of effective Japanese security legislation undercut efforts to promote an active security partnership. This issue, particularly the question of Japan's vulnerability to Soviet-directed espionage, has generally been neglected in existing work on post-war US–Japan relations. Examining it more closely reveals the important role played by inter-agency institutions, most notably the Operations Co-ordinating Board (OCB), in influencing the Eisenhower administration's Japan policy at this time.

Viewing the Lucky Dragon Incident more broadly also reveals an interesting ambivalence in Japan's attitude to nuclear issues. Japan's nuclear allergy was highly selective. It was rooted in a widespread aversion to the testing of nuclear weapons, but at the same time official and public opinion enthusiastically favoured the development of the peaceful use of nuclear energy and Japan's own nuclear power industry. This sentiment gave US officials a valuable tool with which to limit the political damage associated with the Lucky Dragon Incident and developments in the latter half of the 1950s suggest that the Americans had learnt important lessons from the earlier crisis, enabling them to prevent similar tensions in the future. This adaptive capacity suggests that in any balanced assessment of US–Japan policy, it is important to consider, in addition to points of unmistakable bilateral tension, those crises which did not occur. The absence of conflict can sometimes be just as significant as instances of disagreement.

The outline of the crisis

The broad sequence of events surrounding the crisis of 1954 can be set out quite simply. On 1 March, a small private fishing vessel, the Daigo Fukuryū Maru (or Lucky Dragon, No. 5), was about 82 miles east of Bikini Island,[4] a coral atoll that formed part of the Marshall Island chain in the Western Pacific. The ship was far from Japan and fishing in a relatively unfamiliar area. Early in the morning, the crew was startled by a bright flash of light, followed seven minutes later by an enormous explosion. Two hours later, a fine white powder started to rain down on the boat and its crew. It was not immediately clear what had happened. Some of the fishermen could recall that the Marshall islands had been the site for earlier nuclear testing by the United States in 1946, and as recently as 1952, Japan's Maritime Safety Board had warned vessels to stay away from Bikini.[5] However, the Lucky Dragon was well outside the official exclusion zone (some 14 miles according to later reports),[6] and in theory the crew had no reason to be concerned.

In reality, the situation was much more serious. The United States had resumed its nuclear testing programme in the Pacific, and the 1 March explosion, or

'BRAVO shot' as it was officially known, was the first detonation in the 'Operation CASTLE' series of nuclear tests planned for an area that included Bikini as well as a number of other atolls. However, unlike the tests of 1946, which had involved atomic weapons, the CASTLE series was designed to test the latest developments in hydrogen bomb technology, and represented a major and dramatic increase in destructive power. Defined in strictly scientific terms, BRAVO was hugely successful. The anticipated size of the explosion (a fission reaction which in turn triggered a much larger fusion explosion)[7] had been five megatons. However, the US nuclear scientists who had designed the bomb overlooked an important stage in the lithium-based chain reaction and seriously underestimated the final yield: a massive 15 megatons, which was unquestionably at that stage the world's largest ever nuclear explosion.[8] The coral atoll was vaporized in an instant soon to be deposited as atomic rain, or as the Japanese media would later describe it, 'Ashes of Death'.[9] A chance event, rather than conscious planning, had intervened abruptly catching the unsuspecting and hapless fishermen in a radioactive downpour, and in the process creating the basis for intense bilateral tension.

Confused by what they had witnessed, the Japanese fishermen decided to return to their home-port of Yaizu, in Shizuoka Prefecture, before reporting the incident. En route, the men began to display the characteristic symptoms of radiation exposure, including hair loss, sores, loss of appetite, and diarrhoea.[10] When they returned home on 14 March, the men reported to a local physician who downplayed the extent of their condition, suggesting that they would have displayed more serious symptoms if their exposure had been severe. Indeed, such was the doctor's confidence that he reassured the men that they could safely sell their catch to the local market.[11] There was, apparently, no danger of contamination. However, by 16 March, an enterprising local *Yomiuri Shinbun* newspaper reporter had managed to tease out the details of the story, which once published, rapidly transformed a local incident into a major international event.[12]

News of the event prompted a swift response from Washington. On the same day, the Atomic Energy Commission (AEC), the government agency with overall responsibility for the civilian and testing aspects of the nuclear programme, quickly ordered the despatch to Tokyo of Dr John Morton, the director of the Atomic Bomb Casualty Commission (ABCC), together with a group of US Air Force radiation physicists, to examine the affected fishermen, two of whom, with their conditions deteriorating, had already been sent to Tokyo University hospital.[13] Morton, on the basis of seeing the two men (and before heading off to Yaizu to visit the other 21 crew members) issued a public statement pointing out that the men were in better condition than he had anticipated and that he expected them to recover within 2–3 weeks.[14]

Any hopes of a rapid resolution of the problem were dashed by reports from private Japanese researchers that the hull of the Lucky Dragon registered high levels of radiation and, most significantly, that fish stocks in Osaka, including the latest shipment from Yaizu (some of which had already been sold and consumed), were heavily contaminated.[15] Not surprisingly, the news immediately caused a major panic, closing markets not only in Osaka, but also in Tokyo and throughout the country, a trend which was exacerbated when it was learnt that fish had been removed from the Emperor's diet.[16] However, restoring market confidence was the least of America's problems. Far more serious was the widespread press criticism of the United States for allowing testing to take place in the first place, for revisiting (intentionally, according to some reports) the horrors of radiation exposure on a vulnerable and defenceless Japan, and for America's alleged indifference to the fate of the 23 fishermen.

Some of this criticism was overstated and some, it turns out, clearly inaccurate. However, Japanese grievances (at least at the level of public opinion), reinforced by public relations blunders and crass insensitivity on the part of certain US officials, were also compounded by news of the death of the oldest of the crew members, Kuboyama Aikichi, in September 1954. In addition, extended government negotiations over the issue of financial compensation for the fishermen and their relatives further increased tension between the two countries, delaying a final settlement until January 1955, 10 months after the original Incident. Understanding the causes of this tension and the manner in which the issue was resolved provides a basis for assessing alliance relations between the US and its junior partner and the extent to which the Americans were willing to take Japanese grievances seriously.

Testing and nuclear strategy

In order to make sense of US actions in 1954, it is important to appreciate the central role of nuclear weapons in the Cold War strategy of the recently inaugurated Eisenhower administration. Despite the apparent ideological thaw following Stalin's death in 1953, the US leadership remained deeply suspicious of Soviet intentions. With the announcement of the 'New Look' strategy of 30 October 1953, Eisenhower had intentionally endorsed nuclear deterrence as a means of minimizing the enormous economic burden associated with a conventional arms race.

In the public perception, the new doctrine became closely associated with a crude and seemingly uncompromising policy of 'massive retaliation', although as Saki Dockrill has pointed out, the policy was more subtle, encompassing political, economic and psychological policy options while attempting 'to combine a defensive nuclear military policy with an offensive strategy in the non-military field'.[17] In Eisenhower's mind, a credible military deterrent (in effect the risk of mutual atomic annihilation), coupled with a policy of 'studied ambiguity'[18] regarding when and where nuclear weapons might be deployed, was vitally important in allowing the US to guarantee its and the West's security in an increasingly unstable environment. Europe, despite the benefits of the Marshall Plan, gradual economic recovery and the creation of the European Coal and Steel Community (ECSC), remained vulnerable and potentially unstable, and the European members of NATO worried about a possible American withdrawal from the continent.[19] In Asia, the inauguration of the South East Asia Treaty Organisation (SEATO) in September 1954 had done little to allay fears of regional instability and 'falling dominoes' in the form of Communist expansion, especially following the surrender of the French garrison in Dien Bien Phu in May 1954. Against such a background and with senior US policy makers increasingly on the defensive in the East Asia, it is easy to see why the American government considered that nuclear testing was unavoidable. To some in the Administration, including Eisenhower, events in 1954 particularly (most notably the Indochina talks at Geneva in July) suggested that the bomb was not merely a military device and might conceivably carry powerful weight in diplomatic negotiations.

Criticisms and misperceptions

Much of the criticism of the US reaction to the Lucky Dragon Incident, both at the time and subsequently, was focused on a number of issues. The Americans, it was argued, were slow in responding to the crisis and in issuing a formal apology to the Japanese government.[20] They had refused to disclose information on the effects of the explosion and had, therefore, demonstrated little concern for the fishermen's well-being. Moreover, according to the more critical Japanese press reports, the Americans had deliberately and callously triggered an explosion likely to inflict damage on Japan: contrary to official US statements, Washington, it was suggested, had been fully aware of the power of the bomb and may well have been testing a cobalt bomb, a 'dirty weapon', intended to spread radiation over a wide area.[21] In effect, the Japanese were being used as human guinea-pigs in American radiation experiments.[22] At the very least, the US could be attacked for not taking Japan's views and interests seriously and for placing its own agenda ahead of that of its alliance relationship with Japan.

The claim that the BRAVO shot was intentionally harmful to the Japanese is not sustainable. Lithium deuteride rather than cobalt was the core fissile material, and given the exposure, not only of the Marshall islanders, but of US naval vessels in the vicinity of the test area, it is clear that the extensive environmental damage thus caused was the result of miscalculation rather than an attempt to disperse radiation on the high seas. By contrast, the argument that America should have apologized sooner is much more persuasive. It was only on 30 March, two weeks after news of the disaster had emerged, that the US decided to send a formal note to the Japanese government expressing its regret (albeit without admitting any legal responsibility),[23] a shortcoming later freely acknowledged by the then US ambassador, John Allison.[24] However, this should not entirely overshadow the initial US efforts to respond promptly to the crisis. As of 24 March, Robert McClurkin, the acting assistant secretary of state for Northeast Asian Affairs, chaired both the OCB working group on Japan and an ad hoc interdepartmental group, made up of representatives from the AEC and State and Defense Departments, established to deal with the Lucky Dragon Incident. A summary of US government actions after 16 March reveals a series of responses of varying degrees of effectiveness: on 16 March, Dr Morton's name had been passed on to the embassy in Tokyo as a technical consultant to examine the two fishermen in Tokyo University hospital; the following day, the embassy issued a statement indicating that the US government was prepared to provide fair compensation if the facts warranted; and on 18 March, Washington instructed the embassy to inform the Japanese government that the danger zone for future tests had been expanded.

Five days later, on 23 March, the embassy was authorized to inform the Japanese Ministry of Foreign Affairs (MoFA) that the US would reimburse Japan for any medical care for the crew members and relief for family members; the following day, US–Japan working-level meetings were held in Tokyo to try to improve joint co-ordination between the two governments, and the Japanese Ministry of Health and Welfare established an Atom Bomb Inquiry Investigating Committee which the Americans hoped would address the problem of a lack of Japanese internal co-ordination. Further, on 28 March, the US Far Eastern Command flew the 21 fishermen still in Yaizu to Tokyo where they could receive more effective medical supervision.[25] The OCB, it was clear, recognized the need to respond, although it appears to have been divided or at least confused over the long-term implications of the incident.

The charge that the Americans chose not to share technical information with the Japanese is easy to substantiate. In treating the crew of the Lucky Dragon, Japanese medical personnel understandably wished to know the composition of the ash, which appeared to have caused the fishermen's illness. However, the Americans worried that any disclosure of either the content of the fallout or de-tails of the design of the BRAVO bomb would reveal the unique character of the weapon, in particular, that it was a dry thermonuclear device based on a lithium core.[26] Such information, it was feared, would be beneficial to the Soviets and jeopardize the US lead in the nuclear arms race.

While this reasoning might seem overly cautious, it was entirely consistent with existing policy. The timing of the CASTLE series had been deliberately concealed and the testing area made as wide as possible in order to prevent any Soviet ship from obtaining samples of the fallout material, from which Soviet scientists might deduce the design of the new super-bomb.[27] Moreover, as early as 1952, Eisenhower had emphasized the importance of secrecy where the testing programme as a whole was concerned, not only because of the obvious need to prevent important technical information from being disclosed to the enemy, but also to maintain a psychological edge over the Soviets. The President calculated that it would be more of a blow to Russian morale to learn for themselves of America's testing successes than have the information disclosed publicly.[28]

Washington's general preoccupation with maintaining the confidentiality of its nuclear technology was reinforced in its dealings with Tokyo by a deep-seated concern that the Japanese had yet to develop their own reliable internal security and intelligence structures. An extensive report (based on a visit to East Asia by a government team headed by General James Van Fleet) highlighted the main shortcomings. Namely, that the Diet had considered but refused to enact suitable legislation to protect classified military information. More generally, since the end of the Second World War, the Japanese authorities had failed to take adequate measures to safeguard against communist infiltration, whether in the form of North Korean and communist Chinese agents or repatriated Japanese civilians and soldiers indoctrinated during their time, both during and after the war, in communist-dominated areas on the Asian mainland.

Moreover, in interrogating these repatriates, the Japanese had shown only a limited willingness to share information with the US military and intelligence services and refused to allow American personnel to question the repatriates from either the PRC or the USSR. Japanese authorities had provided valuable political and economic information derived from their 'own secret and small-scale interrogation reports', but had 'failed to produce enough of the data desired by the United States military, including information pertaining to United States citizens thought to be held by communist countries.'[29] Even with increased working-level co-operation between US and Japanese security personnel and the provision of American financial assistance to train Japanese officials in US intelligence techniques, there was little evidence of any major progress on this issue. By early 1955, Washington still considered that Tokyo had failed to adequately grapple with the problem of internal security.

This weakness appears to have been acknowledged by the Japanese government. Certainly, officials in MoFA, shortly after the Lucky Dragon Incident, were quick to acknowledge that 'in regard to the issue of maintaining secrecy . . . there is in our country, no appropriate legal foundation'.[30] Moreover, 1954 also provided striking evidence of some of the shortcomings of Japan's domestic security system. In the second half of January, Yuri Rastvorov, third secretary in the Soviet mission in Tokyo, but in reality a lieutenant colonel in the Soviet security service, disappeared from his post. Six months later, on 14 August, MoFA's Culture and Information Bureau, together with the Public Security Investigation Agency (Kōan chōsachō) unexpectedly announced that Rastvorov wished to seek refuge in the United States, which Washington rapidly endorsed.[31] It transpired that, behind the scenes, Japanese and American officials had been co-operating to smuggle Rastvorov out of the country and to ensure that the details of his planned defection were not disclosed to the Japanese media. At one level, the incident revealed that Washington and Tokyo were, in particular instances, able to co-operate over security matters.[32] (Some 36 MoFA officials had been assigned to the case).[33] However, the information provided by Rastvorov, following his debriefing, revealed a more troubling general state of affairs and two years later, in May 1956 in testimony before the US Senate, Rastvorov publicly disclosed that an extensive Soviet spy network had been operating throughout Japan.[34] The incident, at the time, prompted US embassy officials in Tokyo to write to the State Department warning that a country lacking a system for managing domestic security might be incapable of developing a modern military, and pointing out not only the shortcomings of the legal system, but also the Japanese government's failure to give serious attention to ways of preventing industrial sabotage.

Rastvorov's revelations

Rastvorov's revelations provide a fascinating insight into the murky world of spying and counter-espionage in Japan at this time. Findings in the US archives reveal the systematic and long-term efforts of the Soviet liaison mission in Japan to penetrate both the Japanese government and American civilian and military detachments in Japan. Rastvorov was the principal Ministry of Internal Affairs (MVD, later to become the KGB) operative in the embassy and as such was involved in recruiting an extensive web of agents throughout Japan. Such agents included American service personnel, White Russian émigrés, Indian and Chinese nationals, and, especially important, Japanese civilians and middle-ranking Japanese government officials, including three relatively prominent members of MoFA. The involvement of the latter was particularly damaging to the Liberal government of Prime Minister Yoshida Shigeru, since the men in question, Higurashi Nobunori, Shoji Hiroshi, and Takamore Shigeru, were all privy to secret government- and, in one instance at least, cabinet-level information. Indeed, the extent to which the Japanese government had been compromised may have been greater than the initial revelations indicated. An untimely suicide by Higurashi (who threw himself out of a fourth-floor window during a police interrogation) may have conveniently protected the identity of other Japanese nationals working for the Soviets, since there may have been further information that Higurashi had yet to disclose.

Rastvorov's information was undoubtedly very valuable to the Americans and President Eisenhower had personally authorized the decision to provide the defector with a safe haven in the United States. In his extensive debriefing with US military intelligence officials, Rastvorov identified not only Soviet intelligence operatives in Japan, but also provided valuable background on similar individuals operating in the United States. Also, he was able to highlight the methods used by the Russians to recruit Japanese prisoners of war in Siberia following the end of the war, a number of whom successfully worked as double-agents within the offices of the US occupation after their repatriation. Similarly troubling to the Americans and the Japanese was the revelation of two separate covert operations sponsored by the Soviets: a money-laundering scheme and a narcotics ring, both centred around Kobe and Osaka and involving more than 80 individuals. Undoubtedly there were limits to the effectiveness of Soviet subversion in Japan at this time. The Soviet liaison mission in Japan did not enjoy traditional diplomatic privileges and was both short-staffed and apparently underfunded (hence, it seems, the emphasis placed on money laundering). Also, the success rate in terms of penetrating the US military and air force facilities in Japan (the latter was the principal target of Soviet operations) was relatively low. Futhermore, where Japanese organizations were concerned, the Soviets chose to devote a lot of their energies to the private sector, working closely with the Japan Communist Party (JCP), but also recruiting supporters in front organizations and friendly institutions, including Russia-focused research institutes, Japanese press organizations, and groups closely identified with the peace movement.

Given the US insistence on maintaining nuclear secrecy and legitimate worries over Japan's security preparedness, it is easy to appreciate why the Americans would have felt unable to reveal the precise composition of the ash from the BRAVO shot to the Japanese authorities. However, a policy of non-disclosure soon turned into a strategy of disinformation when, on 31 March, Lewis Strauss, the Chairman of the AEC (in many respects the public face of the US reaction to the crisis), suggested at a press conference that the symptoms displayed by the ailing fishermen might be due to the chemical composition of the coral dust from Bikini rather than the result of radiation exposure.[35]

Taken at face value, Strauss's crude assessment seems absurd and hardly likely to have convinced either public opinion or the scientific community in Japan, particularly given the country's first-hand experience of the effects of radiation-related illness. A more charitable interpretation might conclude that the Americans, confronted by the dilemma of not being able to reveal the composition of the dust while also not wishing to antagonize Japan by suggesting publicly or privately that they could not trust the Japanese government to handle secret information, had settled necessarily on a poor compromise solution. Advancing a patently implausible explanation would allow the US to avoid debating the radiation issue, while Japan's direct experience of caring for the victims of Hiroshima and Nagasaki would allow the Japanese to devise their own effective treatment regime for the Lucky Dragon crew. If the 31 March press conference was the only instance in which the coral argument was used, it might be simplest to characterize the remark as an off-hand, poorly judged statement. However, as late as 22 April, the OCB was itself recommending that the US 'seek to attribute continued illness of Japanese patients to chemical effects of coral dusting rather than radioactivity per se',[36] lending weight, perhaps, to the notion that this was a calculated second-best solution, albeit a highly imperfect strategy.

Whatever the precise motivations behind such statements, it is clear why public opinion in Japan would have felt understandably suspicious of American intentions. Yet, at the same time, there is no doubt that US officials in Japan recognized that the issue risked running out of control and were conscious of the presentational and symbolic side to the bilateral relationship. Reports from Tokyo warned against taking Japan for granted as a strategic ally,[37] senior embassy officials attended Kuboyama's funeral,[38] and Allison, whatever his own regrets about not issuing an apology immediately, sought to convey the urgency of the situation to his superiors back home.[39] Moreover, there is little reason to question the sincerity and good intentions of the Americans sent out to examine the afflicted fishermen. A detailed MoFA report, commenting on the visit by Dr Morton and the ABCC inspection team to Yaizu, noted that the US officials had behaved 'extremely courteously', while other reports on the Yaizu visit pointed out that the Americans had offered to provide treatment for the fishermen, only to have this offer rejected by the local doctors. This in turn generated expression of displeasure from the Americans, prompting a hostile local Japanese response and some of the more critical and 'inaccurate' press reports, all adding up to mutual US–Japanese misunderstanding which, although difficult to resolve quickly, MoFA was taking pains to settle as smoothly as possible.[40]

The MoFA report is particularly relevant because, in general, it confirms the US perception that local conditions in Yaizu were a source of much of the original bilateral tension. On 22 March, Merril Eisenbud, the director of the Health and Safety Laboratory of the AEC, arrived in Japan, en route to Yaizu in order to inspect the hull of the Lucky Dragon for signs of radiation exposure. Commenting in general on his visit, the minutes of a joint meeting of the embassy and Far Eastern Command held in Tokyo to assess the state of the crisis, noted:

> The Japanese, while accusing the US of desiring to use the injured as 'guinea pigs,' are in fact doing this themselves. Although it is generally agreed that the hospital in Yaizu is unable to provide adequate treatment for the crew members, professional jealousies and bickering by the local doctors have so far prevented their movement to Tokyo . . . The press is continuing its emotional outbursts and otherwise responsible scientists and other prominent individuals are indulging in a similar vein.[41]

Moreover, almost a month later there were no signs of any improvement in the situation. At a meeting of the Embassy–FEC consultative group, it was clear that the Americans were growing increasingly frustrated by continued inaccurate press reporting and the apparent refusal to acknowledge earlier US offers of assistance:

> Mr. Leonhart . . . summarized the happenings of the last two weeks. He stated that Drs. Eisenbud and Morton left a few days ago after three weeks of Japanese non-co-operation and refusal of US offers of assistance. He referred to stories appearing in the April 21 press stating that the patients were getting worse and asking for assistance from any quarter. Mr. Leonhart pointed out that we have been permitted to examine only two patients thoroughly, that we have never been given full information on the patients' condition, that the Japanese have failed to give us promised clinical data and that the offers of assistance by Drs. Morton and Eisenbud and more recently by Dr. Lewis, Chief of Medicine on the Atomic Bomb Casualty Commission, have been ignored.[42]

US irritation with the local reaction quickly extended into a broader criticism of the Japanese government. American frustration was not based on a substantive disagreement with senior government officials, but rather on a sense of poor internal co-ordination in the Japanese government itself,[43] and a belief that the Yoshida and his government were not doing enough to correct the inaccurate and damaging press reports.[44] To what extent was this frustration justified? As far as public and press reaction to the nuclear issue was concerned it seems fair to assume that much of the reporting was overly speculative, attributing the worst intentions to the Americans.[45]

There is some evidence to suggest that the Japanese authorities compounded the crisis and that some senior figures in the government, out of domestic political considerations rather than any particular concern for the well-being of the fishermen, may have deliberately sought to exploit the tension with the United States. In general, the Yoshida government's response appeared slow, unfocused and at times contradictory. Shortly after the crisis broke, a Japanese inter-ministerial committee consisting of the principal civil servants from six ministries was established to co-ordinate the government's response. Meanwhile, in the Diet, the government maintained a united position, with the Foreign Minister, Okazaki Katsuo, refusing to condemn the US tests.[46] Yet these early Japanese efforts took place in March. As the American files reveal, by April, the government had still failed to counter the spate of damaging press reports. This problem continued throughout the remainder of the year. Senior officials in Washington, while apparently able to reassure their counterparts in Tokyo, were losing the public relations battle with Japan as a whole, a shortcoming which the Americans attributed, in part, to the absence of strong Japanese leadership. As one US report in October noted:

> The complex emotional reactions of the Japanese, particularly as sensationally represented in their press, to United States actions and policies, the threat of nuclear warfare, and the growth of Communist power in Asia have tended more and more to prejudice United States-Japanese relationships. . . . While the Japanese Government has demonstrated a sense of trust and confidence in the willingness and determination of the United States to assist in the realization of Japan's legitimate national aspirations, the failure of the Japanese Government to exert strong leadership, to resolve intra-conservative factionalism and to combat intellectual and neutralist tendencies affords a latent threat to Japan's political stability and consequently to its ability to co-operate effectively with the United States and the free world.[47]

The Japanese government's inability or reluctance to manage the problem might simply have been due to institutional inertia, a shortcoming exacerbated by a tendency to send confusing signals to the Americans. For example, Japanese press reports in late March highlighted internal ministerial tensions in the Japanese government as MoFA officials struggled unsuccessfully to persuade their Education and Health and Welfare Ministry colleagues to encourage Japan's doctors and scientists to work with US officials in a joint treatment programme for the crew members of the Lucky Dragon.[48] Similar tensions surfaced the following month when the Kyodo wire service leaked news of a forthcoming report from the Ministry of Health and Welfare criticizing American medical personnel for failing to provide treatment for the crew members despite alleged repeated requests from Japan for assistance. Given past US offers of help, it is no surprise that Allison responded immediately to this news, contacting Okazaki, the foreign minister, to protest against the criticism in the strongest possible terms. For its part, MoFA responded quickly, admitting that the report was irresponsible and damaging to bilateral relations, while noting that it would be held back from publication for revision and that in future MoFA officials would assist the Health and Welfare Ministry in its press briefings.[49]

Notwithstanding the MoFA's damage control, there were other issues which continued to expose serious internal divisions on the Japanese side. By late May, the problem of financial compensation had emerged as a source of disagreement between the two governments. Bilateral negotiations revolved around Japanese pressure for indirect (but at the same time unquantifiable) damages and US irritation at Japan's refusal to agree to a rapid settlement,[50] differences which can in part be attributed to the hard-line position of Andō Masazumi, the minister of state heading Japan's inter-ministerial committee who, as a former purgee, may have 'had personal political motives for publicly rejecting' US offers of compensation and whose combative approach was popular with Japanese opinion.[51] Andō's stance was, as Sakamoto Kazuya has pointed out, one among several different views within the government. Although senior MoFA officials privately informed US embassy personnel that they disagreed with the tactics over compensation,[52] the issue continued to exacerbate an already tense relationship throughout 1954. When Allison was finally able to persuade his superiors in Washington to agree to an increased settlement of $1,000,000 some on the Japanese side ratcheted up the tension by demanding an additional $1,000,000 in payment, citing as justification the additional time that had elapsed since the start of the compensation talks. Even though both Yoshida and Okazaki privately informed Allison that the increased demand was excessive and not in Japan's long-term interests,[53] the Japanese government appeared powerless to resist pressure from both interest groups (mainly fishermen) and individual ministers (Andō and Hori, the minister of agriculture) for the additional payment and eventually (in January 1955) the US agreed to a $2,000,000 settlement.

Andō, it should be stressed, was not the only senior Japanese official willing to play to the public gallery. On 9 and 10 August, Ikeda Hayato, a senior government official and protégé of the prime minister, on two separate occasions (a press conference and a national meeting of all the local branches of the Liberal Party) claimed in off-the-record remarks, critical in tone, that the June–July Geneva conference demonstrated the failure of America's 'roll-back strategy' of resisting communism in Vietnam, and that in light of this Japan should distance itself from the US and move closer towards the Soviet Union.[54]

The remarks generated little interest in Japan, but were picked up by startled US embassy personnel. A shocked Allison wrote to Washington, noting that Ikeda's remarks suggested that Japan was an unreliable ally, unprincipled and willing to sell itself to the highest bidder.[55] It is not immediately clear what motivated Ikeda. Ishii Osamu has suggested four competing explanations: the remarks may have been internally directed and a way of deflecting criticism of the Yoshida administration from both the Japanese left and right wings, by ostensibly distancing the government from the United States. Less plausibly, the reference may have been merely a slip of the tongue, as Iguchi Sadao (the Japanese ambassador in Washington) suggested to Robert Murphy, the US undersecretary of state. Alternatively, Ikeda may have been motivated by purely personal considerations. Yoshida, at this stage, was politically beleaguered and there was widespread speculation that he would soon be eclipsed by rival conservative politicians: Ikeda may have been attempting to distance himself from his political mentor while also appealing to other conservative factions. Finally, the critical remarks may have been externally focused. By implying that Japan's commitment to its partnership with the US was vulnerable, Ikeda may have been angling for further economic assistance from the Americans. This interpretation would be consistent with Allison's analysis.[56] Whatever the reason behind Ikeda's comments, there is little doubt that many Japanese conservatives believed that criticizing the United States was politically advantageous and a way of boosting their electoral chances. Treating the alliance in a cavalier fashion for immediate electoral and personal gain would clearly have done little to strengthen bilateral relations against an already volatile and tension-fraught background.

Scientific shortcomings

It is important to keep in mind that Japan was not alone in registering intense alarm following the Bikini test. Even before the full circumstances of the Lucky Dragon Incident had become known, the simple magnitude of the new super-bomb had raised fears world-wide. In Britain, Churchill, the then prime minister, faced considerable pressure in the Commons from a Labour opposition demanding to be informed of the details of the test and calling for a ban on further testing. The Prime Minister himself was deeply disturbed by the weapon, worrying that a single comparable device detonated off the coast of Britain might saturate the country with radioactive fallout. By April, Pope Pius XII and Albert Schweitzer had expressed grave concern and Prime Minister Nehru of India had joined the chorus of voices advocating a moratorium on testing.[57] However, there were particular elements of the Japanese experience which made the reaction in Japan more pronounced than elsewhere. The bombing of Hiroshima and Nagasaki was obviously a critical factor, but so too was the process of interaction with American authorities, particularly representatives of the ABCC, in the years after 1945. This experience had given the Japanese powerful reasons to discount the findings and advice of the US in matters relating to radiation exposure.

The critical controversy was the debate over the effects of residual radiation. While it was accepted that massive, instantaneous radiation exposure following the detonation of an atomic bomb would have lethal results for humans, there was no such certainty about the biomedical and genetic effects associated with living in an environment in which background levels of radiation may have increased markedly as a result of an explosion. Shortly after the war ended, a number of Japanese scientists, some with experience in researching radiobiology, had begun to explore this question, increasingly sceptical (on the basis of their own field-work) of US reassurances in 1945 that residual radiation was not harmful. Their efforts were reinforced when the Japanese Welfare Ministry organized a long-range study of the genetic effects of the Hiroshima and Nagasaki bombings. The study led to a series of findings, but at the time, because of occupation censorship, these were not published.[58]

Frustrations and suspicions associated with censorship were aggravated by the approach adopted by US researchers exploring the issue of residual radiation. In 1947, the AEC had launched its own programme to examine the long-term effects of the atomic bombing, to be carried out by ABCC officials in Japan.[59] However, as Sue Rabbitt Roff has pointed out in her highly detailed study, the project was crucially flawed from the very start because of suspect methodology and the distorting professional ambitions of the US scientists engaged in the project. Further, economic pressures and federal government desires to persuade American public opinion of the safety of the emerging nuclear power industry in the United States also limited the scope of the enquiry. US officials were anxious to avoid any suggestion that background radiation might be in any way harmful, a finding, which, it was feared, would encourage a rash of claims for compensation from individuals living close to nuclear power plants.[60] Linked to this was a general desire by the American authorities to allay public fears that a possible future conflict involving nuclear weapons would be catastrophic. In the early years of the nuclear era, as part of the developing civil defence programme and in order to support claims that a nuclear war was winnable, the US government sought to persuade the American public that an atomic attack was survivable by detailing practical steps for guarding against the dangers of radiation.[61]

In light of these serious shortcomings, it is understandable why, both in 1954 and subsequently, the ABCC was viewed with suspicion by some in Japan. Bound up in this distrust was a set of emotional issues, which almost inevitably ensured that the American scientists would receive a cool reception. From the perspective of the ABCC, examining the survivors of the atomic bombings was purely a scientific exercise lacking a humanitarian dimension. For the affected civilians, by contrast, there was the much more immediate and personal need to receive treatment and care from the informed and technologically sophisticated Americans. Since the US government had designed, built and deployed the bomb, surely it would be fair to assume that it could, if not should, help those who had been exposed to its effects.

Over time, State Department officials (including Allison) did recognize the need to provide assistance to the Japanese, but this appears to have been motivated largely by a desire to reduce antagonism towards the ABCC and also to encourage more individuals to participate in the biomedical research programme. Moreover, this initiative came late in the day.[62] In 1954, the ABCC had no adequate facilities for examining patients, other than a small and understaffed diagnostic clinic.[63] The first serious efforts to co-operate with the Japanese government occurred only in November 1955, involving mainly the provision of ABCC data, the offer of medical consultations for A-bomb survivors, and the creation of a Japanese Advisory Council (JAC) to the ABCC.[64] Co-operation increased gradually as the Japanese, in conjunction with the development of their own healthcare programme, agreed in 1957 to refer increasing numbers of patients to the ABCC.[65] However, the degree of common effort should not be exaggerated. It was only in the early 1960s that a joint document (endorsed by both the ABCC and the Japanese government) was issued, one of the earliest cases of the publication of results simultaneously in Japanese and English. However, even in this instance, the study employed the same flawed assumptions of the initial American studies.[66]

From the perspective of Japanese public opinion, it would be easy to conclude that the unhelpful and misleading American approach on the residual radiation issue was directed at Japan. Proof, in effect, that US interest in a co-operative alliance relationship was synthetic rather than genuine. Yet, this would be to misinterpret a general weakness in American policy as a specific failing in the bilateral relationship. It is important to recognize that much of the US nuclear programme, in both the testing and in the development of nuclear power, placed the concerns of the Federal government and the Cold War demands ahead of the interests of individuals and communities, within and outside the United States. American civilians as much as foreign nationals were caught in the literal and the broader environmental fall-out associated with the intense political and strategic pressures to develop the power of the atom. It is worth emphasizing that nuclear tests continued within the continental United States after the CASTLE series, often involving cases where the AEC deliberately minimized or distorted the health-risks associated with testing.[67] Japan had not been singled out for special treatment, whatever Japanese popular fears and press reports may have suggested.

Naturally, this raises the larger question of how much of the US nuclear programme was based on self-deception and a refusal to scrutinize inconvenient scientific findings and how much rested on a wilful disregard of the dangers associated with nuclear testing in general. The problem is a complex one and cannot be resolved here. However, setting the events of 1954 in this context helps to clarify the motivations and reactions of the Japanese and American participants. State Department officials in Tokyo, for example, confronted by the pressures of daily diplomacy, were unlikely to have had any reason to question the advice they were receiving from their scientific advisers in Washington. Moreover, neither would they have been privy to the wider detailed debate taking place between physicists and radiobiologists, a controversy which, after all, would take more than a decade to resolve.[68] Under these circumstances, it is perhaps reasonable to argue that the Lucky Dragon crisis was virtually unavoidable. Contrary to the suggestion of some commentators at the time that the US could have side-stepped much of the controversy if it had acted in a more straightforward fashion,[69] a combination of chance events and conflicting global pressures and local sensibilities inevitably triggered a major diplomatic incident.

Resolving the crisis

Any balanced assessment of America's handling of the Lucky Dragon Incident needs to consider what more the Eisenhower administration could, or should have done, to dampen bilateral tensions. Senior US government figures, including the president, were well aware of the delicate state of relations with Japan in 1954, but to some extent their hands were tied. The very weakness of the Yoshida administration and the confused state of Japanese domestic politics acted as a constraint, preventing a rapid solution. A stronger government in Tokyo, it could be argued, would have been better placed to defuse some of the more strident press criticisms of the United States, as well as taking firmer action to ensure a speedier resolution of the compensation issue than eventually occurred.

Yoshida's problems, in part, simply reflected the continued decline in popularity of the Liberal Party, a steady trend which had been continuing since 1949.[70]

April 1953 saw the start of the fifth Yoshida Cabinet (the previous premier had been Ashida Hitoshi who had served for only six months, from March to October 1948) and by the beginning of 1954, the government appeared to be nearing the end of its natural life.[71] By the spring, a damaging 'shipbuilding scandal' had been exposed, in which two of Yoshida's senior faction members, Satō Eisaku and Ikeda Hayato, were implicated. By the end of April, it seemed inevitable that Satō would be arrested, but at the last minute, the Ministry of Justice, citing executive privilege, intervened and prevented the Public Prosecutors Office from carrying out the arrest. Satō's political career was saved, but the reputation of the government was seriously tarnished.[72] The government's poor public image was further undermined by a damaging political fight over its attempt to introduce legislation limiting the autonomy of local police forces and creating a National Public Safety Commission. The legislation was bitterly opposed by socialist politicians and the controversy erupted into fighting in the Diet and the forced detention of the speaker of the Lower House in an effort by the socialists to prevent an extension of the Diet session, needed to pass the legislation. The new measures were only enacted following police intervention and a socialist boycott of the Diet proceedings.[73] Amidst all this controversy, Yoshida had been forced to postpone until November a planned visit to Europe and the United States, which he had been hoping to make during the summer.

It would be tempting to explain Yoshida's problems and the absence of stable government in Japan as simply a reflection of the prime minister's personal unpopularity. 'One-man' Yoshida was seen as arrogant and a popular target for critics on both the right and the left, either for appearing too dependent on the United States, or for attempting to introduce legislative measures which the socialist and communists viewed as illiberal and anti-democratic. However, Yoshida's difficulties reflected a deeper set of problems. As the intense conflict over the new police legislation revealed, much of the polarization between the forces of the left and right during 1954 revolved around the question of the US-imposed post-war Constitution and the legacy of the occupation. To the right, the Constitution was seen as an alien document, imposed from outside and at odds with Japanese culture and tradition, and a broad swathe of conservative politicians were strongly in favour of constitutional revision. For the left, by contrast, the Constitution represented a bulwark against the past, preventing any return to the militarism and reactionary trends of the 1930s while safeguarding the values of freedom and democratic government.

Under these conditions, one might have imagined a United States government inclined to support moderate left-of-centre political opinion, individuals committed to the democratic process, but also critical of the autocratic character of Soviet or Chinese communism. Yet, such forces did not exist (at least not in a prominent, influential capacity) and the left–right split in Japan never resembled such a neat, analytically convenient dichotomy. The JCP, weakened by doctrinal differences and Japanese public opinion's distrust of its radicalism, had experienced a massive decline in political influence. Between 1949 and 1953 JCP Lower House Diet seats dropped from 35 to one.[74] The socialists, on the other hand, had seen their electoral fortunes steadily improve after 1949, and while Liberal support had fallen consistently over this period, it was offset by the increase in the popularity of the non-Liberal conservative parties.[75] Moreover, left and right continued to be fiercely divided over ideological issues and there was no sign of a consensus on the structures and institutions which should govern Japanese political life. [76]

Under these conditions there was little, if anything, that Washington could do overtly to promote political stability within Japan. However, behind the scenes, the US employed a range of measures designed to strengthen Japanese ties with America as well as attempting to counterbalance the appeal of the left and the alleged effects of Soviet-directed propaganda initiatives. The Fulbright and Smith-Mundt exchange programmes brought Japanese teachers and researchers to the United States; the United States Information Agency (USIA) established information centres in Japan's major cities which were widely used by Japanese citizens (14 centres existed in 1954); Voice of America broadcasts were frequently relayed over the domestic network; indirect support was provided for the translation and publication of English-language material in Japanese; prominent Japanese individuals were contacted in an effort to promote the US position; USIA funding subsidized anti-Communist periodicals and films; and unattributed written material was provided to Japanese writers and editors in an effort to encourage favourable commentary in the media.[77]

Many of these initiatives reflected the legacy of the Psychological Strategy Board (PSB), set up during the Truman administration and the forerunner of the Operations Co-ordinating Board. In April 1952, planners from the CIA and the State and Defense Departments had begun work on designing a psychological strategy directed at Japan, which by early January 1953, led to the approval of PSB D-27.[78] Although the precise content of this plan remains unclear, by 1954, senior figures in the administration recognized the limits of America's own propaganda machinery, and in October officials in Washington wrote to Allison bemoaning the 'diminishing objectivity in Japanese vernacular press reporting', while arguing that PSB D-27 was insufficiently detailed and would, therefore, be reassessed by the OCB.[79]

Despite the shortcomings of the early PSB initiative, there was one area in which a concerted public relations campaign might work in America's favour. Ever since Eisenhower's 'Atoms for Peace' speech before the United Nations in December 1953, in which he proposed that the nuclear powers provide fissile material for peaceful purposes to a new International Atomic Energy Agency, the United States had been well placed to promote the non-offensive merits of nuclear energy. In terms of the relationship with Japan, this could take the form of working with the Japanese government to develop a civilian nuclear power programme. Early in the post-war period, the Japanese scientific community was ready to pursue research into nuclear issues,[80] and by 1954, shortly after news of the Lucky Dragon Incident had emerged, US officials recognized that sharing nuclear technology with Japan might help contain the crisis. An OCB report of 22 March, for example, recommended that the US should offer to build an experimental nuclear reactor in Japan, pointing out that 'a vigorous offensive on the non-war uses of atomic energy would appear to be a timely and effective way of countering the expected Russian [propaganda] effort and minimizing the harm already done in Japan'.[81]

During 1954, the US embassy in Japan launched a series of initiatives promoting the virtues of nuclear energy, which appeared to be positively received by Japanese public opinion. A small atomic energy exhibition in Tokyo, for example, attracted large crowds,[82] while a similar display in Toyama, between April and June, also passed peacefully – 'no hostility and no incidents resulted' – and attracted more than 800,000 visitors.[83] Seminars, lectures, films and displays were organized in Tokyo and

> attracted very favorable response and hearty participation by responsible Japanese scientists and intellectual and civic leaders. Over 100,000 people have been directly reached by these activities, which included ward by ward showing of atomic energy films and insertion of these films in a mass 'peace' rally in Tokyo.[84]

USIA and embassy officials in Japan were quick to stress the benefits of promoting peaceful nuclear power, arguing that 'the great majority of Japanese are receptive to US information on the peaceful uses of atomic energy, provided that it is presented creditably and with due respect for Japanese sensibilities.'[85] Moreover, US efforts were well received by both official and public opinion. In October, the Japanese government made clear to the US that it would respond positively to a planned proposal to establish a small, experimental reactor in Japan for educational purposes,[86] and by early 1955, it was clear to the Americans that the Japanese authorities were focused on developing, with US support, their own nuclear power programme. As a State Department intelligence report noted, 'The Japanese reacted most favorably to hints that the US might assist in a reactor development programme in Japan and have appropriated funds and despatched experts to this country and Europe in an effort to further their atomic energy development.'[87]

In general, the Americans recognized the importance of working in close co-operation with the Japanese authorities in the area of peaceful development of nuclear energy, and by late 1955 there were signs that the distrust that had been so prominent during 1954 had begun to abate. Promoting nuclear energy was a sustained initiative in which US officials took pains to provide reliable information, and as a USIA report from Tokyo observed:

> The Agency's largest and best exhibit on atomic energy opened in Tokyo, November 1, under joint sponsorship with Yomiuri newspaper and with opening messages from the President and other high US and Japanese officials. This exhibit is complete, accurate and clear enough to satisfy a discriminating scientist. It will tour Japan for at least a year and should make a lasting impression on intellectuals and public alike.[88]

Extolling the virtues of nuclear energy was, it should be stressed, only a partial means of tackling Japan's nuclear allergy. Testing remained a controversial issue (both in Japan and world-wide), and in August 1955, some 30 million Japanese signed a petition calling for a total ban on nuclear testing.[89] Yet the United States remained committed to developing its nuclear arsenal and in early 1956 announced plans to carry out a new series of thermonuclear tests in the Pacific. Surprisingly, the American announcement provoked little immediate press commentary in Japan, partly because Washington leaked the news of the tests gradually (the embassy in Tokyo had informed MoFA well in advance), and also because the Diet was out of session, ensuring that the socialists and groups most strongly opposed to testing were poorly placed to respond swiftly. Also, America was not alone. The Russians had recently carried out nuclear tests and the British had publicized their own plans to carry out tests in Australian waters. Moreover, the past two years of association with the development of the peaceful uses of nuclear power may have encouraged Japanese opinion to feel less isolated and singled out in terms of exposure to the harmful effects of testing. As Allison noted in a cable to Secretary of State Dulles, 'Japan has been brought into international "atomic community" as participant – no longer stands on outside as unwilling observer or "innocent victim".'[90]

Nevertheless, US officials were taking no chances in preparing for the tests. The experience of 1954 had clearly impressed on them the need to pay close attention to Japanese sensibilities. Jeff Parsons, in the US embassy in Tokyo wrote to Washington to recommend a series of precautionary measures including providing funding to cover the expenses of Japanese ships forced to make detours to avoid the test site; acknowledging US willingness to provide ex-gratia compensation if any damage should result from the test; and inviting the Japanese government to participate in a scientific survey to check for the possible contamination of fish in the region of the tests. Even with such measures, Parsons feared that reaction in Japan would almost certainly be negative. State Department personnel were very conscious of the risk of a repetition of the events of 1954, but at the same time displayed an almost fatalistic expectation that events might spiral out of control again. In Parsons' words:

> It now appears inevitable that test series will create in Japan serious political and propaganda problems even without repetition of the Fukuryu Maru incident . . . Probably needless to point out that should unforeseen incident occur as a result of tests (e.g. contamination of fish or injury to fishing craft) reaction here would be immediate and explosive and our efforts to counteract after the fact would very likely be almost completely unsuccessful.[91]

Washington appeared to take the State Department's advice seriously and sought to defuse the crisis in advance. An official note was issued to the Japanese authorities, incorporating some of Parsons' suggestions as well as highlighting past international initiatives by the Eisenhower administration to limit the spread of nuclear weapons and monitor the effects of radiation.[92] In the end, the embassy's fears were not confirmed, and in general the Japanese response to the tests was relatively muted, or at least mixed. While politicians and press reports criticized the United States, there was no wave of critical editorials and front-page attention comparable to 1954, and some papers, such as *Yomiuri Shinbun*, even highlighted the 'over-nervousness' of some Japanese to the issue of radioactivity.[93] Moreover, the Japanese government, although opposed to the tests in principle, attempted to allay fears in advance and went out of its way to head off any damaging political repercussions. For example, prior to the tests, the Japanese authorities announced publicly that they would seek to co-ordinate test arrangements with the United States. Similarly, the Health and Welfare Ministry was careful to point out that the radioactivity ingested in the Bikini tests of 1954 had not been sufficient to warrant destroying fish stocks, and a Japanese survey vessel, staffed by scientists, was sent to the test area to monitor the results of the explosion.[94]

In the wake of the Lucky Dragon Incident, it is difficult to determine precisely the extent to which US actions alone averted further crises over the nuclear issue, either in 1956 or subsequently. Both governments, it seemed, had learnt valuable lessons from the events of 1954 and were concerned to avoid exposing the bilateral relationship to unnecessary strain. At the same time, testing remained a contentious issue during the second half of the decade. For example, the administration of Kishi Nobusuke (prime minister after February 1957), was concerned about the global risks associated with nuclear fallout and publicly pushed for an end to, or at the very least a suspension of, testing both in the Pacific and in the continental United States.[95] Moreover, the Diet periodically issued resolutions calling for an end to testing and in favour of nuclear disarmament. In response, the United States tended to discount the wider health hazards, while restating the importance of strategic readiness and technological sophistication.[96] However, senior American policy makers remained well aware of the sensitivity of the nuclear issue in Japan. Eisenhower, at the suggestion of his secretary of state, was careful to write publicly to Kishi setting out the US position in favour of continued testing,[97] while Dulles himself took pains on occasion to demonstrate American appreciation of the Japanese position.[98]

It is striking to note that in 1958 there was a near repeat performance of the 1954 disaster. During nuclear tests near Eniwetok in the Marshall islands, two Japanese Maritime Safety Bureau ships, despite being well outside the test zone, were exposed to radiation levels sufficiently high to cause a considerable drop in the white blood-cell counts of some of the crew-members.[99] At the time, US officials, including the ambassador in Tokyo, Douglas MacArthur II, were very conscious of the risk this posed to bilateral relations. However, remarkably, 'the tests were concluded without arousing serious Japanese opposition or creating serious friction between the United States and Japan'.[100] The absence of tension was noteworthy not only because of the irradiation of the Japanese sailors, but also in light of the Soviet Union's announcement of its unilateral suspension of testing and the publication by the United Nations Scientific Community of a report analysing the effects of radiation, two events which, one imagines, might also have swung public opinion against the United States. Yet, while the Japanese remained 'opposed to nuclear testing, their opposition [was] now largely passive in character'.[101]

Part of the reason for the lack of a Japanese reaction may have been the altered international political context in which testing was taking place. Since 1957, Eisenhower had publicly become much more actively committed to seeking a solution to the question of testing. In April 1958, the President had proposed setting up an international committee of experts to explore ways of monitoring and enforcing a possible international test ban, and by August he had announced that the United States would temporarily halt testing for a year if the Soviets agreed to do the same.[102] In April 1959, Eisenhower went one step further and proposed to Khrushchev a limited ban on atmospheric testing. While agreement between Moscow and Washington on a partial test ban treaty would only be reached in 1963 during the Kennedy administration, it is conceivable that Japanese opinion had been encouraged by the earlier US initiatives, although it would be surprising if this were the only factor accounting for the subdued Japanese reaction to the Eniwetok test. It seems reasonable to conclude that the US initiative to encourage the development of a peaceful nuclear power industry, as well as American efforts to inform Japanese public and official opinion of future tests, while taking precautions to guard against future disasters, may have removed some of the tension and distrust that was prominent in 1954.

None of this, of course, detracts from the very real failings of the United States in handling the Lucky Dragon Incident initially. However, these earlier shortcomings were linked to issues that went beyond the bilateral relationship, most notably Cold War strategic priorities, institutional hubris, scientific shortcomings, and the blinkered approach to testing in general as well as the pressure to develop the nuclear industry within the United States. Added to this were the crucial ingredients of weak leadership and domestic political instability in Japan, caused in part by the ideological tension associated with the post-war constitution. Responsibility for the crisis, therefore, rests with governments both in Japan and the United States, and in certain important respects predates the decisions of the Eisenhower administration. Consequently, although it is legitimate to attack particular American actions in 1954, Washington's handling of the bilateral relationship, when viewed in a wider context, should be interpreted less critically.

Notes

1 This article represents a much-abbreviated version of an original piece, first published in J. Swenson-Wright, *Unequal Allies: United States Security and Alliance Policy Toward Japan, 1945–1960*, Stanford, California: Stanford University Press, 2005. I am very grateful to Stanford for permission to include this article here.

2 R. Dingman, 'Alliances in crisis: the Lucky Dragon Incident and Japanese–American relations,' in W. I. Cohen and Akira Iriye, eds, *The Great Powers in East Asia: 1953–1960*, New York, NY: Columbia University Press, 1990, p. 188.

3 R. Buckley, *US–Japan Alliance Diplomacy, 1945–1990*, Cambridge: Cambridge University Press, 1992, p. 58.

4 R. Rhodes, *Dark Sun: The Making of the Hydrogen Bomb*, New York, NY: Simon and Schuster, 1995, p. 542.

5 R. Lapp, *The Voyage of the Lucky Dragon*, London: Frederick Muller, 1958, p. 23.
6 Eisenhower Library (hereafter EL), Abilene, Kansas, White House Office (WHO), National Security Council (NSC) Staff, Operations Coordinating Board (OCB) Central Files, Box 8, 'US Position with Respect to Injury and Damages resulting from Pacific Nuclear Test', 30 March 1954
7 Dingman, 'Alliances in crisis', p. 188.
8 Rhodes, *Dark Sun*, p. 541.
9 Ibid., p. 542.
10 Lapp, *Voyage of the Lucky Dragon*, pp. 43–9.
11 Ibid., p. 67.
12 Ibid., p. 75.
13 R. Hewlett and J. Holl, *Atoms for Peace and War, 1953–1961: Eisenhower and the Atomic Energy Commission*, Berkeley, CA: University of California Press, pp. 175–6.
14 Lapp, *Voyage of the Lucky Dragon*, p. 108.
15 Ibid., pp. 76–86.
16 Ibid., p. 111.
17 S. Dockrill, *Eisenhower's New Look National Security Policy, 1953–1961*, London: Macmillan, 1996, p. 4.
18 Ibid., p. 66.
19 Ibid., p. 93.
20 'Kojireta Nichibei kankei', *Asahi Shinbun*, 9 April 1954, p. 1.
21 Hewlett and Holl, *Atoms for Peace and War*, p. 176.
22 Lapp, *Voyage of the Lucky Dragon*, p. 105.
23 EL, WHO, NSC Staff, OCB Central Files, Box 8, 'US Position with Respect to Injury and Damages Resulting from Pacific Nuclear Test', 30 March 1954
24 J. Allison, *Ambassador from the Prairie, or Allison Wonderland*, Boston, MA: Houghton Mifflin, 1973, p. 265.
25 EL, 'US Position with Respect to Injury and Damages Resulting from Pacific Nuclear Test'.
26 Hewlett and Holl, *Atoms for Peace and War*, p. 176.
27 Ibid., p. 170.
28 Ibid., p. 14.
29 National Archives, Washington DC (hereafter NA Washington), Van Fleet Report, 1954, Record Group (RG) 330, Box 11, 'Japan', undated section of draft report
30 Diplomatic Record Office, Tokyo (hereafter DRO), Sect. 11, A'-0134/2/0335–342, Ōbei ikka kankei hikitsugu jikkō', 29 March 1954.
31 O. Ishii, *Reisen to Nichibei kankei: pātonāshippu no keisei*, Tokyo: Japan Times, 1989, p. 212.
32 Allison, *Ambassador from the Prairie*, p. 263.
33 Ishii, *Reisen to Nichibei kankei*, p. 212.
34 Ibid., p. 212–3.
35 Lapp, *Voyage of the Lucky Dragon*, p. 127.
36 EL, WHO, NSC Staff, OCB Central Files, Box 8, 'Outline check list of US Government actions to offset unfavourable Japanese attitudes to the H-bomb and related developments', 22 April 1954.
37 EL, WHO, NSC Staff, OCB Central Files, Box 48, OCB working group on NSC125/2 and NSC125/6, meeting minutes, 26 August 1954.
38 Dingman, 'Alliances in crisis', p. 202.
39 Ibid., p. 193.
40 DRO, Sect. 11, A'-0134/2/0335–342, 'Ōbei ikka kankei hikitsugu jikkō', 29 March 1954.
41 NA Washington, Office of Northeast Asian Affairs (ONEAA), RG59, Lot 57D149, Records of the Bureau of Far Eastern Affairs, alpha-numeric file on Japan, 1941–1953

[sic], minutes of the tenth meeting of Embassy–FEC Consultative Group, 24 March 1954.

42 NA Washington, Records of the Bureau of Far Eastern Affairs, ONEAA, RG59, Lot 57D149, alpha-numeric file on Japan, 1941–1953 [sic], minutes of the twelfth meeting of Embassy–FEC Consultative Group, 21 April 21 1954n.

43 NA Washington, WHO, NSC Staff, OCB Central Files, Box 8, John MacDonald to Elmer B. Staats, 'Japanese Fishing Boat Incident,' 14 April 1954.

44 NA Washington, minutes of the twelfth meeting of Embassy–FEC Consultative Group, 21 April 1954.

45 The Americans were not alone in criticizing the Japanese media's response to the crisis. In London, Hugh Cortazzi, a junior in the Foreign Office, noted in an internal minute on the Bikini crisis the 'Japanese hysteria over the death of Mr. Kuboyama and the anti-American tendencies of the Japanese press'. NA Kew, F0 371/110462, FJ 1241/3, 'Bikini Atom bomb Explosion', 2 October 1954. Similarly, some weeks earlier, Cortazzi had observed, again in connection with Bikini:

> Waves of anti-American feeling have occurred periodically in Japan since the signing of the Peace Treaty . . . [These] outbursts tend to be exaggerated by the press and in the Diet and do not reflect accurately the feelings of ordinary Japanese in the countryside. Nevertheless they are dangerous because they provide emotional material for extreme left and extreme right . . . Japanese medicine and science generally tend to be out of touch with latest developments and the accuracy of the observations of Japanese Scientists is open to question. It seems clear that on many of the occasions on which tuna fish have been condemned as contaminated and accordingly destroyed, the scientific observations leading up to this decision have been unreliable. Reports of 'atomic rain', 'atomic cows' and even 'atomic milk' have been caused more by emotional fears than real observations.
>
> NA Kew, FO 371/110462, FJ 1241/2, 'Bikini A-Bomb Explosion', 16 September 1954.

46 Dingman, 'Alliances in crisis', p. 194.

47 EL, 'OCB Progress Report on NSC 125/2 and NSC 125/6,' 27 October 1954.

48 'Bikini hisaisha o meguri – gakusha, jishusei o shuchō,' *Asahi Shinbun*, 23 1954, p. 7.

49 K. Sakamoto, 'Kakuheiki to Nichibei kankei – Bikini jiken no gaikō shori,' in *Kindai Nihon Kenkyūkai*, 1994, p. 250.

50 Dingman, 'Alliances in crisis', p. 197.

51 Ibid., p. 200.

52 Sakamoto, 'Kakuheiki to Nichibei kankei', p. 255

53 Ibid., p. 257.

54 Ishii, *Reisen to Nichibei kankei*, p. 138.

55 Ibid., p. 139.

56 Ibid., p. 140.

57 Ibid., p. 274.

58 S. R. Roff, *Hotspots: The Legacy of Hiroshima and Nagasaki*, London: Cassell, 1995, p. 70.

59 Ibid., p. 63.

60 Ibid., p. 44.

61 Ibid., p. 47.

62 Japanese authorities also dragged their feet on this issue. It was only in 1957 that the Japanese government, in response to pressure from survivors, enacted a Law Concerning Medical Care for A-bomb Victims. Yet, the level of support was minimal and followed some 'twelve years of total neglect'. See S. Tachibana, 'The quest for

a peace culture: the A-bomb survivors' long struggle and the new movement for redressing foreign victims of Japan's war', *Diplomatic History* 19, 2 (Spring), 1995, p. 337.

63 Roff, *Hotspots*, pp. 114–15.
64 Ibid., pp. 140–1.
65 Ibid., p. 172.
66 Ibid., pp. 191–2.
67 Hewlett and Holl, *Atoms for Peace and War*, pp. 154–8.
68 Roff, *Hotspots*, p. 184.
69 See, for example, Lapp, *Voyage of the Lucky Dragon*, p. 129.
70 H. Borton, 'Politics and the Future of Democracy in Japan' in H. Borton (ed) *Japan between East and West*, New York: Harper, 1957, p. 10.
71 Ishii, *Reisen to Nichibei kankei*, p. 204.
72 Ibid., p. 205.
73 Borton, op. cit., pp. 15–6.
74 EL, WHO, NSC Staff, OCB Central Files, Box 47, 'OCB progress report on NSC 125/2 and NSC125/6', 27 October 1954.
75 Borton, op. cit., pp. 10–11; M. Kōno, *Japan's Postwar Party Politics*, Princeton, NJ: Princeton University Press, 1997, pp. 65–6.
76 EL, 'OCB Progress Report on NSC 125/2 and NSC125/6', 27 October 1954.
77 Ibid.
78 Ishii, *Reisen to Nichibei kankei*, pp. 113–7.
79 EL, WHO, NSC Staff, OCB Central Files, Robertson to Allison, 22 October 1954.
80 NA Washington, RG319, G-3, Operations, 1950–51, Box 118, 'Review of policies governing Japanese research in nuclear physics and related fields and stockpiles of radioactive materials in Japan', 28 February 1950.
81 EL, WHO, NSC Staff, OCB Central Files, Box 8, 'Japan and atomic tests', 22 March 1954.
82 EL, WHO, NSC Staff, OCB Central Files, Box 8, Working Group on NSC125/1 and 125/6, 5 May 1954.
83 EL, WHO, NSC Staff, OCB Central Files, Box 8, 'Tokyo trade fair', 5 November 1954
84 Ibid.
85 Ibid.
86 EL, WHO, NSC Staff, OCB Central Files, Box 48, Working Group on NSC 125/2 and NSC 125/6, 6 October 1954.
87 EL, WHO, Office of the Special Assistant for Disarmament (Harold Stassen), Records, 1955–58, Box 5, 'Recent effects of increasing nuclear capabilities on US allies', Intelligence estimate, 72, 16 February 1955.
88 EL, WHO, NSC Staff, OCB Central Files, Box 48, USIA Contribution to OCB Working Group Paper on Japanese Intellectuals, 4 November 1955.
89 J. Weisgall, *Operation Crossroads: The Atomic Tests at Bikini Atoll*, Annapolis, MD: Naval Institute Press, 1994, p. 304.
90 EL, WHO, Stassen Records, 1955–58, Allison to Secretary of State, 14 January 1956
91 *FRUS 1955–57*, vol. XX, p.343.
92 NA Washington, RG59, PPS Office Files, Lot File 66D487, 'Note to Japanese government concerning Pacific nuclear tests', 23 March 1956
93 EL, WHO, Stassen Records, 1955–58, Box 5, 'Press coverage of the nuclear tests', 27 June 1956. The detail here is based on an extensive embassy summary and translation of Japanese articles dealing with nuclear testing.
94 EL, WHO, Stassen Records, 1955–58, Box 5, Allison to Secretary of State, 6 March 1956; Windsor Hackler to State Department, 24 May 1956.
95 EL, WHO, Stassen Records, 1955–58, Box 7, Horsey to Secretary of State, 17 September 1957.

96 EL, DDE Papers as President, AWF, Dulles-Herter Series, 'Memorandum for the President – reply to Prime Minister Kishi's telegram on nuclear tests', 28 September 1957.
97 Ibid.
98 EL, WHO, Stassen Records, 1955–58, Box 6, MacArthur to Secretary of State, 23 April 1957.
99 EL, WHO, Staff Research Group, Staff Notes, 397, 25 July 1958.
100 NA Washington, NSC 5516, RG 273, NSC files, 1948–60, OCB Report on US Policy Toward Japan (NSC 5516/1), 8 April 1959.
101 Ibid.
102 M. Bundy, *Danger and Survival: Choices about the Bomb in the First 50 Years*, New York: Vintage, 1988, p. 332.

8 The revision of the US–Japan security treaty and Okinawa

Factional and domestic political constraints on Japanese diplomacy in the 1950s

Robert D. Eldridge

Introduction

As a result of Article Three of the 1951 Allied Treaty of Peace with Japan, Okinawa was politically separated from Japan and placed under the continued administration of the United States for an undetermined period. Although Japan was recognized as having 'residual sovereignty', administrative rights over Okinawa did not revert to Japan until 1972, more than 20 years after the peace treaty went into effect.[1]

Little known is the fact that initially the United States, led by the Department of State, seriously considered leaving Okinawa with Japan. This, however, was not realized due to the strong opposition of the US Joint Chiefs of Staff.[2] Likewise, little known is the fact that in the late 1950s, in light of the increased opposition in Okinawa and mainland Japan to continued American administration of the islands, the US government again seriously considered returning Okinawa and even launched a study on base consolidations with the remainder of the islands to be returned to Japan on that basis.[3] The plan was called the 'enclave concept', but for a number of reasons, including costs and vulnerability to attack, the final report by the US army recommended against pursuing this plan. President Dwight D. Eisenhower accepted the findings and decided not to return Okinawa. Immediately after this, the revised Security Treaty, which did not include Okinawa in its area of responsibility, was signed on 19 January 1960.

This chapter examines why Okinawa was not returned to Japan during the revision of the Security Treaty in the late 1950s by exploring the debates within the US and Japanese governments, and between the two governments, with a focus on the discussions of the Department of State, Joint Chiefs of Staff, the Japanese Ministry of Foreign Affairs (MoFA), and the ruling Liberal Democratic Party (LDP) in Japan. It will show that the decision to not include Okinawa (and Ogasawara) in the Treaty area, while welcomed (if not highly desired) by some on the US side for geostrategic reasons, was in fact more a result of factional and domestic politics within Japan than of any one outright US demand. In other words, factional politics brought an early end to the possibility of including Okinawa within the Treaty area, even before it became a point of bilateral negotiation. In retrospect, this was unfortunate for those who wished to see Okinawa returned early because during this time, unknown to the Japanese side, the US government was already seriously studying the possibility of returning administrative rights. Had Japan been more proactive about playing a more involved role in the security relationship at that time, the US might have been more willing to compromise on Okinawa.

Most studies about Okinawa have, surprisingly, ignored the Security Treaty revision debate, despite its having had a major impact on Okinawa's continued separated status.[4] On the other hand, the bulk of the literature on the Security Treaty does not shed enough light on the interrelated Okinawa question or the connection that US bases in Okinawa (in terms of nuclear weapons and free use of the bases) had with US–Japan security policy.[5] This study will attempt to bring the two perspectives together to analyse an unknown aspect of Japanese diplomacy in the 1950s. In particular, it will clarify US security requirements in Japan and Okinawa as well as Japanese intentions with regards to the security relationship and understanding of its own limited defence capability. It will also look at Okinawan disappointment with the decision not to return Okinawa or include it within the Treaty area.

The draft treaty area and the question of Okinawa

Pressure for revising the 1951 Security Treaty had been building throughout the 1950s in Japan, a fact which US officials, in particular the new Ambassador to Japan, Douglas A. MacArthur II, were very much aware. Meeting with Prime Minister Kishi Nobusuke, shortly after his arrival in Japan in February 1957, MacArthur was already thinking about the need to revise the Treaty; later, he sought to relay Kishi's similar desires on this matter on the eve of the prime minister's visit to Washington in June that year. It would not be until October of the following year, however, before actual negotiations began due to the need to develop a consensus on the Treaty revision within each government and between them.

MacArthur took advantage of the time to prepare a draft Security Treaty in February 1958. This had become particularly important, as the political situation in Okinawa was deteriorating with the election of an anti-US administration candidate in the Naha mayoral elections the month before. With this, the Secretary of State, John Foster Dulles, called for a readjustment of the US position, which included the study on the enclave concept.[6] MacArthur, for his part, responded by preparing a draft Treaty of Mutual Co-operation and Security, arguing that the US government had to be ready to present a mutual treaty to replace the 'present one-sided arrangement' and that Japan was probably ready for a treaty that was 'really mutual, provided we limit proposals to our minimum essential interests'.[7] For the mutual defence clauses, the Treaty area was to be limited to the Western Pacific (that is, Japan and the Article Three islands in the peace treaty).

MacArthur described the definition of the Treaty area as the 'crux of the matter' and denied that for a treaty to be truly mutual, Japan would have to come to the aid of American forces if the continental United States or its territories elsewhere in the Pacific were attacked.[8] Given the Japanese interpretation of its constitution and domestic Japanese politics, MacArthur observed that such a condition might prevent the conclusion of a mutual security treaty. Instead, MacArthur presented a new argument, which provided the key to unlock the stalemate that had hindered political–military relations for most of the 1950s:

> If we are to have Japan as a partner and thus be able to continue to use certain of her military and logistical facilities which are very important to us, it is *not* essential for Japan to be committed to come to our aid except within a fairly limited area. This is the area where it is very important for us to have Japan committed to act in the event that either we or the Japanese are attacked . . . .I believe it is consistent with the Japanese interpretation of their Constitution and with our basic national interests.[9]

Premised on this argument, Article Four of MacArthur's draft defined the Treaty area as the territory under the administrative control of Japan and the island territories of the Western Pacific referred to in Article Three of the Peace Treaty with Japan under the administrative control of the United States of America. The Ambassador, in other words, sought to include Okinawa and Ogasawara in the Treaty area.

The reasoning for this inclusion became clearer in a 5 June telegram from MacArthur to Dulles. MacArthur informed Dulles that Kishi wished to have confidential discussions with MacArthur on revising the Security Treaty. MoFA was preparing for these talks in an attempt to seek an adjustment in the security relationship, including prior consultation and use of US forces based in Japan for hostilities in the region. Regarding the Treaty area, the Ambassador believed the US should propose from the outset that it would include the Japanese islands and the Article Three islands stating that 'This will be a substantial step forwarding terms of engaging Japan's responsibility for mutual defence outside the area of the Japanese home islands . . . and would be, I think, strongly in our interest'.[10] In a warning to the State Department, MacArthur argued it was clear that the Japanese government would oppose any commitment to a broader treaty area that required them to send the Self-Defence Forces (SDF) abroad due to the present interpretation of the Constitution and the public's unwillingness to support such a commitment.[11] In light of this, according to the Ambassador, the Japanese would interpret such a commitment as an indication that the US did not really desire treaty revision. Because of Kishi's improved political standing following his victory in the elections of May 1958 when the LDP won a large number of seats, and his pro-US stance, MacArthur encouraged Dulles to strike while the iron was hot to bring about a 'long-term, durable alignment with the United States and the free world'.[12]

In this context, on the basis of a July request by Kishi and Foreign Minister Fujiyama Aiichirō to start negotiations on full Treaty revision rather than a series of partial changes, and on an understanding reached by Fujiyama and Dulles in September to go ahead with negotiations, talks officially began in early October in Tokyo. During the first round of talks on 4 October, MacArthur submitted the draft that he and officials in Washington had been working on since February.[13]

MacArthur explained that it had been prepared in an attempt to meet the various suggestions raised by Kishi and Fujiyama, and it reflected the common interests and interdependence between Japan and the United States in security, economy, and other areas. Regarding the Treaty area, and particularly Article Five (responding to an attack on Japan), MacArthur stated that the phrase 'territories or areas under the administrative control' referred to the four main islands of Japan (Hokkaido, Honshu, Shikoku, and Kyushu); Article Three Peace Treaty islands now under US administrative control (over which Japan had 'residual sovereignty'); and islands in the Pacific administered by the United States (such as Guam, Saipan, and the Marshall Islands).[14] The ambassador emphasized at the same time that the US draft would not impact on America's rights under Article Three of the Peace Treaty, meaning that it was not actually returning administrative rights at this time. US Embassy negotiators pointed out to their Japanese counterparts during a discussion on the Treaty area of Article Five that while an attack on Okinawa or Ogasawara would bring it into effect, Japan would be at least partially responsible for their defence since they were under US administration. This would be, the US team added, consistent with Kishi's position in the Diet.[15]

Political problems with the Treaty area

In fact, this draft, which expanded the Treaty area to the Pacific, presented problems for the Kishi government, both within the ruling party and in the Diet. Perhaps because of the fact that the Treaty area was the most important issue and that without a resolution it would be difficult to move forward, Fujiyama visited MacArthur on 22 October to consult him on the government's explanation of the Treaty area in the Diet. According to MacArthur's memorandum of the conversation, Fujiyama told him that a small group was carefully studying the Treaty draft, but in the meantime a formal meeting should be held in order to demonstrate publicly that the negotiations were not stalled, as was implied by press criticism of Kishi.[16] Fujiyama added that currently he had no substantive comments to make, but that he wanted to clarify what actions Japan would be expected to take with regards to Article Five, which, along with Article Six, was the key provision of the Treaty. MacArthur replied that as in the case of mutual defence arrangements with other countries this question had often arisen and urged the Japanese not to attempt to answer these 'hypothetical questions . . . since specific defensive measures and actions would have to depend on circumstances'.[17] The ambassador then went on to explain that the US understood Japan would have to act within the current interpretation of its Constitution, which did not permit the overseas despatch of its forces. Nevertheless, MacArthur believed the Treaty would still provide a degree of mutuality: Japan, for example, would be able to make a contribution by providing its bases to US forces in the event of an armed attack on the Treaty area or on US forces outside Japan. The ambassador ended by suggesting that the Japanese could clarify their wish to provide US forces with the use of facilities in Japan as a substantial part of their contribution.

Vice-Foreign Minister Yamada Hisanari, who was one of the principal negotiators, called on MacArthur a week later for a general discussion of the Security

Treaty and explained that the inclusion of US possessions in the Pacific and even the Article Three islands in the Treaty area could cause difficulties.[18] Yamada was alluding to problems that had emerged during the autumn in the Diet. In late September, the former prime minister Yoshida Shigeru publicly criticized movements towards revision of the Security Treaty and the scaling down of US forces in light of the perceived communist threat in East Asia.[19] Yoshida, who had negotiated and signed the original Security Treaty (and had made the original offer of bases to the US),[20] told visitors such as MacArthur, Fujiyama, and just about anyone who would listen that there was no need to revise the Treaty that he 'made.'[21] Complicating matters, Yoshida was also strongly anti-Kishi and their rivalry would make the process of intra-party consultations difficult. Because of Yoshida's sentiment, Ikeda Hayato and other former loyal members of the Liberal Party (which Yoshida had once headed) likewise argued that it was too early to revise the Treaty.

In addition to the fundamental question of whether or not to pursue Treaty revision, a large, divisive debate had emerged over the wisdom of including Okinawa and Ogasawara in the Treaty area. On 4 October, the Associated Press correctly reported that US authorities said Okinawa and Ogasawara would be included within the Treaty area.[22] The story indicated that the State Department endorsed the view that Okinawa and Ogasawara should be included in the Treaty area and that on the basis of US recognition of Japan's residual sovereignty over the islands, Japanese participation in their defence would make the new treaty more mutual.[23]

Kishi probably did not need any convincing, as he was also in favour of including the Article Three Islands in the Treaty area, and it was around this time that he decided to make his views known. In a Cabinet meeting on 23 October, the day after the second meeting between US and Japanese negotiators, Kishi explained that if Japan were constitutionally able to exercise joint defence of Okinawa, Japan would be able to increase its influence over Okinawa. This would dilute American exercise of administrative rights over the islands and suggest the possibility of Okinawa's early return.[24] Kishi reiterated these views in the Diet Budget Committee on 30 October, emphasizing that Okinawans were Japanese.[25]

While in retrospect Kishi's view was both practical and forward-looking in that it would theoretically lead to the reversion of Okinawa and Ogasawara, his statements and those of others in his government (such as the Defence Agency)[26] caused a backlash within Nagata-chō, the political centre of Japan, and amongst some in the media. The *Asahi Shinbun* accused the Kishi government of playing a dangerous game and asked 'What's the hurry?' in a December editorial.[27] Earlier, it had reported that the Japanese government was considering a joint defence treaty in which Japan would assist US forces and thus commit itself to the defence of Okinawa and Ogasawara.[28] The Japan Socialist Party (JSP), which did not recognize the US–Japan Security Treaty or even the Self-Defence Forces, objected, believing that an alliance would develop between the United States, Japan, Taiwan, South Korea, and the Philippines centring on Okinawa in a virtual North-East Asia Treaty Organization.[29] This, according to the JSP, would entrap Japan in 'America's wars' throughout the region.[30] Likewise, Kawashima Shōjirō and the pacifist Miki Takeo, both of the LDP, criticized Kishi's views stating that a 'military alliance' would evolve if Okinawa were to be included.[31] Miki continued to oppose Kishi, eventually resigning his position as minister of economic planning at the end of December and later boycotting the vote on the revised Treaty in the spring of 1960 due in part to the desire for a stronger prior consultation clause.[32]

In the light of the concerns generated by the inclusion of Okinawa and Ogasawara in the Treaty area, Fujiyama announced at a meeting between leaders of the government and ruling party at the Prime Minister's official residence on 4 December that the government had decided not to include the islands. This announcement reportedly surprised those in attendance, although there had been some stories in the press the evening before that Fujiyama and Kishi had come to 'a meeting of the minds' on this question.[33] Miki stated his support immediately, but Ikeda Hayato, Satō Eisaku (Kishi's younger brother), and Kōno Ichirō all expressed their opposition, saying that Okinawa had to be included. In particular, Kōno was most outspoken on this question.[34]

It was not only Miki who opposed Okinawa's inclusion, but also former prime minister Ashida Hitoshi and former Imperial Navy admirals, and now Diet members, Nomura Kichisaburō and Hoshina Zenshirō. While not faction leaders themselves, the latter two possessed enormous influence in this debate because of both their military background and their known close connections with their American counterparts, including the then Chief of Naval Operations (and subsequently Chairman of the Joint Chiefs of Staff) Admiral Arleigh A. Burke. The two former admirals in particular believed that the US nuclear umbrella, essential for Japan's security, should not in anyway be curtailed in the area of the Article Three islands. They feared that including Okinawa within the Treaty area could limit the US ability to introduce nuclear weapons there.[35]

Kōno was not initially interested in the push for Treaty revision, but believed that if negotiations were to take place, Okinawa and Ogasawara should be included.[36] Moreover, indicative of political and personal rivalries, Kōno may have been using this issue as an attempt to prevent Kishi's re-election as LDP president.[37] On another level, Kōno's pride was injured by Fujiyama's failure to consult him on this issue and sought to embarrass Fujiyama by having the Prime Minister withdraw his support for Fujiyama's plan to separate Okinawa and Ogasawara.[38] After the meeting, Nakasone Yasuhirō, a member of Kōno's faction, told Fujiyama that Kōno had been expecting the foreign minister to visit and was hurt that he had not.[39] It is unclear what the two discussed when Fujiyama finally called on Kōno, but according to a journalist, Fujiyama's failure to prepare the ground thoroughly would cost the Kishi government 'six months' in the end.[40] A new and more divisive debate on whether to include Okinawa or not, fuelled by personal and political rivalries, began enveloping the Kishi government.

As Kōno's protégé, Nakasone led the opposition to Fujiyama's plan to have the Treaty area as the only territories to which Japan's administrative rights extended.[41] In a radio interview shortly after, Nakasone stated:

Japan has residual sovereignty over Okinawa and Ogasawara and they are Japanese territory. It is a natural that they are included in the Treaty area and that Japan assume responsibility for their defence. The people of Okinawa co-operated with, and fought alongside, the Japanese military. It would be wrong to forget about them.[42]

Facing this criticism, Fujiyama set about consolidating opinion within the LDP. In his memoirs, Fujiyama recorded that he was not sure of the truth behind the intra-party opposition he and Kishi were facing. 'I did not know', he wrote almost 20 years later in 1976, 'if they were really interested in the Security Treaty debate, or if they were concerned about the political instability caused by the police bills and/or were already planning for the post-Kishi period.'[43] Kishi, too, lamented that he had no idea what his opponents either in or outside of the Party were thinking.[44]

As a result of these complicated intra-party dynamics and divisive public debates, not to mention the crisis caused by the failed Police Duties Bill (an attempt to increase the powers of the police), Fujiyama stated publicly on 15 December that the government would monitor public opinion before making a decision on defining the Treaty area.[45] Privately, however, it seems that Fujiyama, who had never seriously considered including Okinawa in the first place, had long since made up his mind.

The US Embassy, of course, had been carefully following these movements and was being regularly updated by both Fujiyama and Kishi. On 3 November, a few days after Yamada's talk with MacArthur, the Ambassador wrote to the State Department with a new draft of Article Five. Explaining that the changes in the wording were necessary due to Japanese reservations, MacArthur removed the word 'Pacific', but made clear the inclusion of the Article Three islands and sought to broaden the concept of the Treaty with regard to international peace and security.[46] MacArthur was certain that at the next meeting with Fujiyama, the Japanese side would raise questions on the Treaty area and propose exclusion of all US-administered territories, except Okinawa and Ogasawara. The Ambassador urged that if such a proposal were made, the US side should accept it. Noting the confusion in the Japanese press over the extent of Treaty area, MacArthur added that the sooner the US side could delimit the Treaty area, the sooner the confused debate – one that he felt was 'not helpful to our interests' – would end.[47] In fact, MacArthur went on to say that he believed Kishi and Fujiyama had been reluctant to ask the US side specifically about the Treaty area until they knew whether the US understanding matched their own.[48]

For the Japanese government, and MacArthur, the principal issue was still Okinawa's inclusion, which the Ambassador believed Kishi desired and would try to justify publicly on the grounds of Japan's residual sovereignty. No one at the Embassy, however, was certain about how things would develop. As a result, in the same memorandum, the ambassador urged the Department of State to consider the possible exclusion of Okinawa (despite its earlier preference for inclusion). Inclusion was not essential to US purposes, MacArthur explained, as long as America was able to enjoy a 'reasonably dependable and long-term military security arrangement entered voluntarily by Japan'.[49]

In response, the Acting Secretary of State, Christian A. Herter, stated that the US should await an overall Japanese response before considering any concessions as this would weaken America's bargaining position. After speaking with Department of Defense officials, Herter explained that they were also concerned that limiting the Treaty area to Japan and the Article Three islands might lead to pressure to restrict the use of American bases to support operations.[50] If the Japanese were to request the limited area, Herter explained that MacArthur should first make clear to Japan that other treaties concluded by the United States in the Pacific region were aimed at defending the free world and were not limited to the defence of a particular country: 'A treaty with Japan, which is aligned with [the] free world and occupies [a] predominant position in area, should not contribute less since we assume Japan has [a] vital interest in preserving [the] free world position in the Pacific'.[51] Although from the US perspective this required Japan to reciprocally defend the US, such a debate was theoretical in light of the practical reality of the existence of Article Nine of the Japanese Constitution. Therefore, to make the Treaty appear mutual, Japan would have to allow the US access to its bases in Japan as anything less would be 'unacceptable to Congress and American people'.[52]

Upon receiving this message, MacArthur decided to wait for Japan's views, which came several weeks later on 26 November when MacArthur met secretly with Fujiyama. Concluding that the opposition to Okinawa's inclusion within the Treaty area was very strong, Fujiyama told MacArthur that he and Kishi had decided that it was best from both the Japanese and American viewpoints to limit the Treaty to the Japanese home islands, and requested that the decision be quickly considered in Washington.[53] Fujiyama acknowledged there were weighty arguments in favour of including the islands, not least of which came from the Okinawans themselves, who had petitioned the Japanese government. He had also learnt from the troubled police bill of the importance of marshalling public and party support before making a final decision.[54] Because the Treaty area question was 'the most critical point of the treaty revision for Japan', it would be necessary to proceed with caution. Fujiyama explained that the inclusion of US island possessions in the Pacific would raise major questions of constitutional interpretation and would gain neither Diet nor public approval. Furthermore, Fujiyama continued, the government had originally favoured the inclusion of the Article Three islands in the Treaty area, but after discussions within the LDP and with principal newspaper editors and leaders of public opinion, Kishi had come to realize that his government would not be able to obtain the necessary support for their inclusion.[55]

In reporting his conversation with Fujiyama, MacArthur told Dulles that he was doing so not only because the foreign minister requested it, but also in his eyes, the Treaty area was the key to the entire problem and until it was agreed it would be impossible to proceed. His staff had been working on the issue since Admiral Harry D. Felt, commander-in-chief, Pacific, had urged in a 6 November telegram that the Article Three islands be excluded from the Treaty area. 'In light of developments since that time,' MacArthur continued, he strongly concurred with the Admiral's recommendation only if the US reached a satisfactory agreement with the Japanese government regarding the other important points, including the use of bases, the consultation formula, and the administrative agreement.[56] Further emphasizing his point, MacArthur concluded by reiterating the voluntary and long-term security arrangement with Japan, including use of Japanese bases and facilities in the event of conflict in East Asia regardless of whether Japan was a direct participant or not. He believed that these objectives could be met regardless of the inclusion of Article Three islands in the Treaty area.[57]

Nevertheless, aware that the Diet debate could go in any direction, particularly in the light of Fujiyama's speech on 15 December to the Anpo Jōyaku Mondai Konwakai (Security Treaty Problem Discussion Group) about the importance of public opinion, MacArthur noted in a 24 December telegram that, despite these problems, it was still possible that the Japanese government might find it feasible to include Okinawa and Ogasawara. 'Their inclusion would add another element of mutuality', he explained, but 'in our opinion . . . it is not essential because the really valuable Japanese contribution to mutuality rests in the provision of US bases and logistical facilities in Japan and in common action in defense of Japan.'[58] MacArthur, it appears, had been forced to change his position from hoping to see Okinawa included in the Treaty area to desiring its exclusion, because of LDP infighting and the debates in the Diet and the public realm.

Reaching agreement

A month later on 24 January 1959, Dulles, ill with cancer and frustrated with the pace of the negotiations, wrote to MacArthur stating that he assumed substantive negotiations would not be resumed until Tokyo took the initiative and Kishi obtained unified LDP support on key Treaty issues.[59]

Dulles' telegram confirmed the strong US preference for the Treaty area to include the Pacific; if the Japanese continued to reject that position, the US should limit the Treaty area to territory under the administration of Japan as the inclusion of the Article Three islands were not considered desirable or essential from the US viewpoint.[60] In light of the above, Dulles explained that Article Five should be rephrased as follows: 'Each party recognizes that an armed attack directed against the territory or areas under the administrative control of Japan would be dangerous to its own peace and safety and declares that it would act to meet the common danger in accordance with its constitutional processes.'[61]

Kishi was also painfully aware that 'intra-party faction strife' had discredited Japan abroad and paralysed its foreign policy, and told MacArthur that he hoped to complete negotiations and reach an agreement on the three major foreign policy issues, including the renegotiation of the US–Japan Security Treaty.[62] Kishi, who had called for early LDP presidential elections, was re-elected a week later on 24 January. His government was now in a stronger position to pursue bilateral negotiations. Nonetheless, factional differences remained deep and any co-operation would be viewed as only a temporary alliance in the LDP's kaleidoscope of personalities and politics.

Meanwhile, Fujiyama was attempting to consolidate views within the Party and made a number of public speeches around the country and spoke again at an Anpo Jōyaku Mondai Konwakai-sponsored event on 12 January. Again, he avoided clarifying his views on the inclusion of the Article Three islands in the Treaty, noting the complete difference of views on whether the Ryukyus and Bonins should be included in the Treaty area. The government, he suggested, would carefully decide its policy on the question after ascertaining the trend of public opinion.[63]

While these comments suggested that the islands would not be included, nevertheless, the foreign minister did present a new opinion, which did not go unnoticed by the US. This was that the 'problem of regaining administrative rights over these areas is one that has nothing to do with the present treaty. It is a problem on which Japan should constantly negotiate with the US side through diplomatic channels regardless of whether these areas are included in the treaty area.'[64]

In a telegram a week later, MacArthur explained to Dulles that he had repeatedly informed both Kishi and Fujiyama that the US would not be in a position to complete negotiations for the new treaty or initial any agreement until he was certain it would have LDP support and that Kishi could successfully guide it through the Diet. At the same time, MacArthur acknowledged that press and public opinion had substantially improved. Nevertheless, MacArthur noted that there were 'now increasing indications that certain elements within the GOJ may press for inclusion' of the Article Three islands. Aware of mainland American concerns, MacArthur nevertheless believed he could 'gain support for treaty area covering territory only under administration of Japan.'[65]

It does not seem that MacArthur needed to do so, however, for the time being. In statements in the Diet, Kishi and Fujiyama explained that they viewed the question of the inclusion of the Article Three islands as separate from the revision of the Treaty. In his testimony to the Lower House Budget Committee on 4 February, Kishi stated 'I think the Security Treaty problem and the problem of the return of the administrative rights are two separate things. However . . . we must naturally save the people from any fear that excluding these islands from the Treaty area might lead to disregarding the national desire of the Japanese for the islands' earliest possible return.'[66]

By the end of February, Fujiyama had been able to pull the various factions together on moving ahead with revisions of the Security Treaty in line with the government's approach, although a new debate had emerged on the need to revise the Administrative Agreement.[67] Discouraged at the new round of partisanship, MacArthur told former Chief Cabinet Secretary Ishida Hideo, a close ally of Miki, that the actions of certain LDP anti-mainstream politicians in treating the question of Treaty revision 'as partisan football to be kicked about in an effort to embarrass Kishi' have created a negative impression in Washington.[68] Such actions, the ambassador continued, 'did not inspire confidence in [the] integrity of persons who were trying to exploit this issue for their personal advantage to [the] detriment of over-all long-term US–Japan relations'.[69]

Shortly after, MacArthur reported on a conversation with LDP Secretary General Fukuda Takeo, in which the latter explained there would be 'solid support' for revision by the Kishi, Satō, Ono, and Kōno factions, with the Miki, Ishibashi (Ishida), and Ishii factions agreeing to Treaty revision.[70] The only substantial obstacle was the Ikeda-Yoshida faction, but Fukuda stated that he believed Ikeda would have no choice but to co-operate in the face of overwhelming support for the Treaty. That same day, MacArthur met privately with Fujiyama for further discussions on the Treaty negotiations. Fujiyama assured the ambassador that he would 'oppose any attempts' by politicians to include the islands in the Treaty area.[71]

The following week on 8 April, the LDP adopted its set of principles on the Security Treaty, which stated that the Treaty area would 'cover the whole territory of Japan. However, areas which are not presently under Japan's administration will be excluded from the treaty area for the time being. Those areas, however, should be included in the treaty area automatically when administrative rights over them are returned to Japan.'[72]

Later that month, MacArthur informed State that Fujiyama and Yamada had submitted to him on 28 April the 'complete Japanese "package"'.[73] Explaining that he would forward the revised draft incorporating Japanese modifications as well as his own comments in separate telegrams, MacArthur noted that the Japanese government had in fact agreed to every point of substance in the US position including a treaty area limited to Japan and excluding Okinawa and Ogasawara. He added he would be able to direct events in such as way so as to make the proposal appear as the Department of State had hoped.[74]

Agreed minute on Okinawa's status

Although it looked as if it would be fairly smooth sailing, the Kishi government once again ran into problems during deliberations on the draft treaty in the Treaty Sub-committee of the LDP Foreign Affairs Research Council in the autumn. According to a report on the deliberations, 'a minority of the membership, largely inspired by Kono . . . caused a succession of stormy meetings.'[75] One of the main disputes was the future status of Okinawa and its relationship to the revised Treaty.

As a result of the submission of the sub-committee's report, Fujiyama asked for clarification of some points, such as the prior consultation formula, the status of the Article Three islands, the exact definition of the phrase 'Far East', and the question of indirect aggression.[76] To do so, Fujiyama called on MacArthur on 21 October and explained that the LDP had requested the government to gain US understanding that although the islands were not in the Treaty area, Japan would not be barred from contributing to their safety in the event of an emergency after consulting with the US, which would retain defence responsibility. According to MacArthur, Fujiyama did not see a need for a new agreement per se, but that he might propose that a Japanese government statement be recorded in a 'negotiating minute' expressing 'its interest in the safety of [the] people' of the islands to satisfy the LDP.[77]

The US believed this issue had already been resolved and Fujiyama's request regarding Okinawa threatened to reopen a whole series of debates between the two governments, and also between the State Department and the US military. In a 17 November reply to MacArthur, Herter affirmed that while the State Department recognized the desirability of publicly clarifying the Treaty arrangements to avoid different interpretations, Fujiyama's points were nonetheless problematic. Reiterating the concerns set out in the Department's 16 May telegram to the Embassy, Herter explained that the desire to avoid a formal note or minute on the Article Three islands remained rooted in the belief that Japan's interest in the islands could be reflected in a less formal manner. As an alternative, Herter suggested that the Japanese government might point out that the consultation formula will 'provide [an] opportunity for it to reflect and even act upon Japanese concern for [the] safety' of the inhabitants of the islands if the islands were attacked.[78]

Yamada met with MacArthur shortly after this on 19 November to propose a draft text for the agreed minutes that he hoped would be made public.[79] The proposal sought to recognize that Okinawa would come under Article Five of the new Treaty when administrative rights were restored to Japan. MacArthur reacted negatively to Yamada's request, arguing that he would be 'obliged to oppose any such formulation', and urged him to drop this matter.[80] It is not clear what Yamada thought of this rebuff, but according to MacArthur's memorandum of the conversation, the Vice Minister eventually agreed to recommend its withdrawal to Fujiyama.[81] Yamada argued, however, that it was important that an agreed public minute be reached expressing Japanese official concern for the safety of Okinawans in the event of an attack.

Reporting this to the State Department on 20 November, MacArthur explained that 'while I believe I have killed Japanese efforts to have an agreed minute regarding inclusion of Ryukyus in [the] treaty area after the restoration of administrative control, I also recognize that they must show some interest in the security of the Ryukyuans since the latter are Japanese nationals.'[82] The ambassador recommended that the US accept this formulation as it did not harm US interests.

A month later, after consulting with Herter and Secretary of Defence Thomas S. Gates, Jr, the State Department responded by explaining that it preferred no reference to Okinawa, but if such an exchange were essential to ratification then MacArthur could accept the agreed minute based on revisions to be drafted by the State Department.[83]

Simultaneously, Fujiyama had been pressing Ambassador MacArthur for a response reaffirming Kishi's interest in the welfare of Okinawans as being an essential component of Treaty revision.[84] MacArthur responded that he preferred no minute or reference to the islands, but that if Kishi felt it necessary, the US would agree on the basis of the revisions that he had given Fujiyama. On 22 December, MacArthur received word from Kishi that indeed he felt it was necessary for some public reference to the future well-being of the people of Okinawa since the islands were not included in the Treaty area.[85] Kishi stated that the US revisions were acceptable. Eventually, an agreed minute on the Article Three islands was agreed upon on 15 January 1960, a mere four days before the signing ceremony at the White House.[86]

Conclusion

The decision of the Kishi government, based primarily on political reasons, not to request that Okinawa be included in the Treaty area was inopportune for those who wished to see Okinawa's return, particularly given that the US was then reviewing the possibility of returning administrative rights to Japan. Further, Ambassador MacArthur, America's lead negotiator, was also initially in favour of including the islands in the Treaty area. As historian Sakamoto Kazuya has written, if Kishi could have achieved the return of Okinawa at the time of Treaty revision, it would have been a stunning diplomatic success, making his record all the more impressive and the Treaty more broadly acceptable.[87] Nonetheless, the Kishi government's insistence on an 'Agreed Minute on the Article Three islands' made up for this failure, albeit only slightly, and was another important step in the reversion process and thus probably should not be overlooked.

The non-inclusion of Okinawa had an indirect effect on the reversion process, which would not be realized for another decade. The revision of the Security Treaty and the exclusion of Okinawa, ironically, placed a great strain on America's long-term Okinawa policy. On the one hand, because Treaty revision placed greater restrictions on the use of US facilities in mainland Japan, the strategic importance of Okinawa, where the US had unrestricted rights over military bases (including the introduction and storage of nuclear weapons), increased dramatically in the 1960s. The Joint Chiefs of Staff were, therefore, even more reluctant to return Okinawa. On the other hand, because the Treaty excluded Okinawa, Okinawans came to desire reversion to Japan more strongly than ever (as symbolized by the creation of the Council for Reversion of Okinawa Prefecture to the Fatherland, Okinawa-ken Sokoku Fukki Kyōgikai in 1960, during the Treaty ratification deliberations in the Diet). With these two forces in opposition to each other, the status quo regarding Okinawa gradually unravelled with policy makers finding it increasingly difficult to manage Okinawa policy and bilateral relations.

Although he did not directly write about or predict this paradox, the importance of a resolution to the Okinawa problem did not escape MacArthur's attention at the time. On the eve of the signing ceremonies, MacArthur, looking back over the latter half of the 1950s, satisfyingly reviewed the progress made on redressing the 'series of grievances and complaints' in the relationship, most notably the need for a new Security Treaty. 'We can, I believe, take real satisfaction that good solutions have been reached with respect to virtually all of [the serious issues] except the return of administration in Okinawa.'[88] MacArthur was correct in his assessment. As the revision of the Security Treaty was the single most significant point of contention between the two countries during the 1950s, the resolution of the Okinawa problem would become the most challenging bilateral issue in the 1960s.

Notes

1 Amami and Ogasawara were returned in 1953 and 1968 respectively. See R. D. Eldridge, *The Return of the Amami Islands: The Reversion Movement and US–Japan Relations,* Lanham: Lexington Books, 2004 and R. D. Eldridge, 'Ogasawara to

Nichibei kankei'in D. Long (ed.) *Ogasawaragaku koto hajime*, Kagoshima: Nanpō Shinsha, 2002, pp. 244–70.

2   See R. D. Eldridge, *The Origins of the Bilateral Okinawa Problem: Okinawa in Post-war US—Japan Relations, 1945–1952*, New York: Garland, 2001.

3   For a recent detailed study, see R. D. Eldridge, '40-nenmae Togo keikaku ni manabu,' *Ryūkyū Shinpō*, 19 January–2 February, 2001. Also see Gabe Masaaki, *Nichibei kankei no naka no Okinawa*, Tokyo: San'ichi Shobo, 1996, pp. 121–28; Nicholas E. Sarantakes, *Keystone: The American Occupation of Okinawa and US–Japan Relations*, College Station: Texas A & M Press, 2000, p. 110. Sarantakes makes a convincing case for military opposition to returning Okinawa at this time. This study, however, will focus on the Japanese side of the debate, as there never really were direct bilateral negotiations on the return of Okinawa in the latter half of the 1950s. It would take another decade before that happened.

4   The exception is Watanabe Akio, *The Okinawa Problem: A Chapter in US—Japan Relations,* Melbourne: Melbourne University Press, 1970.

5   The exceptions are G. R. Packard, III, *Protest in Tokyo: The Security Treaty Crisis of 1960*, Westport: Greenwood Publishers, 1966; Hara Yoshihisa, *Sengo Nihon to kokusai seiji: Anpo kaitei no seijii rikigaku*, Tokyo: Chūō Kōronsha, 1988; Hara Yoshihisa, *Nichibei kankei no kōzu: Anpo kaitei o kenshō suru*, Tokyo: NHK Books, 1991; and Sakamoto Kazuya, *Nichibei dōmei no kizuna: Anpo jōyaku to sōgōsei no mosaku*, Tokyo: Yūhikaku, 2000.

6   Eisenhower Library, Abilene, Kansas (hereafter EL), 'Personal letter from Dulles to MacArthur', John Foster Dulles Papers, 1952–1959, Folder: Strictly Confidential M(1), Box 3, General Correspondence and Memoranda Series, 10 February 1958.

7   National Archives, College Park, Maryland, Central Decimal File, 794.5/2–1858, Record Group 59, Records of the Department of State (hereafter RG 59 CDF), Letter from the Ambassador to Japan to the Secretary of State, 18 February 1958.

8   Ibid.

9   Ibid. Author's emphasis.

10   RG 59 CDF 611.94/6–558, Telegram 3202 from Ambassador to Japan to Secretary of State, 5 June 1958.

11   Adding to the political pressure against use of the SDF abroad, a non-binding resolution passed by the House of Councillors called for the banning of their despatch abroad.

12   RG 59 CDF 611.94/6–558, Telegram 3202 from Ambassador to Japan to Secretary of State, 5 June 1958.

13   RG 59 CDF 794.5/10–558, Telegram 743 from Ambassador to Japan to Secretary of State, 5 October 1958

14   Ibid.

15   RG 59 CDF 794.5/10–1358, Telegram 792 from Ambassador to Japan to State Department 13 October 1958.

16   RG 59 CDF 794.5/10–2358, Telegram 882 from Ambassador to Secretary of State, 23 October 1958.

17   Ibid.

18   RG 59 CDF 794.5/10–2958, Telegram 911 from Ambassador to Japan to Secretary of State, 29 October 1958.

19   Fujiyama Aiichirō, *Seiji waga michi: Fujiyama Aiichirō kaisōroku*, Tokyo: Asahi Shinbunsha, 1976, pp. 93–4.

20   See R.D. Eldridge and A. Kusunoki, 'To base or not to base: Yoshida Shigeru, the 1950 Ikeda mission, and post-Treaty Japanese security conceptions,' *Kobe University Law Review*, 33 (1999); Miyazawa Kiichi (trans. R.D. Eldridge), *Secret Talks between Tokyo and Washington: The Memoirs of Miyazawa Kiichi, 1949–1954*, Lanham, MD: Lexington Books, 2007, pp. 21–3.

21   Fujiyama, *Seiji waga michi*, p. 94.

22 Yoshizawa Seijirō, *Nihon gaikōshi, 29 kōwago no gaikō (I) tairekko kankei (ge)*, To-kyo: Kajima kenkyūjo shuppankai, 1973, p. 37.
23 Nakayoshi Yoshimitsu, *Nihon fukki undōki: Watashi no kaisō kara*, Naha: Okinawa Times, 1964, p. 67.
24 Ibid., p. 68; Yoshizawa, *Nihon gaikōshi*, p. 37. Also see Watanabe, *Okinawa*, p. 125.
25 RG 59 CDF 794.5/10–3158, Telegram 929 from Ambassador to Japan to Secretary of State, 31 October 1958. Kishi at this time also made clear his view that 'under the present interpretation of the constitution, troops could not and would not be sent outside of the home islands.' Ibid.
26 Nakayoshi, *Nihon*, p. 69.
27 Watanabe, *Okinawa*, p. 125; 'Anpo kaitei wa isogu na', *Asahi Shinbun*, 8 December 1958 (evening edition).
28 *Asahi Shinbun*, 6 October 1958, cited in Watanabe, *Okinawa*, p. 125.
29 Watanabe, *Okinawa*, p. 125.
30 On the general views of the Socialist Party, as shown in Diet interpellations in late September, see RG 59 CDF 794.5/10–158, Telegram 708 from Ambassador to Japan to Secretary of State, 1 October 1958. Also see Sone Eki, 'Anpo kaitei ni tsuite: shakaito no tachiba kara," in Nihon Shinbun Kyōkai (ed) *Anpo kaitei no mondaiten*, Tokyo: Nihon Shinbun Kyōkai, 1959, pp. 81–104.
31 *Asahi Shinbun*, 25 November 1958 evening edition, and Fujiyama, *Seiji*, p. 95.
32 Miki Mutsuko, *Shin nakuba, tatazu: Otto Miki Takeo to no 50-nen*, Tokyo: Kodansha, 1989, pp. 152–4.
33 Okada Tadao, *Seiji no uchimaku*, Tokyo: Yuki Shobō, 1959, p. 174; Nakayoshi, *Nihon*, p. 70.
34 Okada, *Uchimaku*, p. 174.
35 RG CDF 794.5/11–2858, Telegram 1115 from Ambassador to Japan to Secretary of State, 28 November 1958.
36 Okada, *Uchimaku*, p. 175.
37 According to Yamada Hisanari, Kōno clearly admitted that his opposition was based on trying to prevent Kishi from 'making a third run as LDP President'. Fujiyama, *Seiji*, pp. 97–8.
38 Okada, *Uchimaku*, pp. 176–9.
39 Ibid., p. 178.
40 Ibid., p. 178.
41 Fujiyama, *Seiji*, p. 95; Nakayoshi, *Nihon*, p. 70.
42 Cited in Nakayoshi, *Nihon*, p. 70.
43 Fujiyama, *Seiji*, p. 95.
44 'Shōgen: 1960-nen Anpo Kaitei', *Chūō Kōron*, 92, 7, p. 193.
45 Fujiyama stated on 15 December that 'since the current negotiations were started, whether to include the Okinawa and Bonin Islands has been the focus of arguments at home over the treaty defense area problem. The people of Okinawa, as Japanese nationals, are supporting the inclusion of Okinawa in the area. On the other hand there are some people in Japan who oppose this for fear that if this included Japan will be involved in war relative to the US-ROK and US-Taiwan treaties. About this problem there are other pros and cons based on various points of views. After all, I think this should be decidedly prudently after seeing the future trends of public opinion.' See RG 59 CDF 794.5/1–259, Despatch 737 on Foreign Minister's Speech on the Pending US–Japan Mutual Security Treaty, 2 January 1959.
46 RG 59 CDF 794.5/11–358, Telegram 948 from Ambassador to Japan to Secretary of State, 3 November 1958.
47 Ibid.
48 Ibid.
49 Ibid. For more on Okinawa's relation to the Security Treaty, particularly in the con-

nection with the 1951 Treaty, see Nishimura Kumao (ed). *San Furanshisuko heiwa jōyaku Nichibei anpo Jōyaku*, Tokyo: Chūōkōron Shinsha, 1999, pp. 59–82.

50 RG 59 CDF 794.5/11–358, Telegram 706 from Secretary of State to Ambassador to Japan, 3 November 1958.
51 Ibid.
52 Ibid.
53 RG CDF 794.5/11–2858, Telegram 1115 from Ambassador to Japan to Secretary of State, 28 November 1958.
54 Ibid.
55 Ibid.
56 Ibid.
57 Ibid.
58 RG 59 CDF 794.5/12–2458, Telegram 1302 from Ambassador to Japan to Secretary of State, 24 December 1958.
59 RG 59 CDF 794.5/1–2459, Telegram 1028 from Secretary of State to Ambassador to Japan, 24 January 1959.
60 Ibid.
61 Ibid.
62 RG 59 CDF 694.00/1–1759, Telegram 1425 from Ambassador to Japan to Secretary of State, 17 January 1959.
63 RG 59 CDF 794.5/1–2659, Despatch 815 on Fujiyama Speech on Security Treaty Revision, 26 January 1959.
64 Ibid.
65 RG 59 CDF 794.5/2–959, Telegram 1584 from Ambassador to Japan to Secretary of State, 9 February 1959.
66 RG 59 CDF 794.5/3–1159, Despatch 1008 from Ambassador to Japan to Secretary of State, 11 March 1959.
67 RG 59 CDF 794.5/3–1659, Telegram 1785 from Ambassador to Japan to Secretary of State, 2 March 1959; RG 59 CDF 794.5/3–259; also see Telegram 1878 from Ambassador to Japan to Secretary of State, 16 March 1959.
68 RG 59 CDF 794.5/4–159, Telegram G-564 from Ambassador to Japan to Secretary of State, 15 April 1959.
69 Ibid.
70 RG 59 CDF 794.5/4–359, Telegram 2012 from Ambassador to Japan to Secretary of State, 3 April 1959.
71 RG 59 CDF 794.5/4–359, Telegram 2005 from Ambassador to Japan to Secretary of State, 3 April 1959.
72 RG 59 CDF 794.5/4–1659, Despatch 1178 on LDP 'Principles for Revision', 16 April 1959.
73 RG 59 CDF 794.5/4–2959, Telegram 2232 from Ambassador to Japan to Secretary of State, 29 April 1959.
74 Ibid.
75 RG 59 CDF 794.5/10–1959, Telegram 482 from Ambassador to Japan to Secretary of State, 19 October 1959.
76 RG 59 CDF 794.5/10–2259, Telegram 1241 from Ambassador to Japan to Secretary of State, 22 October 1959.
77 Ibid.
78 RG 59 CDF 794.5/10–2259, Telegram 1217 from Secretary of State to Ambassador to Japan, 22 October 1959.
79 RG 59 CDF 794.5/11–2059, Telegram 1607 from Ambassador to Japan to Secretary of State, 20 November 1959.
80 Ibid.
81 MacArthur met with Yamada again later that evening at which time the Vice Minister

informed MacArthur that Kishi and Fujiyama had agreed to withdraw the proposal. Ibid.

82 Ibid.
83 RG 59 CDF 794C.0221/12–1959, Secto 31 from Paris, 19 December 1959; see also RG 59 CDF 794.5/12–2059, Telegram 1956 from Ambassador to Japan to Secretary of State, 20 December 1959.
84 RG 59 CDF 794.5/12–2259, Telegram 1979 from Ambassador to Japan to Secretary of State, 22 December 1959.
85 Ibid.
86 RG 59 CDF 611.947/1–1560, Telegram 7626 from Secretary of State to High Commissioner, Ryukyu Islands, 15 January 1960.
87 Sakamoto, *Nichibei Dōmei*, p. 201.
88 RG 59 CDF 033.9411/1–960, Telegram 2205 from Ambassador to Japan to Secretary of State, 9 January 1960.

9 Breaking the deadlock

Japan's informal diplomacy with the People's Republic of China, 1958–9

Caroline Rose

By its very nature, the diplomacy conducted between the People's Republic of China (PRC) and Japan in the years before normalization took place in 1972 must be characterised as unofficial or informal. In the absence of diplomatic relations, Sino-Japanese interaction took place through private channels and was heavily constrained by US pressure on Japan to limit contacts and trade with the communist government for strategic reasons. Nonetheless, the three trade agreements that the Chinese and Japanese concluded in the early- to mid-1950s had the tacit support of their respective governments. Further, cultural exchange was also sponsored by each side under the rubric of China's 'people's diplomacy' and Japan's *seikei bunri* (separation of politics from economics), thereby lending a distinctly official flavour to the relationship. However, Sino-Japanese relations were constantly buffeted by the changing domestic and international environments of the time, not least rising Cold War tensions, so that, after a relatively short period of calm in the early 1950s, by the late 1950s the relationship deteriorated sharply, leading to the cessation of trade and cultural exchange in the wake of the Nagasaki flag incident in May 1958. It was only in 1960 that the relationship began to show signs of improvement (if these are to be measured by levels of trade), with the beginning of 'friendly trade' and then Liao–Takasaki (LT) trade.[1] Cultural exchange also began to resume in the early 1960s.

The difficulties that arose in the relationship between 1958 and 1961 originated from domestic changes in both countries and responses to regional developments. Domestically, changes were afoot when Kishi Nobusuke became prime minister in 1957. Kishi's pro-Taiwan stance did not endear him to the PRC, which was going through domestic political changes too, leading to the radicalization of Chinese domestic policy and an attendant hardening of policy towards Japan. Regional issues of the late 1950s included a heightening of tension in the Taiwan Strait, the beginnings of the Sino-Soviet split, and the proposed revision of the US–Japan Security Treaty, all of which had an impact on Sino-Japanese relations.

This chapter is concerned with the evolution of informal lines of communication between Japan and China in the late 1950s, and focuses on the means by which Japanese governmental and non-governmental groups were able to maintain links with their Chinese counterparts during a period of uncertainty and instability in domestic and regional politics. In particular, the focus is on the period from May 1958 to late 1959, when relations were at their lowest ebb, marked by virtually no trade and very little people exchange. The informal diplomacy of the previous seven years gave way to a series of sporadic, ad hoc meetings in the form of visits to China by individual Japanese politicians of ruling and opposition parties, political party delegations, Japan–China friendship groups, trade union representatives, businessmen, and academics. The aims of such visits from the Japanese side were, variously, to ascertain the PRC's thinking vis-à-vis Japan, to explore the possibility of reopening trade and cultural relations, and also, for the left at least, to discuss the possibility of diplomatic normalization. For the Chinese, the aim of receiving such visitors was to continue to apply pressure on the Japanese government and create a body of opinion in Japan that would be favourable to normalization with China.

The chapter looks at the activities of Japanese individuals and groups involved in the efforts to reopen relations with China and analyses their role within the broader context of Japan's informal diplomacy. It suggests that the ongoing use of informal channels during this relatively short period of time was an important step in the evolution of Japan's post-war China diplomacy. The basic assumption is that the interaction that took place between China and Japan in the early 1950s enabled a certain level of, albeit low-level, informal contact to be maintained during the low point of 1958–9. When the domestic and international environments were right for higher level contact to resume, the links were still more or less in place. This 'very informal' diplomacy was not the result of a consistent policy line on the part of the ruling LDP, but was largely due to the efforts of disparate groups and key individuals who tried to maintain contact with China for a variety of reasons. By the same token, the Chinese government welcomed (indeed, actively encouraged) contact with certain groups, particularly those involved in the peace movement in Japan, for their own domestic and foreign policy reasons.

May 1958: the Sino-Japanese rift and Japan's initial responses

As a result of the 2 May 1958 Nagasaki flag incident, in which a Japanese pulled down a PRC flag at a Chinese stamp and papercut exhibition in a Nagasaki department store, the PRC government announced the cessation of trade and exchange with Japan. The volume of trade between the two countries and the number of visitors to and from each country diminished rapidly during the period 1958–1960.[2] This is not to say that the levels of trade before the events of May were particularly high if compared to Japan–US trade volumes, but Japan's China trade was nonetheless symbolic of a strategy which sought to resume trade with China as a means of developing some independence from the US (which preferred to see Japan building its trade links with South-East Asia) as well as rebuilding the Japanese economy. Thus, increasing levels of trade between China and Japan up to 1957, and the efforts made to expand trade by pushing for de-regulation of various products from those prohibited under the CoCom regulations, were indicative of the relative success of this strategy.[3] By 1956 Japan's trade with China represented 29.8 per cent of its total trade with North-East Asia.[4] Similarly, although the numbers of visitors per year between China and Japan never totalled more than 1500 (both ways) in the 1950s, nonetheless Japanese visitors to China exceeded those of any other nation during this period, and were well-received in China, which used this human capital as part of an official policy to 'use people for government business' (yimincuguan).

The events leading up to the Nagasaki flag incident have been discussed in detail elsewhere and need not be recapitulated here.[5] Suffice to say that a combination of (Chinese and Japanese) domestic, regional and international factors contributed to the breakdown of the relationship in 1958. China's reaction to the Nagasaki flag incident had not been anticipated on the part of the Japanese government. Kishi stated in his memoirs that China's cessation of relations was 'completely unexpected.'[6] Many, however, had predicted a deterioration of the trade relationship in the wake of the recognition issue which had caused the fourth trade agreement to fail.[7] In addition, the Chinese government had been indicating openly for some months its growing dissatisfaction with the Kishi cabinet and its foreign policy as a whole. When Kishi became prime minister in February 1957, the PRC government initially argued that that his policy would not differ from that of his predecessors (in terms of not seeking recognition of China), but criticism and personal attacks against Kishi began to appear in mid-1957 once Kishi's pro-Taiwan stance became clear. Shortly after Kishi's visit to Taiwan in June 1957, Zhou Enlai announced to Japanese journalists that 'Kishi is deliberately creating difficulties for China, damaging her relations with Asiatic countries and slandering her in order to curry favour with America.'[8] Thereafter, anti-Kishi tirades became a common theme in the Chinese media, reaching a peak in the middle of 1958 with the Nagasaki flag incident, and continuing into 1959.[9]

That the rupture between the two countries caused chaos in Japanese government circles would be to overstate the situation, but it was viewed seriously and steps were taken to attempt to resolve the problem, or at least understand the reasons behind China's actions. The Ministry of Foreign Affairs' (MoFA) interpretation of the incident at the time was that this U-turn in China's previously friendly attitude was a temporary situation, a Chinese strategy aimed at affecting the outcome of the forthcoming general elections in Japan, specifically with a view to oust Kishi as prime minister.[10] The change in attitude was also perceived as part of China's switch to a hard-line foreign policy which attended the push for self-sufficiency in the form of the Great Leap Forward. MoFA's initial, internal statement on China's announcement to halt trade talked of the need to reaffirm the Japanese government's adherence to its basic policy of not recognising China, but to 'take steps to conduct trade and cultural exchange with Communist China to the maximum extent possible within the framework of this basic policy'. The MoFA statement rejected China's accusations of Kishi's unfriendly policy as 'totally groundless', claiming instead that the Kishi government had 'earnestly and enthusiastically been trying to promote trade and strengthen friendly relations'. MoFA accused China of 'deliberately bringing up an issue that has no direct relations with trade' and of aiming to 'create a rift between the people and the government on the eve of the general election'. China's approach, according to MoFA was 'tantamount to the interference in the domestic affairs of this country'. Referring specifically to the incident at Nagasaki, the statement went on to explain that the incident had been 'perpetrated by a single thoughtless person' and the Japanese government had expressed its profound regret. It concludes with the unequivocal view that 'it is to be deplored that the Chinese Communists should exploit, with exaggeration, the act by an individual for political purposes.'[11]

Using similar language to the MoFA internal document, LDP Secretary General Kawajima Shōjirō issued a statement on 10 May rejecting China's decision as 'internal interference aimed at the elections.'[12] It was hoped that once the elections were over, the situation would calm down. The official Japanese position was clarified by the Foreign Minister, Fujiyama Aiichirō, on 20 June when he announced the decision to take an 'active wait-and-see' policy *(sekkyokuteki na seikan seisaku)*. When it became clear that China's hard-line policy was to continue even after the June elections, the Japanese government began to rethink its strategy, while maintaining, on the surface, a strict adherence to the 'wait-and-see' line.[13]

Given the apparent lack of contact between the two sides during this hiatus, there are, understandably, very few studies of Sino-Japanese relations which consider the events of 1958 to 1959. However, a close reading of diplomatic records, newspapers and weekly magazines, party publications and friendship group newsletters shows that not all contact was severed in May 1958, and a number of Japanese governmental and non-governmental groups and individuals were engaged in a series of 'behind the scenes' efforts to restore some normality to the relationship. As noted above, the number of visitors to China dropped rapidly in 1959, but the fact that the Chinese government continued to allow a certain level of contact is indicative of its reluctance to allow its links with Japan to lapse completely – even if the links were to be used only as a channel through which to reiterate the Chinese government view on Kishi or to announce the various conditions for a resumption of trade. These links were important for the Japanese government too, since they provided an opportunity to communicate indirectly with China's leading politicians and to find out China's 'real intentions', something that vexed both the JSP and the LDP.

China's cessation of trade and cultural exchange in May 1958 caused great dismay and concern to businessmen and other groups in Japan who had been hopeful of an expansion of trade in 1958–9 and who looked forward to the possibility of Japan's diplomatic recognition of China in the wake of Japan–Soviet Union normalization in 1956.[14] The rupture was felt most acutely by those small and medium-sized Japanese businesses which had benefited from trade with the mainland since the early 1950s, and which had already suffered from the lapse of the third trade agreement, and the collapse of the fourth trade agreement in April.[15] The opposition parties, in particular the JSP, were active in attempting to reopen the lines of communication with the Chinese. High-profile visits of Upper House JSP member Sata Tadakata in July 1958 and Secretary General Asanuma

Inejirō in March 1959 did not, however, bring about a change in China's Japan policy as hoped. On the other hand, the visits did contribute to an understanding of the position of the Chinese government. Friendship groups, cultural groups, and unions in Japan also expressed concern about the developments and became active in a people's movement aimed at raising awareness and putting pressure on the Kishi government to adopt a more pro-China policy.

Thus, during the period a fairly constant stream of, albeit, low-level, limited contact was maintained by various groups and individuals. By late 1959, the Chinese position was beginning to soften and some in the LDP perceived that the time was right to engage more directly with Beijing. The revival of trade became a possibility after the visits to China of Ishibashi Tanzan in September, followed by Matsumura Kenzō in November. The visits of these important LDP representatives, acting in a private, informal capacity, offered greater hope for a return to the pre-1957 status quo in China–Japan relations, although it took a further year for a more formal agreement on trade to be discussed in earnest. From the point of view of Japan's evolving foreign policy, the period between May 1958 and late 1959 offers a valuable insight into the role of both unofficial (that is, non-governmental) and official (that is, LDP, MoFA) actors, working in an informal capacity.

The movement to break the deadlock in Sino-Japanese relations

Before describing in more detail the nature of the visits and negotiations undertaken by Japanese groups and individuals during the 1958–9 deadlock, it is worth noting that the role of informal mechanisms in Japan's policymaking on China (and vice versa) has long been recognized in the academic literature. Studies of specific events in Sino-Japanese relations, such as the resumption of diplomatic relations in 1972 for example, have taken into account the role of non-governmental actors such as business and other interest groups, the media, and friendship groups. Individuals with particular expertise and networks are also considered important, as are informal groupings within political parties (for example the pro-China lobby in the LDP, or the left wing of the JSP). Of particular use to this study is Nishihara Masashi's typology of informal contact-makers which helps to categorize the sort of activity undertaken between Chinese and Japanese groups and individuals during the period May 1958 to November 1959.

Nishihara considers three types or levels of informal diplomacy. Level one is informal diplomacy conducted at an official level but unannounced – that is, activities that have government backing, but are undertaken in secret. Those involved are not necessarily diplomats, but the activity does have the support of the home government and is designed to 'test the water' with the other country. The results of the communication are not made public so as to avoid loss of face, or harm to the home country's interests should the negotiations or activities fail. This level of informal diplomacy is considered the most important, given that it is government-driven. Level two is unofficial and unannounced, undertaken when relations between two countries are in a particularly bad state. Activities are undertaken by private individuals or government officials, but without any sort of 'negotiating status'. Those involved are usually trusted on both sides and have a good network of contacts. This level of informal diplomacy is most likely to take place when relations are at their most tense and the aim of intermediaries is to promote negotiations between the two parties. The intermediaries report back to the home government and if they are judged to have been of some use the government might give them negotiating status, thereby 'upgrading' them to level one. If they are not judged to have been useful, they are largely ignored by the home government. Level three refers to activities that are unofficial and announced. This level of informal diplomacy would occur when relations between two countries are in a poor state and there are attempts to improve the atmosphere through visits undertaken by, for example, opposition party visits, friendship groups and influential people. This level of informal diplomacy is deemed the least important since it is undertaken by the private sector; but it can help to create a basis for levels one and two.[16]

Nishihara argues that most interaction between two states will involve all of these types of activity at different times, and that activities undertaken at levels two and three can provide a means by which to improve a relationship when it is experiencing particular difficulties. This corresponds to the findings of this chapter, where activities undertaken, particularly at level three, helped to keep the two sides communicating and provided a basis from which to restore relations. The visits of Japanese friendship groups, and opposition party and union delegations, to China, though not entirely successful in themselves, nonetheless helped to pave the way for some improvement in the relationship, for example through the opening of consideration trade, or reopening of cultural exchanges. In addition, visits by influential LDP individuals, acting in a strictly unofficial capacity, also helped to return the relationship to some level of normality by the end of 1959. While the LDP made some use of level one (official, unannounced) and level two (unofficial and unannounced) channels to try and reopen relations, there is little evidence that these were successful.

Japan's informal diplomacy (unofficial and announced) between 1958 and 1959 can be split broadly into non-governmental and quasi-governmental activities. Non-governmental activities included the attempts of opposition party delegations (in particular the JSP), friendship groups, business interests, and unions to break the deadlock in the relationship, while quasi-governmental activities refers to the strategies of the LDP to gather information about China's aims, and the visits undertaken by LDP members acting in a private capacity.

Non-governmental activities

The JSP had built up close links with the Chinese leadership in the mid-1950s and its frequent delegations were generally well-received in both countries.[17] The visit of a delegation led by Asanuma in April 1957, for example, was described by the British Embassy in Beijing as 'the most important delegation to have visited China for some time'. The delegates were often able to meet with the very top leaders, Mao Zedong and Zhou Enlai, indicating the value with which the Chinese viewed them. Of course, such visits enabled both sides to score political points; the British Embassy reported that for the Chinese the April 1957 visit was 'an unqualified political success' since the JSP gave China its full support on all outstanding questions (for example, trade agreements, fisheries, and restoration of diplomatic relations).[18] For the JSP, successful visits helped to gain or maintain popular support at home, and provided hope that diplomatic normalization might well be engineered by the socialists. After the breakdown of relations, however, not even the JSP was given preferential treatment, and, despite its best efforts, the party had little success in bringing about a reconciliation with China.

The first visit to China of a JSP representative after the Nagasaki flag incident took place in July 1958, and was headed by Upper House JSP member Sata Tadakata. The visit was not a formal mission, but an informal visit of one or two individuals with the aim of talking frankly about problems.[19] Sata met Liao Chengzhi, Sun Pinghua and Xiao Xiangqian – all pro-Japan hands with some political influence – but not with any of China's top leaders. The British Embassy view was that the delegation received a cool welcome, and this was confirmed in the JSP's meetings on Sata's return, where the Chinese attitude was viewed as distinctly chilly. Sata presented his report to various JSP committees on his return, and also to Foreign Minister Fujiyama and other MoFA representatives with whom he had also met secretly before his departure.[20] He was criticized in the press and by the LDP for returning only with a list of six conditions from the Chinese stating what was expected of the Japanese government in return for an improvement in relations. He was also the subject of criticism within his own party, particularly from the right (for example Nishimura Eiichi).[21] Three of the conditions set out by China had already been enunciated by Zhou Enlai in July and required the Japanese government to stop pursuing an anti-China policy, to stop trying to create two Chinas, and to stop hampering Sino-Japanese normalization (these became the three conditions for a resumption of trade). The three additional conditions presented to Sata related specifically to the resolution of the Nagasaki flag incident and included a demand for the punishment of the individual who removed the flag, an apology mission from Japan, and a statement from the Japanese government indicating a willingness to co-operate on the issue of China–Japan normalization. Only then would the Chinese government accept a formal visit from the Japanese government to discuss the future of Sino-Japanese relations.[22]

The hard-line attitude of the Chinese galvanized the JSP to incorporate into their people's movements in 1958 and 1959 a commitment to reopen Sino-Japanese relations.[23] However, the next important visit to China of a JSP delegation, headed by Secretary General Asanuma in March 1959, failed to achieve any major breakthroughs and Asanuma's visit was perhaps overshadowed by the outcry surrounding his assertion that US imperialism was the 'common enemy' of the Chinese and Japanese peoples. The joint statement issued during Asanuma's visit (in which the JSP agreed to support Zhou Enlai's conditions for a resumption of trade), and the position taken by the Chinese, did signal, in the view of the

MoFA at least, some moderation of China's 'intransigent attitude'.[24] Furukawa notes, too, that the Chinese reiterated that they were willing to allow some private cultural exchange to take place in the form of a private Chinese delegation to Japan 'as soon as circumstances allow'.[25] These concessions did not represent a shift in Chinese thinking, and did not provide the JSP with the domestic political boost they had perhaps sought in anticipation of the gubernatorial and upper house elections.[26] It seemed that the Chinese were keen to explore links with other Japanese groups, not least friendship associations, business groups, and, increasingly, unions.

Friendship groups, in particular the Japan China Friendship Association (JCFA), played an important role during the 1958–9 period.[27] The JCFA's largely JSP and JCP membership tends to lead to its dismissal as a quasi-political party and its influence is not considered very great. Describing the group's activities in the 1960s, Chae-Jin Lee argues that although it was the most important conduit for people's diplomacy in the 1960s, exerting pressure on the LDP through statements and demonstrations, ultimately 'the association did not exercise appreciable influence over the LDP and its government'.[28] The same could be said of its activities in the 1950s, but the JCFA (and other organisations like the Japan China Cultural Exchange Association) were useful when a supplementary channel of communication was needed. In addition, the JCFA had a genuine interest in maintaining friendly relations with the Chinese and although their activities often took on a highly political and partisan stance, especially as the peace movement and anti-Security Treaty (*anpo hantai*) protests developed in the late 1950s, it nonetheless played a role in maintaining an awareness in Japan of the Japan–China problem and adding to the pressure already placed on the LDP by opposition parties, peace groups, unions and so on.

The group's stance on the Japan–China problem was made clear immediately after the flag incident took place at a department store in Nagasaki on 2 May 1958. It began at district level with the Nagasaki branch, which had been responsible for setting up the exhibition, issuing a statement on 3 May, followed by a protest meeting on 10 May.[29] The Tokyo headquarters of the JCFA issued a statement on 6 May and called an emergency meeting of the standing committee for 7 May where it took the decision to launch a nationwide protest movement and submit a petition to the government. In the meantime, negotiations taking place in China between Chinese and Japanese businesses were being cancelled one after another. Chinese delegations in Japan (for example, dance troupes, peace delegations, and sports exchanges) were being recalled, and by 11 May, the Chinese government had announced that all economic and cultural exchange was to be halted.[30] The JCFA, in agreement with other pro-China groups in Japan, established a joint committee, called the National Committee to Resolve the Urgent Situation in Japan–China Relations, which met on 20 May.[31] The committee addressed the major bilateral issues: the (failed) fourth trade agreement, the (lapsed) fisheries agreement, and the Nagasaki flag incident; and called upon the Kishi government to resolve all the problems in addition to progressing with diplomatic normalization with the Chinese government.[32]

The activities of the JCFA and other pro-China groups continued throughout the rest of 1958, boosted by the involvement of other organisations and, in particular, unions. In early July, the JCFA remarked on Sōhyō's 'recent acknowledgement of the importance of the critical situation between China and Japan' and met with Sōhyō representatives on 7 July to discuss the union's decision to adopt an official policy on China–Japan relations. The JCFA welcomed Sōhyō's decision and asked for its co-operation to strengthen the overall movement to restore China–Japan relations. Sōhyō suggested that there was a need for greater co-ordination between the various pro-PRC organisations.[33] The JCFA's ultimate aim was to push for normalization with mainland China. The Tokyo branch tried to broaden its activities to include workers, women's associations and youth groups and was keen for the local branches to undertake the same sort of grass-roots initiatives.[34] In so doing the JCFA was certainly attempting to implement a PRC-style people's diplomacy by building up support for a breakthrough in China–Japan relations on the one hand, and by developing anti-Kishi sentiment on the other.[35] Its movement reached a peak in September and October 1958 with a month-long series of activities arranged centrally and locally to promote China–Japan friendship. These activities included meetings, petitions, fund-raising efforts, seminars, leafleting and so on. It culminated in a national meeting held in Tokyo on 8 October attended by an estimated 10,000.[36] While these activities were taking place at home, a 12-member delegation from the JCFA, headed by Matsumoto Jiichirō, was on its way to China to attend the 1 October National Day celebrations. Other organisations invited to China at this time included the National Committee for Normalization of China-Japan Relations, Sōhyō, and the Metalworkers' Union.

The JCFA and other pro-China friendship groups maintained a fairly constant pressure on the Japanese government to open up China-Japan relations throughout the following year, but their activities tended to be subsumed under the larger people's movement of the JSP and Sōhyō and their anpo hantai campaign. In February 1959 Sōhyō and the National Committee for Normalization of China-Japan Relations organised a meeting in Yotsuya, attended by the JCFA and an estimated 30,000 people. In April 1959, the JCFA organised a meeting of 26 pro-China organisations and produced a seven-point plan to be presented to the government.[37] The JCFA continued to gain support from the Chinese and were once again invited to China to attend the 1 October celebrations in 1959, a visit marked by the sudden death of one of Japan's most fervent pro-China activists, Uchiyama Kanzō.[38]

Although the concrete achievements of the JCFA and other pro-China groups are hard to discern, it is clear that their efforts to rebuild some level of trade and exchange were not totally in vain. For example, Matsumoto Jiichirō managed to secure fishing rights for the Japanese during his 1958 visit,[39] and the JCCEA delegation to China in May 1959 (headed by Nakajima Kenzō) produced a joint communiqué on cultural exchange with China, as a result of which plans were made for the visit of Japanese drama group (linked to the JCP) early the following year.[40]

While the opposition parties and friendship groups acted more as channels through which the Chinese side could communicate its intentions, Japanese business groups and unions functioned by attempting to apply pressure more directly on the Japanese government to reopen trade. Passin argues that in the 1950s Japanese businessmen became 'one of the most important pressure groups in the country for relaxation of trade barriers, easing of travel restrictions, and full recognition of Communist China.'[41] However, although the companies affected by the cancellations of trade put pressure on the government to resolve the situation, and greeted China's three principles 'with a determined effort . . . to comply and to create the political conditions that would meet Chinese demands', in reality they had limited success in restoring trade.[42] The main pro-China trade-related groups, such as the Japan China Trade Promotion Dietmen's League (JCTPDL), the Japan International Trade Promotion Association (JITPA), and the Japan China Export Import Association (JCEIA), were persistent in their efforts to lobby the government. The latter group, established by the Ministry of Trade and Industry (MITI) in 1955, enjoyed a membership of nearly 400 small and medium-sized enterprises and it was mainly these companies that felt the impact of China's cancellation of contracts.[43] In late 1958, eight pro-China trade groups applied further pressure on the Japanese government to reopen relations with China, and even decided to take direct action by writing to Nan Hanchen, chairman of the China International Trade Promotion Committee (CITPC), to request a resumption of trade. A representative of the Japanese delegation tried to meet with Nan during the Asia–Africa Economic Conference in Cairo in December 1958 to discuss the possibility of reopening trade,[44] and in December it was announced that a Japanese trade delegation would attend the Wuhan/Guangzhou trade fair in January 1959.[45] Nonetheless, despite the fairly constant pressure applied by these business groups in the latter half of 1958, they were unable to persuade Kishi and his government to shift away from the 'wait-and-see' policy, and their activities subsided in early 1959.

It was the unions, particularly Sōhyō, that managed to secure some trade concessions from China, known as 'consideration trade' (hairyo bōeki). This was agreed during the visit to China in February 1959 and saw the reinstatement of an, albeit small, volume of trade in lacquer and chestnuts, which nonetheless represented a symbolic development for those Japanese businesses which had suffered from the loss of their Chinese suppliers.[46] Other unions became involved in the movement to restore trade, and achieved some success. The National Committee of Labour Unions for the Promotion of International Trade held its first meeting on 4 September, and was attended by approximately 100 people including representatives from the Steelworkers' Union, the All-Japan Shipbuilding and Engineering Union, and the All-Japan Metalworker's Union. The meeting agreed on a resolution to restore relations between the two countries, support cultural and people exchange, seek normalization, ratify the fourth trade agreement, and urge the Kishi government to respect the PRC flag and give it legal protection.[47] Sōhyō undoubtedly played the most high-profile role during the period, although its activities are sometimes conflated with those of the JSP, given their close links. The

Chinese government, however, tended to deal with the two separately, particularly when it became apparent that the JSP was not able to bring about the breakthrough that the Chinese had hoped for.[48] The British Embassy in Japan remarked upon the Chinese preference to use Sōhyō to improve relations in the wake of Sata's ill-fated visit to China in July 1958, and Asanuma's visit in 1959.[49] The LDP also noticed the amount of attention the Chinese paid to Sōhyō, noting that they (and not JSP delegates or business groups) were able to secure promises of trade.[50]

Quasi-governmental activities

The LDP's 'active wait-and-see' policy was adopted soon after China cancelled trade and cultural exchange, but it was hard to discern the 'active' part of that policy. The government maintained the view that problem should be dealt with purely as a trade issue, in keeping with the underlying policy of *seikei bunri*. Indeed, the LDP referred to the problem as the 'Japan–China trade problem', and the government repeated at frequent intervals its desire to expand trade with China. Despite this, the LDP indicated its intention to dissolve (but actually just withdrew from) the JCTPDL in June 1958.[51] The LDP was also consistently opposed to any suggestions from the JSP that a cross-party committee be established to discuss how to resolve the problem, and did not appear to respond to the growing chorus of disapproval of the government's China policy from business interests and trade promotion associations.[52] On the other hand, a great deal of behind-the-scenes activity suggested that the government was in fact keen to prevent the problem from escalating.

The LDP and MoFA maintained a keen interest in the visits of individuals, opposition party group, union members, and friendship organisations to elicit information about China's stance. A number of the more high-profile visitors to China (for example, Sata) were in communication with the LDP and MoFA officials both before and after their visits. In addition, reports from Japanese consuls or embassies (in particular Hong Kong) were lodged with Foreign Minister Fujiyama, paid particular attention to visits to China by opposition party members or businessmen on their way to or from conferences or business trips elsewhere. One memo submitted to Fujiyama reported on the four-day stop-off in Beijing of two businessmen, one JSP member, and one LDP member on their way home from the Stockholm Peace Conference, and there are a number of accounts of similar 'stop-off' visits in late 1958 and early 1959 of different groups or individuals.[53] Such visits are examples of Nishihara's second level of informal diplomacy; that is, unofficial and unannounced. However, there is scant detail of who the individuals met in China or what was discussed. Sata's report of 1958 refers to the Chinese view of such visits, noting that the Chinese considered the Japanese to be 'using all sorts of methods to find out our real intentions, for example, using the opportunity to stop-off in China en-route to or from Sweden, Moscow, Poland, Burma etc.'[54] It is possible that these visits were of use to the Japanese government in testing the water to see if any changes were apparent in Beijing's thinking. Needless to say the LDP maintained a very strict distance from such endeavours, and were often highly critical of what they described as a kow-tow attitude towards China, but their activities show a clear interest in monitoring developments.

In addition to these monitoring procedures, the LDP sought information through its own channels, but in a very low-key way, using official, unannounced (or at least semi-announced), diplomacy. In his memoirs, Kishi mentions a number of plans for visits to China by LDP dietmembers, or discussions with Chinese diplomatic personnel, but the details are vague, and there is little evidence that anything concrete came of these.[55] At a diplomatic level, it seems that the LDP also made attempts to clarify China's intentions, for example via the Chinese and Japanese consulates in Geneva, which had been used in previous years as channels of communication between the two countries.[56] In July 1958 the *Nihon Keizai Shinbun* reported on meetings which had taken place between both consuls in Geneva in an attempt by the Japanese to ascertain the reasons for China's continued hard-line. The need to do so was, according to the report, brought home to the Japanese government once it realised that it had misjudged the original intention of China's changed policy (i.e., to skew the elections), and once it had become clear that the efforts of private groups or initiatives to repair the relationship were enjoying little success.[57] A follow-up report confirmed that high-level meetings had indeed taken place in Geneva, but that they were being conducted informally (*hikōshiki*). The Japanese government continued to pursue this route in August, ostensibly to restart talks with China on the issue of Japanese citizens believed to be missing in China, but the Japanese press considered that such endeavours were also being used to open up communication between the two sides.[58]

However, it was at the unofficial/announced level of diplomacy that the LDP achieved most success. While the LDP, and Kishi in particular, maintained a firm distance from Ishibashi Tanzan's and Matsumura Kenzō's visits to China in September and October 1959 respectively, stressing that they were 'unrelated to the government' and undertaken in a private capacity, they did have the outward 'blessing' of the party. Clearly, the LDP and MoFA expected the delegations to find out as much as possible about the PRC's intentions.[59] Accordingly, both Ishibashi and Matsumura met with top LDP and MoFA representatives before their trips, and reported back on their return.[60] While the visits of these two men caused problems within the LDP, which was becoming increasingly divided on the China problem, they did manage to make some headway in opening up communication between the Chinese and Japanese governments. For example, the communiqué signed by Zhou and Ishibashi in September 1959 was considered, somewhat prematurely perhaps, a major step forward by one American newspaper which suggested that the communiqué 'more or less put the stamp of approval on a full scale campaign of conciliation between China and Japan'. To support this stance, it noted that 'an increasing number of Japanese officials and businessmen have been getting visas to enter China since the communiqué.'[61] Needless to say, this view was not shared by some in the LDP: the Secretary General, Kawajima, was highly critical of Ishibashi's sympathies with the Chinese, and some felt that Ishibashi's visit actually represented a further setback to Japan–China relations, given that the communiqué merely adhered to the Chinese view of the inseparability of politics and economics.[62] Matsumura's visit was similarly criticized by some in the LDP, while others saw it as moving one step closer to improved relations.[63] Zhou Enlai had indicated during his talks with Matsumura a willingness to build up friendly ties with Japan, and the delegation returned to Japan with an invitation for the former Minister of Trade and Industry, Takasaki Tatsunosuke, to visit China.

The LDP's policy on China was fraught with internal differences which explains some of the ambiguity, contradictions, and retractions in the LDP's statements during the period. Divisions within the party grew as the China problem continued beyond the elections of 1958 and then into 1959. In the early stages of the China–Japan rift, top LDP members hinted at the difference of opinion which existed within the party on Kishi's policy. For example, Chief Cabinet Secretary Akagi Munenori, while stressing that he was expressing his personal views, talked at a press conference on 19 June 1958 (on the eve of the government's official announcement of its China policy) of the possibility of sending a special delegation to China.[64] The *Nihon Keizai Shinbun* attributes this view to the growing sentiment within the LDP in favour of a breakthrough in China–Japan relations, particularly amongst people like Takasaki Tatsunosuke, the Minister of International Trade and Industry; and Miki Takeo, head of the Economic Planning Agency. The lack of unity within the LDP was noted elsewhere in the Japanese press. The *Mainichi Shinbun* traces the origin of the internal divide on the China problem back to the policy/ideological orientations of the (more conservative) Liberal Party and the (more progressive) Democratic Party which had re-emerged in 1956 during the negotiations on Japan–Soviet normalization. The former Liberal Party line (formerly held by the Yoshida faction, but now represented by Ikeda Hayato) held the view that it was not necessary to rush into recognition of the PRC in order to enhance trade, and that South-East Asia would be a better place to expand trade. Ikeda and his ilk were not against trade with mainland China per se, but they were against adopting a neutral stance to get close to the PRC as advocated by some progressives and the JSP. Representing the former Democratic Party line, Kitamura Tokutarō (also Matsumura Kenzō and Miki Takeo of the EPA) argued that the China market could not be ignored and that it was essential to recognize the PRC as soon as possible.[65]

On their return from China, the visits of Ishibashi and Matsumura caused considerable disruption within the party, and brought the divisions into the open. In a conversation with US Secretary of State Christian Herter on 19 January 1960, Kishi referred to the two men as having posed difficulties for the Japanese government on the issue of China, since their visits had been exploited by the Chinese.[66] Kishi was clearly aggrieved by the problems Ishibashi and Matsumura caused, since they had brought Kishi's China policy into the spotlight once again, revealing it to be a serious impediment to an improvement in relations with the PRC. Ishibashi's comments about the desirability of Kishi's resignation in the interest of an improvement in relations with China received party censure in October, but his views were shared privately by a number of LDP dietmen. Although Ishibashi would have to wait until after the Security Treaty revision some months later for this to happen, nonetheless the growing fissure in the LDP can be traced back to the dispute over China policy and the intra-LDP debates on Ishibashi's return.[67]

Conclusion

Despite the constraints of the cessation of trade and cultural exchange between May 1958 and late 1959, there was a surprising level of activity in China–Japan relations. In Japan, different types of informal diplomacy were used by different agencies, governmental and non-governmental, all with aim of restoring the relationship to some sort of normality. Some approaches were more successful than others, but it was the unofficial diplomacy of opposition parties, friendship groups, business interests, unions and key individuals within the LDP which managed to keep some lines of communication open and prevented a total breakdown of the relationship.

Non-governmental groups which were active in the friendship and peace movements were unstinting in their efforts to see China–Japan relations restored. This did not refer simply to trade but to demands for diplomatic normalization with China. The membership of such groups as the JCFA, JCCEA and others consisted largely of JSP and JCP members, which explains their often highly political tirades against the Kishi government and its policies. But the importance of the groups to China–Japan relations was that they were able to maintain some informal contact with China. The various friendship groups united after the events of May 1958, joining hands with Sōhyō and Gensuikyō in the *anpo hantai* movement – itself backed by the PRC. In so doing it could be argued that they perhaps deflected attention away from their original aim, but on the other hand they were probably able to raise a greater awareness of China–Japan relations, and scored valuable points with the Chinese too. This 'bandwagoning' had the effect of maintaining some momentum to their calls for a resumption of relations, which may otherwise have been difficult to do as the support of the pro-China trade groups had waned by 1959. The JSP was important in contributing to the people's movement to restore relations with China, but it ultimately failed to bring about the breakthrough it hoped for. The LDP castigated the attempts of JSP missions, particularly Asanuma's March 1959 visit, as kow-tow missions. Yet neither the LDP nor MoFA had been totally opposed to the idea of such visits, since there is evidence that they were in contact with some of the delegates before their departure, viewing them as opportunities to ascertain what the Chinese were thinking. Union representatives seemed to have had more tangible success in gaining concessions from the Chinese, and helped to re-establish albeit limited levels of trade in 1959.

LDP policies on China between 1958–9 were lacking consistency, highlighting the internal struggles within the LDP relating not just to China policy, but to other, perhaps more pressing, issues, such as the Security Treaty revision and relations with the US, and security issues such as Taiwan. The internal divisions between pro-Taipei and pro-Beijing groups in the LDP became much clearer during this period and would soon develop into public, 'official' Diet members' groups in the 1960s.[68] While Kishi was constant in his professed desire to expand trade with the PRC, this proved impossible as long as he was prime minister. Nonetheless, this did not prevent various individuals and groups within the LDP from attempting to resurrect trade, along with their supporters in MOFA and MITI. These efforts should not be viewed as a unified movement, but more as a series of ad hoc attempts in response to various stimuli at different times. The shift from a wait-and-see approach to a gradualist, cumulative approach held out some hope for a resumption of relations, but was too little too late for it to have any effect during the remainder of Kishi's prime ministership. Ikeda Hayato's emergence as prime minister in July 1960, combined with a relaxation in China's foreign policy due to the failure of the Great Leap Forward and the Sino-Soviet split, enabled China and Japan to move quickly towards a resumption of trade relations.

It would be overstating the case to say that the informal diplomacy that charac-terised the interaction between China and Japan between May 1958 and late 1959 had a catalytic effect in bringing about a shift in Japan's official China policy. On the contrary, it sometimes appeared more to expose the divisions of opinion on China within Japan and the LDP in particular. Informal diplomacy was nonethe-less a useful barometer by which to measure the gradual easing of China's hard line in 1959. In addition, many of those involved in the evolving networks of friendship, business and diplomatic links between Japan and China in the 1950s went on to play increasingly important roles in the resumption of trade between the two countries in the 1960s and in the eventual normalization of relations be-tween the PRC and Japan in the early 1970s.

Notes

1 Friendly trade, from 1960, involved China's agreement to trade with only those Japa-nese companies that were deemed to be friendly towards China. Liao-Takasaki trade was named after Liao Chengzhi and Takasaki Tatsunosuke, who signed the agreement in 1962.

2 Two-way trade amounted to $105 million in 1958, dropping to $22.6 million in 1959. 1960 saw a slight increase to $23.4 million, and thereafter the volume of trade in-creased year on year reaching $137m by 1963. See W. Mendl, *Issues in Japan's China Policy*, Basingstoke and London: Macmillan, 1978, pp. 127–8. The number of visitors had reached a post-WWII peak in 1957 with 1243 Japanese visiting China and 140 Chinese visiting Japan. In 1958 this dropped to 594 and 93 respectively, and in 1959 just 191 and 0 respectively. Numbers increased again from 1960 recovering to 1957 levels by mid-1962. Figures drawn variously from National Archives, Kew (hereafter NA Kew) FO371/127285, 133588, 150570 (Political relations between China and Japan); Lian S., *Bainian waijiao fengyunlu,* Shenyang: Shenyang chubanshe, 1995.

3 CoCom refers to the Coordinating Committee for Multilateral Export Controls to which Japan belonged during the Cold War, and which placed restrictions on exports to communist countries.

4 Soeya Yoshihide, *Japan's Economic Diplomacy with China, 1945–1978,* Oxford: Clarendon Press, 1998, p. 43.

5 See for example H. Passin, *China's Cultural Diplomacy,* New York: Praeger, 1963; Mendl, *Japan's China Policy.*

6 Kishi Nobusuke, Yatsugi Kazuo, and Ito Takashi, *Kishi Nobusuke no kaisō,* Tokyo: Bungei Shunju, 1981, p. 213.

7 *Nihon to Chūgoku* 21 April 1958, p. 1. Japan and China had concluded three private trade agreements in the early part of the 1950s (specifically in 1952, 1953, and 1954). The main sticking point of fourth trade agreement was the exchange of trade missions, which both the Japanese and Chinese negotiators felt were necessary to ensure that the agreement fulfilled its potential. This was construed as a step towards diplomatic

recognition of China, and the US, LDP conservatives, and then the Nationalist government of Taiwan raised their concerns. President Chiang Kai-shek was particularly concerned about the possibility that the PRC trade office would be allowed to fly the PRC flag. The Japanese government placated Taipei by emphasising that it would not recognise the right of the PRC trade mission to raise the flag, but in so doing further angered the PRC government which announced that it would not implement the agreement. The Nagasaki flag incident occurred just two weeks later.

8 NA Kew, FO371/127285 FC10323/10 From Peking to FO, 30 July 1957.

9 Articles from the *Renmin Ribao* and official statements from PRC leaders of the time are reproduced in Tian H., *Zhanhou ZhongRi guanxi shi 1945–1995*, Beijing: Zhongguo shehui kexue chubanshe, 1995.

10 The British Embassy in Japan also saw the anti-Japan campaigns and the cessation of trade as a means of influencing 'Japanese commercial interests in particular against Mr Kishi in the Japanese elections', and the view from the British Embassy in Beijing was similar, warning that China's 'naked use of their commercial bargaining position to achieve political ends may serve as a salutary warning to firms in the West', both in NA Kew, FO371/133588 FJ 101310/2, From A.D. Wilson British Embassy Peking to Selwyn Lloyd FO, 23 May 1958.

11 Diplomatic Record Office, Tokyo (hereafter DRO), *Nihon Chūkyō kankei zasshū*, A'-0356, A1.2.18, 10 May 1958, pp. 861–2.

12 *Nihon Keizai Shinbun* 10 May 1958, p.1

13 *Nihon Keizai Shinbun,* 20 June 1958, p.1; *Nihon Keizai Shinbun,* 20 June 1958 (evening edition), p.1.

14 Furukawa Mantarō, *Nitchū sengo kankeishi*, Tokyo: Hara Shobō, 1988, p. 159; *Nihon to Chūgoku,*1 January 1958.

15 Ibid., p. 166

16 Nishihara Masashi, 'Nihon gaikō to hiseishiki sesshokusha', *Kokusai seiji*, 1983, 75, pp. 3–5.

17 The JCP also maintained contact with China (although later broke with the CCP), but this tended to take place via more covert channels, usually through unions or visits of individuals acting in a private capacity.

18 NA Kew, FO 371/127285 FC 10323/5 O'Neill British Embassy Peking to Selwyn Lloyd, FO, 20 May 1957.

19 The media and the JSP were very keen to emphasise the informal nature of the talks. In addition, the JSP urged Sata to publish his report *in his individual capacity,* presumably to enable him to distance his position from that of the JSP. If the report was published under the auspices of the JSP it was felt that this would create the wrong impression of the party as accepting China's wishes. Matsumoto Shichirō. 'Jishu gaikō e no tenki', *Gekkan Shakaitō,* 17, October 1958, pp. 4–9.

20 C. Braddick, *Japan and the Sino-Soviet Alliance, 1950–1964*, Basingstoke, Hampshire: Palgrave Macmillan, 2004, p. 128–9.

21 Nishimura was equally critical of the Chinese, whom he regarded as having ignored the feelings of the Japanese people in making such punitive demands, and as damaging the cumulative policy (*tsumiage hōshiki*) followed by the JSP hitherto. Matsumoto, 'Jishu gaikō', pp. 4–9.

22 *Nihon Keizai Shinbun* 30 August 1958, p.1. The Sata report is reproduced in *Gekkan Shakaitō,* 17, October 1958, pp.18–19.

23 Other aims included bringing down the 'military block system' (i.e., the US–Japan Security Treaty); maintaining the peace constitution and preventing re-militarization; promoting friendship with the USSR; resolving the Okinawa and Northern Territories issues. 'Nitchū bōeki wa dō naru ka', *Gekkan Shakaitō* vol 14, July 1958, pp. 52–3.

24 NA Kew, FO 371/1414254 FJ 10310/7 From Sir O. Morland to Selwyn Lloyd, 3 April 1959. Morland refers to the view held within MoFA that moderation could be seen in

the listing of only three of the six conditions previously stated by Zhou Enlai during Sata's visit to China in July 1958.

25 Furukawa, *Nitchū sengo kankeishi,* p. 169.

26 NA Kew, FO 371/1414254 FJ 10310/5 Chancery, Tokyo to FE Dept. 10310/18/59, 13 March 1959.

27 The JCFA had an original membership of approximately 200 when it was formed in 1950. By 1958 this had increased to approximately 500, with a headquarters in Tokyo and branches in most prefectures. Its mission statement was 'to deepen friendship and mutual understanding between the Chinese and Japanese people, to effect cultural exchange, and to contribute to world peace and the prosperity of both counties.' Its main activities included research and dissemination of information about China and Chinese culture in Japan and vice versa; the exchange of friendship missions; management of cultural enterprise; and promotion of Japan-China trade etc. Nihon Chūgoku yūkō kyōkai zenkoku honbu (hereafter JCFA), *Nitchū yūkō undō shi,* Tokyo: Seinen Shuppansha, 1980, pp. 245–55.

28 C. J. Lee, *Japan Faces China,* Baltimore, London: John Hopkins University, 1976, p. 76.

29 The group was deeply embarrassed by the incident and the Nagasaki branch issued a statement in which it expressed a deep apology to the Chinese government and people, and called upon the Japanese government to treat the matter (and the criminal) seriously. It laid the blame firmly at the feet of Prime Minister Kishi's weak foreign policy, presumably referring to the problems associated with the failed fourth trade agreement and the flag rights issue. *Nihon to Chūgoku* 11 May 1958, p. 1.

30 Lian, *Bainian waijiao,* p. 1053.

31 The Committee was an umbrella organisation for 16 organizations involved in trade or cultural exchange in China, in addition to some which joined specifically for the purposes of restoring links with China in the wake of the Nagasaki flag incident. The groups included Sōhyō, The Tokyo Regional Council of Trade Unions, Japan Publishers Association for Cultural Exchange, Japan Federation of Women's Organisations, Japan Chamber of Commerce and Industry, Japan China Export Import Association, and the Japan China Trade Promotion Association. *Nihon to Chūgoku,* 11 July 1958.

32 *Nihon to Chūgoku,* 21 May 1958, p.1.

33 *Nihon to Chūgoku,* 11 July 1958, p. 1. On 12 July Sōhyō held a meeting and demonstration in Hibiya park in support of a resumption of Sino-Japanese relations. See also *Sōhyō* 18 July 1958, p. 1 for a report on this meeting in Hibiya park, attended (allegedly) by 5,000 workers.

34 For example a meeting was held on 9 August 1958 by the Osaka regional association of union workers and received a congratulatory address from the All China Federation of Trade Unions (*Nihon to Chūgoku* 21 August 1958, p.1). The China–Japan Women's Exchange Association launched a two-day campaign in August and managed to collect 973 signatures and 11,088 yen in aid of China–Japan normalization (*Nihon to Chūgoku,* 1 September 1958, p.1).

35 For an outline of the JCFA's aims see *Nihon to Chūgoku,* 7 November 1958, p.1. For examples of its activities at central and local level see *Nihon to Chūgoku,* 8 November 1958, pp. 6–7.

36 *Nihon to Chūgoku* 1 September 1958, p.1. This is the JCFA figure, but according to the *Nihon Keizai Shinbun* the police figures were 3,400 (9 October 1958, p. 1).

37 JCFA, *Nitchū yūkō undō shi,* 1980, pp. 101–2.

38 Uchiyama Kanzō had spent much of his life in Shanghai and developed a friendship with Lu Xun. On his return to Japan he set up a Chinese bookshop and was one of the leading figures in the Japan–China friendship movement. His death was reported in the Japanese and Chinese press.

39 *Gekkan Jiyū Minshu* 10 March 1959, p.1.

40 *Nihon to Chūgoku* 21 November 1959, p. 2
41 Passin, *China's Cultural Diplomacy*, p.14
42 Ibid.
43 Chinese sources tend to stress the serious setbacks and job losses suffered by, for example, the Japanese steel and chemical industries. See for example Lian, *Bainian waijiao*, p. 1053.
44 *Nihon Keizai Shinbun* 7 December 1958, p. 1.
45 *Nihon Keizai Shinbun* 25 December 1958, p. 2.
46 *Nihon Keizai Shinbun* 18 February 1959, p.1; *Nihon Keizai Shinbun* 19 March 1959, p.1.
47 *Nihon to Chūgoku* 11 September 1958, p. 1.
48 Chae Jin Lee also points out that Sōhyō developed its own links with China (and the USSR) independently of the JSP, and 'exerted significant influence over the JSP's attitude toward foreign countries' (*Japan Faces China*, p.14). This view was expressed within the LDP at the time – for example, the left wing of the JSP is described as being 'dragged behind' Sōhyō in early 1959, *Gekkan Jiyū Minshu* 10 March 1959, p. 1.
49 NA Kew, FO 371/1414254 FJ10310/5, Chancery Tokyo to FE Department, 13 March 1959.
50 'The JSP and China', *Gekkan Jiyū Minshu*, 10 March 1959, p. 1.
51 The reasons for this are explained in an article by Ikeda Masanosuke in *Gekkan Jiyū Minshu*, 15 July 1958, p. 3 as being largely ideological. The LDP felt that the JSP members of the JCTPDL were becoming too political and that the original mission of the league – that is, to promote trade – was being obscured by party politics and socialist ideology. The decision to pull out of the League was apparently made by Ikeda Masanosuke, ironically one of the keenest advocates of trade with the PRC.
52 *Nihon Keizai Shinbun* 12 May 1958, p. 1.
53 DRO, *Nihon Chūkyō kankei zasshū*, A'-0356, 13 August 1958, p. 1024.
54 DRO, *Nihon Chūkyō kankei zasshū*, A'-0356, undated, p. 1027.
55 Kishi, *Kishi Nobusuke no kaisō*, p. 214.
56 I am grateful to Chris Braddick for alerting me to this aspect of the government's informal diplomacy. For example, the issue of missing Japanese in China had been raised via the Japanese and Chinese consuls general in Geneva in 1957. See NA Kew, FO 371/127285 FC10323/8, Peking 331, 26 July 1957.
57 *Nihon Keizai Shinbun* 15 July 1958, p.1.
58 *Nihon Keizai Shinbun* 30 July 1958, p. 1. See also *Mainichi Shinbun* 7 August 1958, p.1 which carries an article indicating that the Prime Minister and Foreign Minister agreed on the need to restart talks with China on the issue of missing Japanese, while at the same time making use of the opportunity to open up Sino-Japanese relations and reopen a diplomatic route. The Chinese response to this approach was one of anger and frustration, since in their view the issue of the missing Japanese had already been resolved. There is reference to this matter in the British Foreign Office despatches from Beijing. See for example NA Kew, FO 371/127285 FC 10323/9, citing NCNA report, 26 July 1957.
59 Kishi, *Kishi Nobusuke no kaisō*, p.215.
60 See K. Radtke *China's Relations with Japan, 1945–83*, Manchester and New York: Manchester University Press, p.128; *Nihon Keizai Shinbun* 30 September 1959, p. 1; *Nihon Keizai Shinbun* 1 December 1959, p. 2.
61 *Globe and Mail* 31 October 1959 reproduced in DRO, *Nihon Chūkyō kankei zasshū*, A'-0356, p. 1423.
62 'Ishibashi hōChū to jimintō', *Sekai*, November 1959, pp. 259–63.
63 For example, Tagawa Seiichi, secretary to Matsumura Kenzō. Tagawa Seiichi, *Nitchū kōshō hiroku – Tagawa nikki – 14 nen no shōgen*, Tokyo: Mainichi Shinbunsha, 1973.
64 *Nihon Keizai Shinbun*, 19 June 1958, p. 1.

65 *Mainichi Shinbun,* 1 August 1958, p. 2.
66 The point of the conversation seemed to be to reassure the US that the visits of Ishibashi and Matsumura did not indicate a change in Japan's policy toward China, and that Japan continued to adhere to its policy of non-recognition while seeking 'some increased contacts in the future with Peiping depending upon developments and particularly upon Communist Chinese actions.' Memorandum of Conversation between PM Kishi and Secretary Herter, Washington, 19 January 1960, *Foreign Relations of the United States 1958–1960,* vol. XVIII, pp. 277–8.
67 'Ishibashi hōChū to jimintō', pp. 259–63.
68 For example, the pro-China politicians who formed the Asia–Africa Problem Research Association in 1965 included such members as Ishibashi Tanzan, Furui Yoshimi, Tagawa Seiichi, Fujiyama Aiichiro, and Ide Ichiro – members of the various delegations to China in the 1950s. See Tagawa, *Nitchū kōshō hiroku,* and Ogata Sadako, *Normalization with China: A Comparative Study of U.S. and Japanese Processes,* Berkeley, University of California, Institute of East Asian Studies, 1988, p. 9.

10 Conclusion

John Weste

Over the past sixty years, Japan's history has been punctuated by several rather striking events, which have sufficed even to capture global attention. Obviously there was international relief and joy with the final defeat and occupation of imperial Japan in 1945. While the world was certainly nervous and fearful of an unreconstructed Japanese revival at some point in the future, Japan was, at least for the moment, out of action and someone else's (namely, an American) problem. It was perhaps with some shock then when, during the late 1970s and the 1980s, Japan emerged as an economic superpower with the capacity to rival the United States. While in some instances admired for its success, Japan was equally reviled by those, often labelled 'Japan Bashers', who claimed that the Japanese cheated at trade and simply did not play fair. Regardless of which side of the fence one sat, Japan had truly captured global attention at the popular level. In between these periods, however, Japan often faded from view, particularly from the popular perspective of the European and American nations. Essentially, Japan was no longer a military threat, assumedly democratic and, while charming in its own curious manner, exotica was enhanced by a reassuring distance. Academic scholarship is equally prone to highlighting specific points or moments at the expense of intervening periods. Obviously this is inevitable: one can hardly know everything and something will always be left out. The contributors to this book, with their focus on Japanese foreign policy and diplomatic history, would certainly argue that the 1950s constitutes one such gap in our understanding of modern Japanese history (and also one in the market).

A great deal of scholarly effort has been devoted to the 1945–52 occupation of Japan, whether that be a study of, to name a few, the formal structures of occupation, the motivations of both the occupiers and the occupied, perceptions of successes and failures, and the interplay between international and domestic forces on the eventual outcome. However, the immediately ensuing years have, understandably perhaps, attracted less detailed attention: the excitement was over. Furthermore, the very end of the decade, as with its beginning, was bracketed by another calamitous event in Japan's foreign relations, the 1960 Security Treaty Crisis, which raised fundamental questions about the nature of the US–Japan military alliance, brought Japanese of both left and right persuasions out on to the streets in huge numbers to protest, and saw the fall of the Kishi government. In the first instance, our current work seeks to, in effect, provide the tomes for these decade-bracketing bookends to sandwich: Japan's foreign policy and relations throughout the 1950s was very active and is worthy of more attention than has thus far been afforded to it.

The second key theme covered by the authors is to analyse the extent to which Japan could independently develop and guide its own foreign policy initiatives. Again, scholarship following the occupation tended to present Japan as passive and generally in thrall to the pre-eminence which was the United States. Japan had devolved to the status of pre-war Manchukuo and was now the puppet jerked by strings threading their way back to a foreign capital, this time Washington. It would be foolish and completely inaccurate to deny the partial truth of this observation. At the very least, defeat and occupation impressed upon the Japanese political and big business elite the need for reliance and, even if temporary, dependence upon the United States. Actions that cut completely across American wishes could not be undertaken, which was a lesson the United Kingdom, for example, did not learn until the 1956 Suez Crisis.

Having said that, however, the contributors to this volume also show that, within acknowledged constraints, Japan was capable of independently seeking to re-establish and reintegrate itself, both within the region and beyond. American support was often helpful, indeed essential, yet it also came with costs, particularly in terms of relations with the communist states of Asia; here, too, Japan sought less formal diplomatic channels to consolidate its position. Success and consistency in Japanese efforts could not be assumed, but nonetheless neither was Japan a passive entity waiting to be worked upon by its American big brother. Equally, while it is crucial to emphasize Japanese vitality in the diplomatic arena and perhaps tempting to find ever earlier evidence for the passing of Japan's American eclipse, it also essential that we acknowledge how utterly irrelevant Japan could also be to the great powers of the time. Tokyo's treasured ambitions, such as membership of GATT and the UN, could be thwarted, denied, toyed with and ultimately discarded as dictated by the interests of foreign capitals, including, but by no means exclusively, Washington, Moscow, London and Beijing. As any would-be actor in a play, Japan could still find itself on the stage only to be dressed as a tree and could not always assume a speaking part. Similarly, the Japanese were rapidly left to understand that the United States was not always a talent scout thrilled with pride and joy at its exclusive new discovery and constantly ready to berate others to ensure a more prominent role in the piece for the supposed prodigy.

More specifically, the decade of the 1950s, as shown throughout this book, was certainly one of transition, and it was within this changing environment that Japan had to engineer its return to the international community. One clear consequence was that pre-war tactics and assumptions were frequently over turned. At the most basic level, Japan could no longer use military force as a means to resolve foreign policy issues; post-war demilitarized and democratic Japan needed complementary mechanisms to win friends, promote regional stability and security, and to affirm its value to its alliance partners. In this sense, an economic role in leading regional recovery was one such option. While the US expressed constant irritation that Japan sought to over-egg this particular pudding to avoid the realities of rearmament, it nonetheless also acknowledged the use of Japan in promoting economic recovery in South-East Asia. Further, it is also striking how quickly the Japanese themselves identified the importance of South-East Asia as a potential market and source of raw materials, as shown by the despatches of businessmen and technical support groups. For the United States, Japan could be distracted from communist-dominated North-East Asia, and Japan could also gain fresh markets and promote capitalist development in nations perceived to be dangerously open to the misguided allures of communism. By emphasizing its economic role, Japan could clearly mark a new-found commitment to pacifism, provide a safe and honourable demonstration of pride for the Japanese people, confirm the domestic eclipse of the former military elite, and simultaneously earn Japan a prominent and core role in the region.

Other clear markers of regional and international transition include the dismantling of the Japanese Empire, gradual colonial independence matched by the decline of the European empires, successful communist revolution, civil war on the Korean Peninsula, and the emergence of the US and the USSR as the two global superpowers. Japan, though certainly not only Japan, had to take new soundings and learn fresh lessons. For example, political independence, whether granted to or taken by the former colonies, created alternative centres of power which could not be ignored. While it was still necessary to consider the views of London, Paris, or Washington in the context of South-East Asia, new states now existed with their own ambitions, dreams of the future, and understandings of wartime legacies and memories: they also had to be consulted and persuaded. The rise of Asian nationalism and growing regional autonomy could be directed against Japan as readily as the US, the Netherlands, Britain, or France.

New doors offered new openings, but also required that Japan rethink the guise in which it approached potential partners and foes. In essence, what was Japan? Admittedly, this query has a lengthy pedigree, but to what extent was post-war Japan, as the key Asian member of the American-led capitalist camp, a Western power, an Asian power, or indeed a unique bridge between the two? How would other nations perceive Japan: an insidious American proxy and lap dog; an untrustworthy, yet irritatingly necessary nation temporarily beaten and shamed into relatively good behaviour; or a genuine friend? Indeed, to what extent would other nations even wish to see Japan rehabilitated, and how would any possible restoration of Japanese power hinder or promote their own national interests? To chart a path through this course was not an easy task, and the chapters within this book point to a variety of potential solutions Japan considered. Japan is clearly the junior partner in the American alliance and that must be accepted. However, we also see a measured Japanese willingness to seek alternatives, for example, by turning to third parties, such as Great Britain, and newly created regional and international bodies, such as the United Nations and ECAFE, in moves to suggest something other than a helpless dependence on the United States. Moreover, in the case of the People's Republic of China, there is also informal Japanese diplomacy, itself borne out of a realization that the United States would not always be there to protect Japanese interests.

Transition is, therefore, a consistent topic in this book, but as always one must be careful to consider the continuities. Within Japan, the elite might well have lost its military component, but the determination to recover and retain a leading role within the region, and also internationally, carries on. Defeat and occupation might have been humiliating, but they did not extinguish aspirations (or in fact assumptions of the right) to hold power and influence. While not nearly the equal of the United States, and presented with the novel challenge of relying upon non-military mechanisms to promote the national interest, Tokyo had little intention of accepting third-class status for itself. Japan was, its elite held, inherently a significant power and a leading Asian nation. It was the means and manifestations of power which showed the greater change, not the end itself, and to win co-operation and the acceptance of this purportedly self-evident fact was the challenge.

The rise of the United States is also seen as one of the great transitions arising from Allied victory in the European, Pacific and Asian theatres of conflict over 1939–45. Matching this American emergence is the collapse of the Japanese Empire, and the gradual fall of the European empires, regardless of how intransigently that trend might have been contested by the home powers. The decline of Great Britain is particularly evident in this regard as it lost not only its colonies to independence movements, but also its leading position in East Asia to the United States. However, it is also important to remember that this decline was neither absolute nor immediate.

In common with Tokyo, London likewise cherished ambitions of remaining a global power and retaining a significant presence in Asia was core to this ambition. While it was evident by the late 1950s that Britain was simply incapable of sustaining the breadth of its global presence, this was by no means clear in the early 1950s. For approximately half of the period considered by this book, Britain's capacity to curtail Japanese ambitions, especially in South-East Asia (but also elsewhere as shown by the constant refusal to grant Japan admission to GATT until 1955), was real, to the vexation of both the US and Japan. Great Britain still had the potential to matter, and should be considered as one further continuity from the pre-war period to the immediate post-war in the context of Japanese diplomatic history. Certainly, Whitehall and Westminster at least did see a useful, but regulated, role for Japan in the former South-East Asian empire. However temporarily, a former colonial power was still able and willing to condition the nature of Japanese engagement with the Asian region.

Japanese diplomatic and foreign policy ambitions over the 1950s are important. It is more than a story of a fledgling nation making its first hesitant steps, as, while not always stepping boldly, Japan did carry significant pre-war legacies into the post-war era. Japan had experience of empire, and was a unified state with a highly developed economy, albeit one temporarily checked by the war and its aftermath. These certain continuities were also matched by change marked by the Cold War, the European retreat from empire, and growing Asian autonomy. Our study of Japan's foreign policy over the 1950s is ultimately an examination of the pursuit of national concerns and charts the steady evolution of Japan's re-emergence in the regional and global communities.

Index